SPLIT DOWN THE SIDES

On the Subject of Laughter

R. D. V. Glasgow

University Press of America, Inc.
Lanham • New York • London

Copyright © 1997 by
University Press of America, ® Inc.
4720 Boston Way
Lanham, Maryland 20706

3 Henrietta Street
London, WC2E 8LU England

Library of Congress Cataloging-in-Publication Data

Glasgow, R. D. V. (Rupert D. V.)
Split down the sides : on the subject of laughter /
R.D.V. Glasgow.
p.   cm.
Includes bibliographical references and index.
1. Laughter--Psychological aspects. 2. Comedy--Psychological
aspects.
3. Self. I. Title

BF575.L3G57 1997 152.4--dc20   96-43223   CIP

ISBN 0-7618-0550-8 (cloth: alk. ppr.)
ISBN 0-7618-0551-6 (pbk: alk. ppr.)

Contents

Acknowledgements

Many thanks to Martin Amis for permission to quote from *The Rachel Papers* and *Money*. The quotation from Ludovico Ariosto, *Orlando Furioso*, translated by Guido Waldman, Oxford University Press, 1974, is reprinted by permission of Oxford University Press. The quotations from *Watt* by Samuel Beckett are reprinted by permission of The Samuel Beckett Estate and The Calder Educational Trust, London, as well as Grove / Atlantic, Inc. Copyright © Samuel Beckett 1953, 1963, 1970, 1976. The quotation from *Murphy* by Samuel Beckett is reprinted by permission of The Samuel Beckett Estate and The Calder Educational Trust, London, as well as Grove / Atlantic, Inc. Copyright © Samuel Beckett 1938, 1963, 1977 and copyright © The Samuel Beckett Estate 1993. I am grateful to Faber & Faber Ltd and Grove / Atlantic, Inc. for permission to quote from Samuel Beckett, *Endgame*. Copyright © Grove Press 1958. The quotation from Giovanni Boccaccio, *The Decameron*, translated by G. H. McWilliam (Penguin Classics, 1972), translation copyright © G. H. McWilliam 1972, is reproduced by permission of Penguin Books Ltd. The quotation from Cervantes, *Don Quixote*, translated by J. M. Cohen (Penguin Classics, 1950), copyright

© J. M. Cohen 1950, is reproduced by permission of Penguin Books Ltd. Excerpts from *White Noise* by Don DeLillo reprinted by permission of the Wallace Literary Agency, Inc. Copyright © 1984, 1985 by Don DeLillo. Published by Viking Penguin, Inc. Many thanks to Dafydd Johnston for permission to quote from his translations of the poems "Cywydd y Gal" and "Cywydd y Cedor" from the volume *Canu Maswedd yr Oesoedd Canol. Medieval Welsh Erotic Poetry*. Many thanks to the Estate of James Joyce for permission to quote from *Finnegans Wake*. The quotations from Petronius *The Satyricon*, and Seneca, *The Apocolocyntosis*, translated by J. P. Sullivan (Penguin Classics, 1977), copyright © J. P. Sullivan 1965, 1969, 1974, 1977, are reproduced by permission of Penguin Books Ltd. The quotations from Plautus, *The Pot of Gold and Other Plays*, translated by E. F. Watling (Penguin Classics, 1965), copyright © E. F. Watling 1965, are reproduced by permission of Penguin Books Ltd. The quotation from *The Rig Veda*, translated by Wendy Doniger O'Flaherty (Penguin Classics, 1981), copyright © Wendy Doniger O'Flaherty 1981, is reproduced by permission of Penguin Books Ltd. Many thanks to Bruce Robinson for permission to quote from *How to Get Ahead in Advertising*. Many thanks to N. F. Simpson for permission to quote from *One Way Pendulum*. I am grateful to Tom Stoppard, Faber & Faber Ltd. and Grove / Atlantic, Inc. for permission to quote from Tom Stoppard, *Rosencrantz and Guildenstern are Dead*. Copyright © Tom Stoppard 1967.

I owe special thanks to Christian Topf of Falmouth for making such an excellent job of the typesetting. I'd also like to thank, in particular, the following people: Janet Anderson, Mark (Jeff) Astle, Walter Bayer, Buddy Bendick, Ingrid Bietz, Rick Bluett, Ollie Briese, Andy (Mrs Marwood) Carey, Karin Claesson, Dave Collier, Tina Grothoff, Sean Hannan, Phil Jenkins, Bronwen Jones, Lisa Jones, Molly Kadarauch, Mirjam Kasperl, Dick Laycock, Frank (Francis) Lee, Bettina Loxley, Kevin Lynch, Akemi Masuko, Fergus McCormick, Ollie Money-Kyrle, Jim Reed, Tim and Christiane Swain, Steve Taylor, Stephen (Tommo) Thompson, Lois Thorley, Stefan Troisch, Bill Weir, Nick Williams, Uwe Willmann, Dom Wollenweber and my colleagues and friends at the Volkshochschule Treptow. The biggest thank you of all goes to my Mum and Dad, Barbara and Wilfred Glasgow, and to my sister Faith.

Introduction

This essay, taken as a whole, is a study of the interrelationship between comedy (defined by the laughter to which it gives rise) and selfhood (understood, simplistically, as my awareness of the seemingly empty fact that I am myself and not somebody or something else). While most people have a fairly clear idea of what is meant by comedy, however, the notion of a self is much more enigmatic and therefore needs illumination. The essay is accordingly divided into two parts, the first of which attempts to clarify what is meant by a self and the second of which applies the resulting schematization of selfhood to the phenomenon of laughter. The two parts are in this way intended to echo one another, contributing both to an understanding of comedy and to the ongoing philosophical question of human identity.

The relative autonomy of the two sub-essays means that those interested only in laughter can in theory skip part one without being utterly at sea in part two. Indeed, part one makes excursions into the physical sciences which may seem spectacularly irrelevant to the theme of laughter (although I hope their relevance will become clear at least in retrospect). Likewise, those concerned only with the more technical question of what it means to be oneself can ignore the following discussion of laughter. The two sub-essays do not strictly presuppose one another, although they do both presuppose this introduction, which offers an explanation why the whole of the essay – parts one and two together – is taken to be worth more than the sum of its parts. What is said about the self in part one serves as a theoretical foundation underpinning and giving depth to the remainder of the book, for the self is seen less as a "topic" of comedy (one among many) than as the precondition for its very possibility.

A self has been defined as an individual that is conscious of the individual that it is and is conscious that it is the individual it is conscious of. It is conscious of itself, that is, and of itself *as* itself. This definition, put forward by Stephen Priest,[1] is helpful and enlightening, but also fatally circular. While telling us that something that is conscious of itself as itself has the property of being a self, it tells us nothing about what it is that has this property. Another definition of the self, proffered by Robert Nozick, moves in similar circles: a self is what is synthesized or created by the act of reflexive self-reference using the token "I".[2] But if the self is what is synthesized by this act of reflexive self-reference, what is being referred to by the reflexive self-reference? The self? What self? What does it refer to itself as? Perhaps as what is synthesized by the act of reflexive self-reference. But what does this act of self-reference refer to? The self of course.... Circular definitions, by (circular) definition, get us so far and no further. Priest concludes his definition: "That is what a self is, whatever it is."[3] Such circularity is not inappropriate for an entity whose defining characteristic involves some sort of circularity or reflexivity. But if this is all that can be said about the self, then this essay is going to waste quite a lot of time not getting anyone anywhere.

Fortunately (I think), it is not all that can be said. The other immediate clue to the nature of the self is that if it is defined as being something that is conscious of itself, it must also have the property of consciousness. The German idealist philosopher Fichte, cited by Nozick, speaks of the self as positing itself and of positing itself as positing itself. But this as it stands will not do. The act of *positing* something is logically interdependent with a concomitant *negation.* Consciousness can only be an undifferentiated blur unless the concepts of which it consists are in some way defined, delimited and thereby distinguished from what they are not. Position presupposes negation, quite as much as the reverse, and my self presupposes a non-self which in turn presupposes a self. Question: which came first? Answer: the chicken or the egg.

It has long been recognized that all knowledge implies an accompanying negation, a differentiation between self and other. Knowledge is relational (knowledge *of...*), it is argued, and the act of cognition necessarily entails an implicit distinction between the object of knowledge and the knowing subject, between whatever it is that is known and the consciousness doing the knowing. But it was the philosopher Immanuel Kant who made the greatest effort to explain *why* this act of differentiation must lie at the heart of our cognition of the world. Our empirical sense of self he understands as coming into being on account of the ability of the knowing subject to distinguish between variations in experience and variations in what is being experienced. As experience can fluctuate without any corresponding change in the thing experienced and conversely the thing can fluctuate without any corresponding change in the experiencing, the subject of these experiences must be endowed with a sense of itself as distinct from its objects. The notion of an objective world cannot be separated from the possibility of alternative experiential routes through it and thus depends upon the distinction between subjective experience and the world being experienced. Kant accordingly claims that "the consciousness of my own existence is simultaneously an immediate consciousness of the existence of other things outside me,"[4] and refutes the Cartesian conception of a disembodied self-consciousness by arguing that the possibility of empirical self-consciousness and the perception of a unified objective world are inextricably bound up with one another.

It is not merely as *conscious* beings that we differentiate ourselves from the world of which we are conscious. Consciousness is never just a disembodied ghost breezing about gathering knowledge of itself. If it were, any empirical distinction between itself and the world would be scuppered for a start. As my consciousness of myself is of a being with a body, the role of the human body and its movements is crucial to the flow of experience: my perceptions constantly change as my body moves, for example, and through my control of my body I can switch the objects of my attention. It is because persons are themselves physical objects, movable at will and located in time and space, that the idea of an objective world can be formed. Movement and will are what enable me to draw the frontiers between myself and the rest of the world, the resistance offered to my volitional activities situating me in a world which is not me. It is as one body located amongst and interacting with other bodies in the world that I am conscious of self and world alike. My self-differentiation is thus also a differentiation of what I *do* from what *is done* to me.[5]

A being which is conscious of itself as itself, therefore, must necessarily delimit or "define" itself by its difference from what it is *not*, from its "other." Structuralist thinkers have indeed stressed that the "value" of any linguistic sign consists in its difference from all other signs in the same system of signification, the meaning of a term like "cup" amounting to an exceedingly long list of negative terms: "not saucer," "not knife," "not table," and so on (but where do we stop?). Concepts are defined not by their positive content, but by what they are *not*. Instead of inhering in the sign itself, meaning is displaced into a series of differences, an approach which has led to the idea that the meaning of any single word is inseparable from the open-ended structures of which it forms a part and ultimately "spreads out" across every other word. In the face of this infinite play of signification meaning can at best only be provisionally pinned down. Admittedly, a full understanding of the meaning of any specific concept, and of the concept of a self (or a subject or a person) in particular, cannot possibly be achieved in isolation from its relations to a whole set of semantically contiguous terms. Any understanding of what it is to be a human being is necessarily a function of accompanying conceptions of the world in which the human being is situated. But – again – where do we stop this search for meaning? While it is relevant (to me) that I am not you (dear reader), is it equally relevant that I am not an element such as boron, an abstract quality such as sagacity, velocity or gross national product, or a fictive figure such as Ned the Lonely Donkey or Postman Plod?

Underlying this infinity of differences – the fact that I am not a teapot, a wardrobe, a tube of tomato purée, a cuddly toy, a pterodactyl, a protracted period of hot weather, an armadillo, any of the Benelux countries, gravity, Yorkshire, a game of limited-over cricket, Doctor Who, Boadicea, or one of the world's top ten darts players – is the purely logical point that "I" am defined by my difference from "not-I." This binary opposition based on negation is the bottom line to any differentiation of oneself from the rest of the world. It is, of course, an artificial construction: "normal" or non-philosophical self-consciousness is unlikely to be explicitly equipped with this ugly concept "not-I," instead taking a synecdochic representative of the global non-self against which to define itself: "you," "them," or perhaps "my surroundings" or "the world." Yet it seems justifiable for our purposes to abstract from these synecdochic non-selves to their lowest common denominator, *the* non-self: like an over-ambitious sporting challenge, it is Me versus The Rest.

The two complementary propositions that I am me and that I am not what is not me (or indeed that any entity is what it is and is not what is not it) may seem just too vacuous to warrant all this attention. They are blatantly tautological. But as the two so-called "laws of thought" (the law of identity and the law of contradiction) they underpin all human cognition. Of the proposition "I=I" Fichte correspondingly writes: "It is the foundation of all knowledge; i.e. we know what it expresses because we know at all... . It accompanies all knowledge, is contained in all knowledge, and all knowledge presupposes it." [6] And Fichte is equally aware of the role played by the non-self as the medium whereby the self comes to self-consciousness. It is only upon being able to distinguish itself from what is not itself (say, a bottle or a rattle) that a baby can know of itself as a self: this primordial encounter with what is not me is essential to my sense of being me. Not that this need be declarative knowledge, expressly formulated. Nor need it imply some pre-natal training in the foundations of logic. "A child," writes the English philosopher John Locke, "certainly knows that a stranger is not its mother, that its sucking-bottle is not the rod, long before he knows that it is impossible for the same thing to be, and not to be."[7] It is a question of principles which are presupposed by consciousness without necessarily ever coming to explicit articulation.

The tautological self-evidence of the propositions means that while culture and upbringing may determine where the boundaries between self and non-self actually lie, the fact that *there must be* a non-self in opposition to which my concept of myself can be placed is an analytical one. The problem in this case lies in differentiating between cognitive universals and particular historical configurations and in resisting the temptation to impart a general validity to what is in fact a local or cultural variable. Nouns such as "identity" and "individuality" are anachronistic when applied indiscriminately to pre-modern contexts; a sense of self need not imply any self-ascription of the sophisticated philosophical term "self" on the part of the conscious individual. The precise terms of my self-definition – how I perceive myself in relation to what is not me – are historically conditioned.

The purpose of this essay is to examine the phenomenon of laughter as a fundamental expression of the human self, understood as that which is aware of itself as itself and as not what it is not. It is concerned with laughter as an unfolding of the relationship – a manifestation of power (or its absence) – between the self and its non-self. It is concerned with the laughter of a subject asserting itself (or failing to) in the face of its object, an identity affirming itself against what is different. It deals, in other words, with the diabolical grimace which Baudelaire, like Hobbes before him, recognized as stemming from a feeling of superiority. Yet both Hobbes and Baudelaire saw the double edge implicit in such a show of power, for the need to display itself is a fatal giveaway of its very relativity. Baudelaire thus took laughter to task as "weakness rejoicing in weakness,"[8] just as Hobbes had explained the "sudden glory" moving people to laughter as "caused either by some sudden act of their own, that pleaseth them; or by the apprehension of some deformed thing in another, by comparison whereof they suddenly applaud themselves. And it is incident most to them, that are conscious of the fewest abilities in themselves; who are forced to keep themselves in their own favour, by observing the imperfections of other men. And therefore much Laughter at the defects of others, is a signe of Pusillanimity."[9] Being an advertisement of strength, laughter is a token of weakness. It is an act of self-assertion that exposes one's vulnerability.

This ambivalence will be seen to permeate laughter through and through, as a phenomenon that both buttresses the fortress of the human ego and sabotages the bulwarks from within. As such, laughter is perhaps best viewed as a signal of fear, the fear that underlies both relative weakness and relative strength, the fear necessarily inherent in the relation between the self and the unmastered or unknown other. The physiological contiguity of laughter and anxiety is indeed betrayed by the relationship in which laughter – as something we may choke on – stands with the throat.[10] While laughter at something dangerous or frightening can signal a release from anxiety, therefore, it is always a less than total overcoming of it.[11] As a mark both of fear and of the vanquishing of fear, it hovers somewhere between alarm and assurance.

If laughter is thus an (unfinished) conquest of the fear structuring the relationship of an identity to what is different from it, this is primarily thanks to the creation of *distance* within this relationship. This may be the retrospective distance between ourselves and danger past, the spatial distance that permits us to observe a threat from a position of safety, or the internalized distance through which we mentally "withdraw" from a situation and view it *as if* dissociated from it. Laughter both presupposes and generates such distance.[12] This need not be explicitly "aesthetic" distance, framed in an institutionalized dramatic production. The more general concept of "play" – as a context conducive to laughter – also incorporates ideas of invulnerability and non-seriousness, as well as (often) make-belief and imitation. Nonetheless, the distance intrinsic to and produced by theatrical comedy allows the latter, like Carnival and ritual festivity, to function as paradigmatic for laughter-provoking situations in general.

In laughter particularly, the notions of distance and of difference are linked by more than just the Latin prefix they have in common: difference from "what is other" converges with distance from threat, for both are essentially connected with the setting of limits, the self-protective delineation of boundaries. Through the context of play, the threat is in some sense made unthreatening and the alien rendered harmless. To the extent that laughter assumes and engenders distance, therefore, it can be understood as a signal and assertion of difference. Clearly, however, laughter may equally be empathetic in nature, an affirmation of identity with its object rather than difference from it. Not all laughter is assertive and derisory: much is affable and congenial, expressing understanding or fellow feeling. Yet even empathy itself presupposes the distance that has to be spanned by the act of empathetic identification: here it reveals difference through the very gesture of affirming identity. This tension between identification and differentiation, between the overcoming and the creation of distance, again bears witness to the duality of laughter.

Indeed, the conceptual interdependence of identity and difference lies at the heart of laughter's capacity both to reinforce *and* to undermine the limits of our selfhood. Fichte makes the age-old point, later to become one of the basic tenets of German idealism, that there can be no distinction without a prior unity, nor any unity without a prior distinction: the assertion, for example, that a and b are "different" implies some shared substratum of identity, while the claim that they are "identical" or "the same" entails an implicit distinction if it is to have any positive content at all. In Fichte's own words, "every opposite is like its opponent in one characteristic (=x), and every like is opposed to its like in one characteristic (=x)."[13] There is always some point, that is, at which the law of identity is infringed, at which I = not-I, at which the self coincides with its other, and so fails to coincide with itself. This point ("x") is the *Grenze* or boundary.[14] The boundary thus has a "double identity"[15] as something which both links and separates self and other, and in its concern with this boundary laughter duplicates this double identity. Laughter in this way incorporates the same duality that allows the assertion and the subversion of identity to be taken as two sides of the same coin.

To determine more precisely *where* the boundaries of the self lie, to reconnoitre that ambiguous no-man's-land where the self is not itself, it is necessary to turn from the plane of rather arid theoretical abstraction on which we have worked so far to more concrete and empirically substantial considerations. Instead of opposing the self to a global non-self which swallows up all semantic diversity in a single binary opposition and reduces the complexity of the world to two morphemes ("a" versus "not-"), the self and non-self can be broken down into a number of distinct *aspects*. Part of the reason for the confusion surrounding the notion of self-awareness has been a tendency to reduce this "self" to a unitary phenomenon, fully explicable in one set of terms. This blindness to multi-levelled complexity has resulted in synecdochic over-simplification, where one part or aspect of the entity is taken for the whole. Symptomatic has been the habit of viewing self-consciousness simply as a transparent self-presence in abstraction of any material embodiment. The following essay will concentrate on seven co-existent and interrelated aspects of the human self. These aspects are more fully elucidated in part one and provide the chapter divisions for the ensuing schematization of laughter in part two.

In short, the self is to be regarded as (1) a bodily entity that thus exists in opposition to the environment in which it is spatio-temporally situated *(Chapter 6: Self as Body)*. But it is not just an inert glob of physical matter; it is also (2) a living organism, a body endowed with "life," a being that is engaged in perpetual conflict with the non-being from which it emerged at birth and which will engulf it again when it shuffles off this mortal coil *(Chapter 5: Self as Living Organism)*. As a communal being, moreover, the self is (3) a persona, a role-player in a network of human interaction, someone identifiable to others and defined by his or her difference from the other social actors. It is in this sense that I am (or have) an identity *(Chapter 8: Self as Persona)*. As (4) a social self, I indeed internalize the order or structure inherent in the social system of which I form a part: embodying the strictures of the system's political, legal and ethical self-interpretation, the self as a social being will seek to demarcate itself from threatening incursions from without, opposing the menace of social and moral otherness or chaos *(Chapter 2: Self as Structure)*. Yet within this system, the self also exists as (5) an autonomous physiological unit, an "individual" with the potential to negate the social order in which he or she participates. This capacity to negate underlies what has often been perceived as the human being's defining characteristic, the ability to question, wonder and doubt, to imagine what is *not* the case *(Chapter 3: Self as Individual)*. Such individuality is not simply a matter of bodily particularity: as (6) a thinking subject, the self necessarily comprises a unique and unilinear experiential route through the spatio-temporal continuum *(Chapter 4: Self as Subject)*. Indeed, its cognitive activity depends upon this so-called numerical identity. However shaky its foundations, this stipulation (I am me and no one else) is the basis for all rational behaviour. As (7) a numerical identity or unity, therefore, the human self implicitly distinguishes itself from the "madness" or "irrationality" of self-division and disunity *(Chapter 7: Self as Rational Unity)*.

The sense of self is evidently reliant upon the establishment of barriers, boundaries and limits separating self from non-self. The perspective represented in this essay is not – as some would claim – that the self is an illusion, but rather that it is a *fiction*, by which is meant not an untruth or lie but a mental construct imposed on something in fact much more mercurial. In the face of the inordinate complexity and subtlety of the human being, the boundaries between self and other are shown to be inherently problematic and indistinct. The clear demarcation that is a prerequisite of human rationality is as arbitrary as any geographical boundary. Comedy is seen as an attempt either to bolster this rather wobbly defensive construction or to offer subversive release from its rigours. Comic laughter spotlights the borderlines between self and other, where I may be you and you me or where I merge with my surroundings and they with me. Shakespeare's *Twelfth Night* embodies this duality, as a realm both of tautology (where "That that is, is," as Feste the Clown playfully burbles, 4.2) and of contradiction (where "Nothing that is so, is so," 4.1). Comedy allows me both to assert myself as myself and to show the ways in which I may not be myself. It is for these reasons that this essay is best regarded not simply as a treatise on laughter, therefore, nor merely as an orthodox monograph on the nature of being a self. It is about the inextricability of the two topics. Just as comedy cannot be fully understood without reference to identity and loss of identity, identity too is given new perspectives when seen through the cross-eyes of comedy. In this context, the notion of acting forms a unique conceptual bridge between the existential and the aesthetic, the fiction of identity and the comic fiction. Before turning in more detail to the various aspects of selfhood just touched upon, it is thus fitting to cast an anticipatory glance at some of the implications of acting as far as identity is concerned.

Acting itself, be it theatrical performance or non-theatrical imposture, constitutes a shedding or suspension of identity: as an actor, one ceases to be merely oneself, instead turning into "someone else" and hiding one's "true" identity or one's "true" motivations and emotions. Of course this transformation is never absolute, for the actor subsists in a state of existential equivocation, both himself and not himself. Theatre consequently permits its spectators to come out with such seemingly contradictory comments as "Kenneth Branagh is Henry V" or "Robbie Coltrane is Falstaff": the all-pervading law of identity is temporarily repealed, and a potentially disruptive interplay of identity and difference is given free rein. It was for this reason that Plato judged the multivocal literary forms of comedy and tragedy to be a menace to the *polis*. Mimesis – seeming to be other than one is – is dangerous precisely insofar as it jumbles the categories of identity and difference, and actors are subversive thanks to their mastery of the art of convincing dissimulation. Yet theatrical performance may easily go one step further, not merely consisting of acting, but also fictionally representing it, depicting roguery, impersonation and even plays-within-plays. Indeed, by turning acting into a theme, it may highlight the pervasiveness of role-playing in general, showing the ways in which we may all (without realizing it) become engulfed in pre-set attitudes towards ourselves and others and slip into modes of being unthinkingly copied or learnt by blind imitation.

While such fictional role-playing or identity-loss may provoke a reflective questioning of what it means to have an identity, however, the theatrical context ensures that it is still from the security of a position of relative enlightenment, which permits us to recognize the acting for what it is and to know ourselves "above" it. The position of ascendancy enjoyed by the spectator creates possibilities for self-affirmation and self-congratulation over against the confusion and self-difference being enacted down below on stage. This dilution of comedy's unsettling potential is intrinsically connected to the actor/audience division; unlike the actors, *we* are ourselves, and in full possession of our "real" identity. It is a dichotomy which much modern avant-garde theatre is at pains to dissolve (say, by addressing or abusing the spectators, or calling for audience participation) but which is most effectively overcome in popular *festivity*, where distinctions between actor and audience, subject and object, are at most secondary. Communal celebration and comedy have indeed in the past been deeply interrelated social phenomena, closely contiguous in their orientation to the issues of cultural co-existence. Yet like much present-day Carnival, comedy involves a radical displacement of Carnival's more subversive energies, as universal farcical improvization – open-ended, participatory and resistant to authority – is replaced by the controlled re-presentation of a closed work of established dramatic literature.

Whereas communal festivity is potentially conducive to a sort of Nietzschean *Rausch* or intoxication, to the Bacchanalian whirl in which we have the feeling that all barriers are falling, comedy thus tends to operate at one remove, be it by representing, enacting or displaying the blurred boundaries of the self or by implicitly or explicitly drawing our attention to the problematic theme of identity. In comparison with the ecstatic folly of Dionysian revelry, the comic theatre on the whole offers its audience a rather moderate madness. Yet laughter's deep-seated ambivalence – as something which may both support and undermine human identity – is at work even in Carnival situations. As historical instances have shown, the "good-natured" merrymaking that may seem to enact the chaotic dissolution of social structure and fixed identity can easily flip over into gestures of collectively self-assertive solidarity *in opposition to* outsiders and outcasts (such as whores or beggars). The very laughter which has the potential to transgress limits and resist control may equally be channelled into the maintenance of identity and the intimidation and exclusion of "deviant" difference. It may be an act of collective oneness or a challenge to authority and to the community: "Which way the laughter is to go will depend on the individuals and societies concerned: jokes have the same structure of ambiguity whether they are the conformist's or the rebel's."[16]

While ordinary consciousness tends to take its own identity and unity for granted and to concur with the boundaries necessary for its continued day-to-day existence, comedy – creating distance and detachment – may at least sow the seeds for questioning these margins, just as certain contexts (revelry, performance, orgy and intoxication, and religious ecstasy) may allow their participants to "lose" themselves and their sense of self. In this questioning function, comedy indeed reflects (or mimics) the philosophical endeavour to understand what it means to have a sense of identity or to be a person.

PART ONE:
THE HUMAN SUBJECT

Chapter 1

Defining the Subject

Our Selves

After an introductory skirmish with the notions of identity and difference, it is time to look more closely at the various ways in which a human self may define itself, before turning to the damp, dank, dark problem patches necessarily pasted over by such a peremptory demarcation as that between self and other. This will put us in a stronger position to assess the habit comedy has of sticking its nose into realms normally characterized by taboo and *Angst*, revealing – be it implicitly or explicitly – the makeshift quality of this attempt at synthetic self-insulation.

Self as structure. Human beings are beings who exist within, and are constituted by, a specific language, a language which is generated and maintained by a language-using social community. One's understanding of oneself, in its verbally articulated form at least, emerges from a process of communication and social interaction, and is indissociable from the organized community and the concomitant system of social meanings presupposed by thought itself. My self-awareness is thus a function of a network of determinant social institutions and is defined by the nexus of commitments and beliefs that determine what is of importance to me, what I value and endorse in concrete interactive situations. As Charles Taylor expresses it, knowing who I am is a matter of knowing where I stand, of being capable of taking a stand.[1] Our sense of self exists as a framework of values and is crucially bound up with a sense of what is good: "To know who you are is to be oriented in moral space, a space in which questions arise about what is good or bad, what is worth doing and what not, what has meaning and importance for you and what is trivial and secondary."[2] The spatial metaphor used here is not without significance, given that boundaries and borders are at issue: our self-definition is a fixing of frontiers. Taylor takes this moral space, with its accompanying commitments and evaluations, to be "onto-logically basic": a person lacking such a framework altogether would be seen as pathological, "outside our space of interlocution."[3]

What *sort* of commitments, then, are of relevance to our self-interpretation? Taylor writes:

> People may see their identity as defined partly by some moral or spiritual commitment, say as a Catholic, or an anarchist. Or they may define it in part by the nation or tradition they belong to, as an Armenian, say, or a Quebecois. What they are saying by this is not just that they are strongly attached to this spiritual view or background; rather it is that this provides the frame within which they can determine where they stand on questions of what is good, or worthwhile, or admirable, or of value. Put counterfactually, they are saying that were they to lose this commitment or identification, they would be at sea, as it were.[4]

In such instances it is one's *group* identity that is at stake, be this based on class, religion, gender, ethical or political adherence, or ethnic or national origin: a sense of self is maintained at the cost of distinguishing oneself from others. In these terms, two levels of self-differentiation are possible. Within the system of orientation, we can define ourselves through our opposition to contradictory commitments. At a deeper level, we may see ourselves as being different from the pathological "outsider," the madman or monster foreign not just to *our* moral space but to moral space in general. This outsider exists – if at all – as a fictive embodiment of chaos, as the devil or rogue-trickster of certain mythologies. The second chapter of this essay focuses on laughter insofar as it may constitute an act of self-assertion in the face both of those with different "identities" from the person laughing (different communal and spiritual allegiances) and of certain fictive incarnations of more general human or semi-human non-identity, those fools, demons and scapegoats representative of primeval non-differentiation.

The idea that our self is a matter of self-interpretation and that this is a function of the language in which it is necessarily couched, coupled with the structuralist notion that language is but a structure of differences without positive terms, has led to a tendency to see the self as (at best) purely relational: "once the conscious subject is deprived of its role as source of meaning – once meaning is explained in terms of conventional systems which may escape the grasp of the conscious subject – the self can no longer be identified with consciousness. It is 'dissolved' as its functions are taken up by a variety of inter-personal systems that operate through it."[5] The French tradition of social anthropology in particular has tended to regard individual selves more as a product of common life than as its determinant and (following Marx) individualism itself as but the ideology of the bourgeoisie. Yet individualism may have its good points too, for it draws attention to a perspective necessary to counter arid anti-humanism. And indeed, the structures of signification exist nowhere but in the minds of the physiologically autonomous human beings who make up the system. While consciousness is therefore inconceivable without a structured network of oppositions and differences, this is not a sufficient condition for its presence. As a purely relational entity, it would have no criteria for recognition of itself *as* itself. Cognition depends upon precisely this *re*-cognition, i.e. upon the recurrence of an identity and the perception of something *as* something.

Self as individual. The human self is thus necessarily both existent and relational. On the one hand, any experience of the world is an interpretative activity founded in the language that the person uses, and the language-user's self-interpretation – or sense of self – is accordingly at the mercy of the modifications and revisions perpetually undergone by the language in question. On the other, those very changes are a direct consequence of the actual deployment of the language by existing individuals. In a chain of circular interdependence, the social whole determines the individual part, who in turn affects the social whole, which determines the individual part...

Julia Kristeva has pinpointed what she terms the *negativity* of the subject as the force galvanizing this ongoing process, "that negativity – drive-governed, but also social, political and historical – which rends and renews the social code."[6] It is a question here of negating the bounds of the system, subverting existent significations, of transgressing and transcending the static structures of meaning. Notably, this "transgressive" reinvigoration has its roots in the human body: "biological operations, ... though invariably subject to the signifying and/or social codes, ... infringe the code in the direction of allowing the subject to get pleasure from it, renew it, even endanger it."[7] The American philosopher George Herbert Mead drew a distinction between the "me," which is the organized set of social attitudes assumed by the individual, and the "I," which is the response of the organism to these attitudes. Both aspects are equally essential to a full expression of the self: any person must adopt the attitudes of the others in the community and enter into a relationship with those others in order to belong to that community as a rational citizen; equally, however, that very interaction entails perpetually reacting to the social attitudes and in this way changing the community of which one is a part.[8] Although the "I" is the agent of negativity, of change and novelty, in Mead's conceptual schema it is a much more rational and less hedonistically transgressive force than Kristeva's subject. To the extent that we *all* as thinking beings have this capacity to react back on the social system which we in a sense embody, moreover, it is only a matter of degree separating us from those great minds whose revolutionary responses to the community's existing thought-systems produce more profound changes. The very act of speaking – a concrete instantiation of the otherwise timelessly abstract structures – indeed means that language is in a process of perpetual renewal. It is constantly being re-deployed in novel contexts and innovatory forms, however unobtrusive this renewal may be. It simply cannot stand still. Again, the relationship of whole and part, society and individual, is one of circular interdependence: "The response of the 'I' involves adaptation, but an adaptation which affects not only the self but also the social environment which helps to constitute the self; that is, it implies a view of evolution in which the individual affects its own environment as well as being affected by it."[9] Which comes first, chicken or egg, whole or part? Yes.

The idea of the self as an individuated organism with a certain sort of autonomy should not be confused with the tradition of individualism. The fact of the human being's separateness from the rest of the beings who make up the system of which he also forms a part is not the same as, and need not in itself imply, any *awareness* of individuality, nor of human particularity and uniqueness. Modern individualism is a culture-specific phenomenon, indissoluble from a whole ideological system, an entire network of economic, historic, social and intellectual circumstances. Stressing that each individual is unique and that this uniqueness is morally significant, individualism as a creed implies a system of values, tending to set store by independence as a moral good and to encourage introspective self-exploration and personal commitment. Modern culture has spawned a brand of individualism in which the human person finds his or her identity by, in the words of Taylor, "declaring independence from the webs of interlocution which have originally formed him/her, or at least neutralizing them."[10] Precisely as a tradition, however, individualism has become cripplingly self-defeating, mass-producing its individualists as stereotypical clones. This over-emphasis on "being oneself" corresponds to the loss of a pre-modern unity of individual and symbolic universes implicit in such belief-systems as totemism, which conceive the individual as part of a powerful *collective* reality incorporating living members of the community, dead ancestors, animals and plants. Modern individualism by contrast sees in this an infringement, if not the destruction, of human uniqueness, and regards the social structures as conducive to alienation rather than to any enrichment of the single identity through identification with the transindividual.

The individualistic tendency has not been irrelevant to the question of comedy, for it has entailed a much greater willingness to assert oneself in opposition to the community, and accordingly to *identify* with those fictive figures who embody such opposition. The third chapter of this essay shows the comedy arising from this category of self-assertion, which may come in a number of forms, including (a) rational, satirical criticism of a society viewed as corrupt or irrational, (b) humour associated with identificatory participation in a subculture or an excluded or disadvantaged social group, and (c) identification with the general representatives of disorder (already encountered as scapegoats to be expelled from the community as potentially subversive) or mockery of the general representatives of order and authority (such as the police). All these forms are inherently ambiguous. The "anti-social" impulse of the first is often an expression of deeply felt social commitments, as regards – for example – justice or human dignity. The second, though defined in opposition to the social whole, is not really a matter of "individualism," since the identity in question is still collective, albeit but a part (or sub-whole) in relation to the community in its entirety. Identification with disorderly figures is just as equivocal. While they may on the one hand be laden with negative signification (as a threat to communal well-being), their apparent independence from any cultural restraint may equally come to represent an idealized individualism or periodic (and thus delimited or controlled) festive transgression. More likely, in fact, is that our reactions to such anarchic figures as Falstaff or Panurge hover between the two poles, an ambivalence of attraction and repulsion, enjoyment and fear.

Self as body. Individuality has been seen to be intimately connected to the autonomy of the living organism; in its turn, bodily existence can itself be understood as a necessary (though not sufficient) condition for having a sense of self. The thinking subject cannot ultimately be divorced from its physical incarnation, as tended to be the case with the pure, rational, bloodless subjects of Enlightenment thought; on the contrary, it is always embodied, a subject-in-the-world, a "body-subject," whose experience of the world is understandable only within the context of a manipulative and perceptive body, and whose experience of this body is only understandable within the context of a world perceived and manipulated by it. The subject does not observe the world as a disinterested spectator, but is constantly acting within it and interacting with it as one physical body among many.[11]

The identification of the self with its body is of course not unproblematic. If I am my body, then am I all of it? If so, what about my wooden limb and my hook? Aren't some parts of my body more essential to my identity than others? Surely I could dispense with my pancreas, my colon, my heart, indeed with any part of my body except my brain, without ceasing to be *me*. Certainly, my consciousness seems so intimately bound up with my brain as to make this appear the most indispensable portion of my body. What I am, it can be argued, is whatever explains the psychological continuity of my mental life: as it is the activities of my brain which account for my mental activities, then I *am* my brain. On such a view, the criterion of my personal identity over time is the spatio-temporal physical continuity of this extraordinarily sophisticated porridge-like glob in my cranium. Of course, I am not only my brain. As Thomas Nagel writes, "I weigh more than three pounds, am more than six inches high, have a skeleton, etc. But the brain is the only part of me whose destruction I could not possibly survive. The brain, but not the rest of the animal, is essential to the self." [12] Nagel does not present this as an analysis of our self-awareness but as an empirical hypothesis about the true nature of the self. I may not know these conditions of my identity; I may not realize that I am my brain, instead believing that my liver or my kidney is where my "soul" resides. Yet this need in no way prevent us from meaningfully applying the term "I" to ourselves or from having a sense of self. We simply do not know everything about the nature of the referent.

If I am my brain, regardless of my awareness of the fact, then need I be *all* of my brain? Is it not possible to be a little more specific about the seat of my consciousness? Neurophysiological speculations have varied widely on this point. A holistic approach emphasizes the difficulties of localizing functions within the brain, claiming instead that every brain region partakes in almost all cerebral functions. Experimental evidence, however, has suggested that consciousness might be a manifestation of the activity of the upper brain stem (in communication with some region of the cerebral cortex), or attributable to the reticular formation (the section of the brain accountable for its general state of alertness), to the hippocampus (central to the storage of long-term memories), or even to the cerebral cortex itself. If speech is regarded as crucial to human intelligence, moreover, then the left cerebral cortex (where the speech centres are sited) is likely to be privileged over the right-hand side of the brain. Yet an excessive zeal in localizing functions may prove misguided. While the cerebral cortex certainly does have distinct parts playing various roles, there is a great deal of interaction between these parts as well as with the rest of the brain: the diverse centres perform different functions, but this is within the self-maintaining activity of a single interacting community. [13]

Certain proponents of artificial intelligence, however, would claim that we can understand the mind without *any* reference to the biology of the brain. Mental operations are describable instead as a sequence of computational processes in a *formal* programme. On the assumptions of such "strong" artificial intelligence, "the mind is to the brain as the program is to the hardware." [14] I am not my brain so much as a formal pattern which happens to be instantiated in it. And indeed the brain does comprise tens of billions of neurons firing away, none of which in itself has a clue as to the "meaning" of what is going on in my mind. The experiences, thoughts and volitions that I have, it is argued, require explanation on a higher level than the hardware level of individual neurons, on a level which touches neither the biochemical processes of the brain nor its physical constitution, but the software, the "programme," the formal organization. The implication here is that "where mind is concerned, the brain doesn't matter.... What matters are programs, and programs are independent of their realization in machines."[15] Mind is thus conceived in formal terms as an algorithm or calculational procedure, and mental activity as nothing more than the execution of a well-defined sequence of operations.

As the American philosopher John Searle objects, a dichotomy is thus prized open between form and substance, programme and instantiation, an age-old dualism rearing its head in a new guise. Searle writes: "If mental operations consist in computational operations on formal symbols, then it follows that they have no interesting connection with the brain; the only connection would be that the brain just happens to be one of the indefinitely many types of machines capable of instantiating the program." For Searle, the working of the mind "is a biological phenomenon, and it is as likely to be as causally dependent on the specific biochemistry of its origins as lactation, photosynthesis, or any other biological phenomena."[16] Indeed, any reductionistic approach which ignores either the physiological, morphological or biochemical modes of understanding the brain in the name of an information-processing model will ultimately fail to do justice to the extraordinary complexity of what is above all a *living* system with a capacity not simply to store information but to learn inductively from experience and to *use* its information to adapt to its environment and maintain itself as a cognitive system.[17] While the proponents of artificial intelligence may claim that the formal or logical structure is what is essential to mind (and mind's relationship to its cerebral embodiment is purely contingent), scientists such as Roger Penrose counter that something about the brain itself helps to explain mind as something which is not just algorithmic. Algorithms do not explain everything about consciousness, Penrose claims, for they are unable ever to ascertain *truth*: the concept of mathematical truth, for example, can never be encapsulated in any formalistic scheme, instead needing something like insight.[18]

Whether or not intelligence in itself can in some manner be refined or distilled to a purely formal, software property, what does seem beyond question is that *human* consciousness necessarily implies a complementarity of the substantial and the formal, the neural and the mental, the brain matter and the pattern. For all the relational qualities inherent in it, human consciousness is *in fact* a brain-bound phenomenon, and although intelligence could conceivably (though infinitely improbably) be transferred into some isomorphic formal system in another physical medium based on electric wiring or exceedingly convoluted stacks of toilet rolls, it would then – obviously enough – cease to be *human* consciousness. Perhaps it is this complementarity which has contributed as much as anything to our schizoid sense of ourselves as both minds and bodies and has tended to encourage a vision of our "soul" or "essence" as in some way non-localizable, and possibly even detachable from our body. The logical possibility of having a perfectly well-developed sense of self without realizing its empirical rootedness in the brain or in any specific organ of the body, together with this illusion of detachability or of a pure disembodied subject, has begot a situation in which my body itself occupies a deeply ambivalent, transitional or mediatory position between "me" and the world. On the one hand it "belongs" to me; on the other it is but one object among an infinitude of others in the world and is as such exposed to the inquisitive or hostile gaze of other people in a way that my "private" self, my innermost thoughts, are not. My "real" self, it might seem, can retreat to some non-localizable cranny of my cranium, sulking anti-socially in order to be alone with its thoughts. Or assuming that I am – in Nagel's sense – my brain and not something else detachable and impossible to pin down, then the rest of my body is still lumbered with a fundamental ambiguity, and is at best only marginally me. Indeed, even if a healthy holism would grant that I am my *whole* body, however fluid and transient this may be, then what about my fingernails, my toenails, the bits of dirt in the corners of them, and all the gunk churning around in my digestive tract? Of course, I may dissociate myself from the grime attached to me, perhaps therefore washing now and again, but where do we draw the line? And what about the way other people see me? Greasy hair might well be seen as an essential component of my identity and identifiability. The sixth chapter of this essay is concerned with the extent to which comedy and laughter constitute an act of assertion (and of insecurity) in the face of the ambivalence of our bodies and their interaction with the rest of the world. It will focus on the margins of the human creature, exploring in particular some of the nooks and crannies mediating self and non-self.

Self as persona. The English philosopher P. F. Strawson also emphasizes the significance of the body in the concept of a person, remarking on the strange fact that one's states of consciousness ("I can see red") are attributed to the very same thing as certain corporeal characteristics and a given physical situation ("I am in my room wearing a baggy jumper"). Strawson maintains that the subject to which we ascribe properties implying consciousness is in fact *identical* with the subject to which we ascribe physical properties. Particular states of consciousness or experiences can only be meaningfully referred to insofar as they are the states or experiences of a person *identifiable* within the spatio-temporal continuum: "States, or experiences, one might say, *owe* their identity as particulars to the identity of the person whose states or experiences they are." [19] Cartesian conceptions of oneself as composed of both a physical and a mental substance are thus derivative or secondary, Strawson argues, depending upon a prior conception of oneself as a *person* with both physical and mental attributes, and the concept of a person is in these terms an unanalysable primitive concept entailing the logical identity of subject and body. It requires subsequent intellectual gymnastics to wrench them apart.

The self is thus inherently identifiable, and its identifiability is inherently bodily. It does not, like a disembodied subject, logically or chronologically precede an objective world and a social community external to itself which it then proceeds to reconnoitre, experience and explore. Even before articulation and conscious reflection, the self is a body-subject which is inseparably involved with other things and other people, and its experience of itself is always acquired via the mediation of its interaction with non-selves. Accordingly, our bodily identifiability is not simply the identifiability of a static material entity, but that of a developing complex of dispositions and behavioural tendencies. We learn the language that allows us to interpret ourselves and the world by being engaged in a process of ongoing interlocution with those who bring us up, and my self develops in dynamic interaction with and in relation to those who share my language. As Taylor points out, selfhood is never atomic and autonomous, but only evolves in relation to certain interlocutors. The social significance of *naming* exemplifies the proximity of identity, identifiability and interlocution: "My name is what I am 'called.' A human being *has* to have a name, because he or she has to be *called*, i.e. addressed. Being called into conversation is a precondition of developing a human identity, and so my name is (usually) given me by my earliest interlocutors." [20] As the most fundamental token of identifiability, a name is essential to our sense of being a person.

The subject experiences itself not directly and in a vacuum but via the mirror of intersubjectivity, seeing itself from the standpoints of individual or collective others. My self-understanding is a function of my understanding of how others understand me, just as my self-naming is a function of what others have named me. Underlying this interdependence of self and other is the non-thematic mimesis structuring our actions from infancy onwards. Our development from babyhood through to adulthood incorporates this imitation and adoption of the roles and attitudes observed in others, including in particular those attitudes pertaining to ourselves. Just as I am identifiable by, and in a sense I am, the name I have been given (and when introducing myself I can truthfully say "I am R.G."), so I am (identifiable by) a peculiar bundle of gestures, attitudes and roles I have mimetically picked up over the years. Even my ability to react negatively or critically to the roles I have – largely unwittingly – been assigned by others can be understood as just another gesture I have learnt; even our thematic self-spectatorship, our introspection and self-exploration, is but another performance.

This perspective has a natural tendency to turn all human doings into a matter of role-playing, exposing the notion of a person's inner or private core as an illusion (for even this inner self can be analysed without remainder into a sequence of social roles). This omnipresent role-playing includes such obvious aspects of ourselves as our profession or vocation (or absence thereof), our social and cultural functions (as parent, lover, neighbour, friend), or our attitudes and beliefs (or absence thereof). It may, moreover, be taken as covering aspects often deemed biologically determined. Freudian psychoanalysis regards our sexual identity, for example, as a socially conditioned function, an unstable position within a network of interaction which is culturally established during the process of the child's insertion into social reality. That our sexual identity is a sort of role has special relevance in the realm of comedy.

As the Cynics recognized a couple of millenia ago, man is an actor, necessarily and unremittingly so. For all its usefulness and aptness, the extreme version of this metaphor can of course be fatally debilitating in its tendency to obscure human *potential*, potential not only to perform in life's drama, nor even to be a spectator, but also to assume some of the responsibilities of a producer, choosing precisely which roles are to be played and what course the action is to take. Regardless of existential possibilities for spontaneity, improvization and choice, however, the point here is that our concept of self is inextricably related to our *persona*, to the roles we are seen to play and we see ourselves as playing, the functions we are seen to fulfil and we see ourselves as fulfilling, the identity by which we are identifiable to others and by which we identify ourselves. We are defined by our situation within a community of other persons and by our difference from them, be this in terms of name, rank, gender, disposition, bodily characteristics, or a whole host of further identificatory criteria.

It may here be countered that this line of argument entails a confusion between identification and identity, between the evidence or criteria employed to discern personal identity and the question of what this is evidence *for*. In the words of Colin McGinn, "there is no guarantee that what we actually use as evidential signs of personal identity will coincide with that which these are signs of. To take an extreme example in which these come apart: we can imagine a society in which judgements of personal identity were always made on the basis of documents the people carried around with them; these documents would be criteria in the epistemological sense, but they are obviously not criteria in the metaphysical sense – or else we would have to say that selves are constituted of documents!"[21] Yet although documents (of all identificatory criteria) stand in the most purely contingent relationship to what we like to regard ourselves as being, even here there is a sense in which we can truthfully – if metaphorically – point to our passport photo and say "That's me!" Indeed, apparently extraneous personal clobber may come to be understood as a part of my identity in much the same way that my favourite tatty pullover, my tattoo or my nose-ring are: they are features by which I allow myself to be recognized. For such a deeply reflexive entity as the self, the distinction between epistemological and metaphysical notions of identity, between criteria for identity and what this identity consists in, becomes too shaky to be applicable. There is an important sense in which a human identity *is* what it identifies itself and others identify it as being.

The eighth chapter of this essay looks at the comedy which may be generated from role-playing, role-swapping, and play with the criteria of identification. While popular festivity – with all its disguise and travesty – sanctions a periodic (and therefore controlled and delimited) swapping of identities, comedy portrays both intentional role-play and the potentially more traumatic or unsettling experience of involuntary identity-loss and mis-recognition. The spectator generally remains protected from the chaos by the reassuring privilege of knowing better and identifying the characters for who they really are.

Self as living organism. The self is not just an inert body, nor is it merely a (changeable) set of identificatory criteria. Self-evidently enough, a sense of self is characteristic of an entity which is *alive* and as such engaged in continual struggle against its opposite, lifelessness. As a living being, therefore, the self is defined by the temporal boundaries separating it from non-being, i.e. by its conception and its death. For all its awesome aspects, it is indeed the possibility of not being which lends being/life its significance, and which generates an existential awareness of what it *means* to be. According to the German philosopher Heidegger, the authentic mode of such awareness is "Being-Towards-Death," which entails not so much a fear (*Furcht*) of actually dying nor gloomily introspective ponderings on the act of popping one's clogs as anxiety or *Angst* in response to the ineluctable possibility of non-existence.[22] In the fifth chapter of this essay, it is the temporal gateways into and out of non-existence – death and sex – which are the objects of attention. The chapter explores how laughter and humour may serve as both a symptom and an overcoming of the *Angst* (or the sheer unphilosophical fear) to which we are prey in the face of these ambivalent margins to our existence, and how the genre of comedy has traditionally embodied a ritualistic triumph over death itself.

But what is the nature of this fight against death, this incessant battle to stay alive? Though seemingly digressive, a brief glance at this question is not amiss, especially as it will prove useful in the subsequent accounts of the self in its capacity as a cognitive being and a rational agent. Keeping alive consists, physically speaking, in continually lowering the disorder or entropy that is within ourselves. The Second Law of Thermodynamics dictates that disorder – quantified in the notion of entropy – is always on the rise over time; if a physical system is isolated from its surroundings, the entropy will necessarily increase until it can go no higher. After this there will be no further change, for the system will have settled in a condition of what is termed "thermodynamic equilibrium." Take a system of gas molecules in some sort of container, all initially confined to one side of the container by a partition. On the removal of the partition, the molecules will tend to space out and fill both halves of the container. The reverse of this process is infinitely improbable (for it would require infinite information to reverse all the changes). This natural proclivity towards disorder can thus be understood as a movement from low-probability to high-probability situations. The quintessential characteristic of life, by contrast, is *order*, for complex living organisms comprise a mind-bogglingly unlikely organization of matter and energy. As such, the workings of brains and the evolution of ever more complicated and highly structured organisms during the earth's history constitute an increase in order which would seem to be in direct conflict with the implacable tendency towards disorder implied by the Second Law.

Yet the contradiction is only apparent. The law of entropy applies only to the *total* system, and there is nothing to prevent an increase in order in one part of a system (say, in one part of a system such as the universe) provided that this is compensated by sufficient disorder elsewhere. One of the absolutely key features of living systems is that they are "open" to their surroundings, existing in perpetual interchange of energy and material with the environment and maintaining themselves by the processes of metabolism and homeostasis. In the words of the scientist Ilya Prigogine:

> When we examine a biological cell or a city, ...the situation is quite different [from isolated systems in equilibrium]: not only are these systems open, but also they exist only because they are open. They feed on the flux of matter and energy coming to them from the outside world. We can isolate a crystal, but cities and cells die when cut off from their environment. They form an integral part of the world from which they draw sustenance, and they cannot be separated from the fluxes that they incessantly transform.[23]

It is this openness that permits the growth or maintenance of order in the organism at the cost of increased entropy in the surroundings.

When we are metabolizing food, for example, it is not so much that we are *acquiring* energy – since energy is conserved and in practice remains roughly constant during adulthood – as that we are *replacing* the energy that we continually dissipate in the disordered, high-entropy form of heat; energy is imbibed in a low-entropy form (as food and oxygen) in order to be "dumped" in a disordered form as heat, carbon dioxide or excreta. The quantum physicist Erwin Schrödinger has referred to an organism's "astonishing gift of concentrating a 'stream of order' on itself and thus escaping the decay into atomic chaos – of 'drinking orderliness' from a suitable environment."[24] By eating and excreting, breathing in and breathing out, we prevent the disorder in our bodies from rising and thus maintain our inner organization. Life is a fight against entropy, an ongoing war against the disorder encroaching upon us from within and without.

Living organisms must accordingly be kept in a state far from thermodynamic equilibrium (for equilibrium precludes the dynamic interaction intrinsic to life). It is the organism's openness to the environment that holds it in this condition of disequilibrium, enabling the disorder generated by the system to be exported to the environment and thereby permitting the maintenance of organization within itself. The living being is in this way fundamentally dependent upon what is external to it, in a sense "incorporating" it in the form of a lack or a need. The idea seems to have been intuited by Hegel, who uses the term "negativity" to designate "the pulsation inherent in all self-movement and animation."[25] It is because it embodies and is constituted by a lack or imbalance that the self-moving organism is impelled to change and to interact with what is around it: "a thing is only alive insofar as it contains its contradiction within itself and indeed consists in this power to embrace and endure this contradiction."[26] If it is unable to maintain this negativity – this imbalance – within itself, then it goes to ground.

Dependent upon its own state of disequilibrium and perpetually open to the threat of disorder, the living organism embodies a reflexive propensity to uphold the order within itself. Yet this property of "self-organization" is by no means exclusive to animal organisms. Take what happens when a pipe pours oil – smoothly at first – into a large industrial basin: if the tap is progressively opened so that more and more oil flows in, the effect is increasing turbulence and randomly proliferating fluctuations. The surface of the liquid seems ever more chaotic. At a critical juncture however – a so-called bifurcation point – one of these fluctuations will fan out and become amplified in such a manner that it ends up dominating the whole system. What had seemed to be mere chaos has given birth to the order of a whirlpool. When a system is forced away from thermodynamic equilibrium, that is, it does not simply break down. Instead, new orders emerge, patterns which can best be modelled not by traditional linear mathematical equations but by

nonlinear ones incorporating the element of *feedback* (where the output
is fed back into the equation as new input).

Ilya Prigogine regards the principles underlying the simpler
examples of self-organization, be it in fluid motions or in certain
chemical reactions (such as the Belousov-Zhabotinsky reaction), as lying
at the heart of organic life itself. Fundamental is that when the system in
question is driven from thermodynamic equilibrium it becomes
unstable, but may then spontaneously – through inner dynamics – tend
towards large-scale self-organization. Prigogine has coined the term
"dissipative structure" to denote such an entity, by which he means a
system that is able to maintain its identity by a process of dynamic
interaction with the flux of its environment: "What seems certain is that
these far-from-equilibrium phenomena illustrate an essential and
unexpected property of matter: physics may henceforth describe
structures as adapted to outside conditions. We meet in rather simple
chemical systems a kind of pre-biological adaptation mechanism. To use
somewhat anthropomorphic language: in equilibrium matter is 'blind,'
but in far-from-equilibrium conditions it begins to be able to perceive,
to 'take into account,' in its way of functioning, differences in the
external world."[27] It is perhaps far-fetched to apply notions of adaptivity
to turbulent flow in a liquid, which after all never produces the sort of
schema or algorithmic compression of information that would enable it
to predict or anticipate future developments in the environment.
Nonetheless, if Prigogine is correct, then the self-organization of
complex biological systems (including human beings) is but an
astonishingly sophisticated version of analogous self-organizing
phenomena such as vortices in fluid motion and chemical clocks. Living
systems lie at the "complex" end of a whole spectrum of open systems.

The circularity implicit in the idea of self-organization can indeed be
applied equally feasibly to the concept of life itself. Animals and even
plants, writes J. Z. Young, "are *agents*, provided with targets and a
remarkably strong inner motor tendency that causes them continually to
strive to achieve the aim of remaining alive." In other words, living
organisms are systems that have the property of acting purposefully,
their purpose being to stay organized, to preserve the distinctive
organization of themselves and their kind.[28] Of course, the idea that the
purpose of life is to maintain life tells us as much and as little about
"what life is" as the concept of self-organization betrays what the "self"
is that is organizing and being organized, or as our initial definition of
the "self" (as something conscious of itself as itself) reveals what that
self is. But it does seem to be at least half the story.

The biologist Humberto Maturana has employed a correspondingly
circular term – that of autopoiesis – to describe cognitive systems in
general. An autopoietic system, according to Maturana, is one which
defines its boundaries through the continuous maintenance of its own

autopoietic organization.[29] Clearly the notion of circularity is paramount: "the living organization is a circular organization which secures the production or maintenance of the *components* that specify it in such a manner that the product of their functioning is the very same organization that produces them." Or again, "a living system defines through its organization the domain of all interactions into which it can possibly enter without losing its identity, and it maintains its identity only as long as the basic circularity that defines it as a unit of interactions remains unbroken."[30] It is irrelevant whether every other measurable property of the system changes in the course of its continuing adaptation to the environment. If its circularity is upheld, *it* survives. If the circularity is disrupted, the system's unity disintegrates and the organism dies.

It is the criterion of circular self-maintenance which implies at least a capacity in the system for *adapting* to its circumstances. As Maturana explains, a plastic, autopoietic system, whose structure can change over time while its identity remains, must necessarily develop or evolve in such a way that its activities are properly coupled to its medium. If not, it will die. A cognitive system is thus an inductive system, functioning predictively and repeating only what works, on the principle that what has happened once will happen again.[31] Such adaptability may work either through learning or through evolution, according as the relevance of our behaviour for self-maintenance is a function of the history of interactions of the particular organism or the evolutionary history of the species. Living organisms combat the tendency towards disorder, that is, both by the use of inherited codes of genetic information embodied in the "memories" of the DNA (which is responsible for the formation of protein molecules and thus for making the organism perform the same activities that have kept it alive in the past and will therefore probably continue to do so in the future) and by means of the neural memories of the brain, which likewise consist of coded stores of information directing future conduct in the light of past experience. The difference is that our brain memory provides us with instructions in response to more recent experiences than our genetic one does.

Cognition is life's trump card versus death, the key to the self-definition and self-maintenance of living organisms. Cognitive processes have been described as "[buying] information with energy" and in this way cocking a snook at the natural world of normal physics;[32] in the words of Maturana, "living systems are cognitive systems, and living, as a process, is a process of cognition."[33] This applies to individual cells and human beings alike. Cognition, which is also *re-*cognition, is vital even at the level of cellular and subcellular biology, where the continued existence of a bacterium (for example) depends on precisely this ability to distinguish its own DNA from that of viral attackers, and to annihilate the DNA which is not appropriately labelled. On such recognition hinges its survival.

Self as numerical identity and rational agent. Maturana describes a cognitive system as one "whose organization defines a domain of interactions in which it can act with relevance to the maintenance of itself" and the process of cognition as "the actual (inductive) acting or behaving in this domain."[34] This circular understanding of life in terms of the maintenance of life is expressive of a long-recognized affinity between life, cognition and self-maintenance. Locke defined the self as "that conscious thinking thing ... which is sensible or conscious of pleasure and pain, capable of happiness or misery, and so is concerned for itself, as far as that consciousness extends."[35] And as Nozick points out, this concern of a self for itself is a specially reflexive sort of concern. In this it forms a significant contrast with such feelings as self-hatred:

> It is not that the self cares especially for itself as a bearer of some non-self-reflexive property, as an especially sterling example of some general property that it happens to have. The self cares especially for itself as itself; I care especially for myself as me. In contrast, self-hatred ... always is based on the self's possession of some denigrated property that is non-self-reflexive (which the self knows reflexively that it has); in self-hatred, the self does not hate itself as itself, but as a possessor of some undesirable (nonreflexive) trait.[36]

This deeply reflexive caring is in a sense gratuitous and purposeless. I care for myself as myself, not because I like myself. I care for myself because that is who I am. I care about my identity because I care about myself. The relation is as immediate and as reflexively circular as my consciousness of myself.

This reflexive caring is evidently connected to the idea of "self-interest" often judged to lie at the heart of rationality. In this respect the self – insofar as it is a self-maintaining cognitive system – is concomitantly a *rational* being. Clearly this concept of rationality cannot be justified by any form of meta-rationality from above ("self-interest is rational because..."). Like induction, it can only be "justified" in circular fashion, by pointing to its success. If we were definitionally incapable of using induction to predict and adapt to our circumstances, even the lowest levels of cognition would be ruled out; if we did not (in some manner) care for ourselves, the whole question of rationality would simply not arise. While an understanding of rationality in terms of self-interest means that it is not a specifically human quality, even primitive self-interest does presuppose the presence of some sort of innate, functional sense of self, for there cannot be self-interest without some distinction between self and non-self. Even the lowliest of creatures must be designed to behave in its own interests, exhibiting rudimentary protective impulses which stop it from eating or savaging itself. Evolutionary forces would otherwise be quick to do away with such kamikaze creatures. Be it bird, bat or baboon, the organism must somehow be able to make a reliable distinction between behaviour that would entail its own destruction and behaviour that would not. It must be able to differentiate between self and other simply in order to be able to favour itself in the course of life's incessant struggle against being chewed up, trodden on or swatted. The very lowest levels of cognition presuppose this pre-articulatory "concept" of a self, and as with consciousness, it is presumably a matter of taste (and anthropocentric pride) just how far down the biological ladder we go before balking at attributing this low-level rationality to a particular organism.

The theory of self-interest is not, strictly speaking, a biological postulate (about what we do do) but a theory about rationality (about what we have most reason to do). It dictates, for example, that (i) for each person, the one supremely rational ultimate aim is that his or her life go as well as possible for him or her; (ii) we each have most reason to do whatever would be best for ourselves; or (iii) it is irrational to do what one believes will be worse for oneself.[37] Insofar as human individuals act in their own interests, it would be claimed, they are acting rationally. Such a contention can be challenged in particular from the direction of morality, a moral theory such as consequentialism telling us that what we have most reason to do is whatever produces the best possible outcomes for everyone, not just ourselves. Whereas the latter is a collective code, the self-interest theory is about *individual* rationality. Being rational amounts to looking after number one. Yet this need not imply conscious decision-taking. The idea that rationality entails a reflective weighing up of a series of alternative modes of behaviour, followed by deliberation and choice, is the product of one specific rationalistic understanding of mind. While it may correspond to certain circumstances, it is unlikely to be applicable to many others. As often as not, rational action proceeds without involving conscious choice.

Nonetheless, the view that rationality consists simply in being able to steer one's action in a strategic or ostensibly purposive way does seem to miss out something vital as far as specifically *human* rationality is concerned. This is not just conformity to a rule of behaviour (such as self-interest or altruism); it includes an ability to formulate the rules that are to be conformed to. As such it is essentially bonded to the human power of speech. Thus arises a possible distinction between "having reasons" and "giving reasons." A slug *has* a reason for avoiding the Dr. Martens boot bearing down on it, yet only human beings are able to *give* or articulate reasons for the avoidance of contact with such a moving object. It might be countered that it is dangerously anthropomorphic to talk of a slug even having reasons: its behaviour can be explained purely mechanically, as a pattern of stimulus and response, rather than teleologically, as oriented towards a goal. This is both right and wrong.

True, the slug's reaction does constitute a series of links in a chain of causality, and it can be conceived in terms of sensory stimulus, neural activity and behavioural response – but so can human behaviour, in theory at least. On a different level of description, the slug's behaviour can be understood purposively (in terms of self-maintenance), albeit purposiveness of a much simpler and less flexible order than human goal-orientation.

If the essence of human rationality resides in the potential *formulation* of rules, then the possession of concepts is of the uppermost importance. At the same time, however, even the most primitive cognitive self-maintenance must incorporate at least some elementary differential "proto-concept" of selfhood. Evidently, human conceptuality is considerably more sophisticated than this – it is a medium of social communication, it can be vocally articulated, and it is infinitely more versatile in its capacity for learning and the acquisition of new concepts. But the difference is gradual, not absolute. Perhaps the key point as regards the traditional idea of rationality is that human language contains in particular the concept of a reason. Armed with the word "because," we are able to reason about rationality, to rationalize our reasons. Whence the ability not just to have, but to give them. Whence, also, the formal or procedural Enlightenment vision of rationality as an objective and disengaged faculty of discursive reasoning, a facility to think in accordance with certain canons of thought, to pass from premises to conclusion. Related to this, moreover, is the application of ideals of rationality to the realm of individual and collective belief-formation. Accordingly, it is irrational to form a belief that is either unsupported by or in contradiction with the evidence at one's disposal, and even more so to believe something that defies logical or mathematical necessity. Simultaneously believing the truth of a proposition and of its negation is the height of such irrationality.[38] Rational cognition depends upon the fact that if something is true, then it is not the case that it is not true.

This point in fact brings us back to the lowest levels of intelligence and thus to the principles underlying rationality *as a whole*, for even rudimentary cognition engaged in the most basic self-maintenance – although not describable in terms of belief – is fundamentally dependent on the tautological self-identity of its "concepts" or categories. The very possibility of experience presupposes the laws of identity and contradiction: everything is what it is, and if a proposition is true, its negation cannot be true. Once again, the bottom line is that I am what I am, $I = I$. A low-level notion of rationality therefore incorporates two mutually interdependent aspects, the cognitive aspect (behaving consistently, or in accordance with the laws of thought) and the volitional aspect (doing what it is in one's interests to do): if there is a hungry jaw or beak bearing down on me (as a worm or an earwig), then it is not the case that I am in a position of safety, and this will affect what I do. It is specifically human rationality that articulates and pontificates about these reasons and laws.

The association of rationality with self-identity entails that the rational human agent is an essentially unitary entity. If there are two of me, it becomes much more difficult to claim that I am what I am. It is a question here not of the self's *qualitative* identity, which pertains to its identifiability as a phenomenon to be recognized, but its *numerical* identity as one and the same thing.[39] Numerical identity is here synonymous with personal unity, and it is infringement of this unity – a fission in our numerical identity – which makes irrationality interesting. Whereas a model of the self as a rationally integrated unit all of whose states are transparently accessible to a central, panoptical scanner can only account for irrationality as a simple *malfunction*, a self composed of a system of loosely organized and relatively autonomous sub-selves which may fail to communicate allows for possibilities of repeated irrationality based – for example – on constitutional structures independent of any motivational intervention on the part of the whole. Belief in a unified self thus coincides with the belief in an intrinsically rational self which has authority over its actions, and this picture of an integrated unity incorporating a system of beliefs and attitudes is indeed vital to our sense of ourselves as responsible agents. Belief in a self composed of a host of homuncular sub-selves striving to assert themselves within a loose organizational confederacy, by contrast, casts doubt on the role of a sovereign, critical rationality acting in the interests of the entire organism. Yet it is this complex constellation of mental, perceptual or behavioural habits that best explains such phenomena as selective insensitivity and self-manipulative focusing. While the "persona" who says "I" may claim centrality as the mind's sovereign, integrative overseer, this centrality is in all likelihood delusive.[40] In this case, our rational unity is a fiction we foster to cover up an underlying *lack* of psychological integration.

The loss of unity may just as easily be temporal as spatial. If we regard ourselves as made different (from an earlier self) by the passage of time (as suggested by such comments as "I'm a different person from what I was five years ago"), then the foundations of long-term self-interest – and of rationality understood in this sense – can be deeply undermined. Of course, the feeling we have that we change with time is a matter of qualitative as opposed to numerical identity, and the self-difference in question is felt to be a mere fluctuation on the surface of an underlying continuity. But need this be so? Am I *really* the same person I was five years ago? The Scottish sceptic David Hume thought not, arguing that the identical self is but a fictional unity imparted to a bundle of ever- changing experiences. And if we do thus become different with the course of time, then what reason have I to act in the interests of a later, different "me"? Long-term self-interest may be sabotaged in the name of the immediate satisfaction of present aims. This conflict between short-term gratification and long-term prudence indeed lies at the heart of human irrationality. When we do silly but pleasurable things like pump ourselves full of alcohol, nicotine or other drugs, we are implicitly distancing ourselves from (or refusing to identify with) the future self who will suffer the consequences.

As a rational agent, therefore, the self is engaged in maintaining a sense of unity, or in plastering over the cracks in this regulative fiction. The rational human self defines itself by differentiating and holding itself apart from irrationality and loss of integration, the act of definition in itself furthermore implying unity; seeing myself as fundamentally rational, I – the one and only me – dissociate myself from visibly irrational conduct. Self-assertive laughter may consequently be directed at behaviour perceived as irrational, or at rationalizations of such behaviour, where the giving of reasons fails to coincide with the having of reasons. Particularly relevant here is Socrates's insight that the ridiculous has its roots in a lack of self-knowledge. If inner opacity and self-division replace rational transparency, then a comic misrecognition of one's own interests and motivations is inevitable. Normative laughter at irrationality and self-deception may here overlap with simple mockery of stupidity or ignorance. Both bribe the onlookers with collusive ego-boosting; both amount to applause for the onlookers' own superiority. The seventh chapter of this essay focuses not only on self-deceptive irrationality, however, but also on more graphic manifestations of split selves, self-conflict, and the potentially disconcerting sense of personal disunity and identity- loss. At the same time, of course, laughter itself – a collective barking and yelping capable of utterly incapacitating those in its grip – hardly seems a model of rational conduct. Mightn't the oft-mentioned ambivalence of the phenomenon betoken some degree of conscious or subconscious identification with the madness of personality disintegration or proliferation?

Self as subject. Kant approached the question of unity from a slightly different angle, asserting as an epistemological principle that for there to be a series of experiences of an objective realm and an accompanying empirical self-consciousness it must be the case that there is but *one* consciousness doing the experiencing. The diversity of elements inherent in experience must – for each subject of experience – be united in a single consciousness, and the subject of experience must be one and the same in all its workings if it is to be a subject at all. This unity Kant designates the *transcendental unity of apperception*, a much-discussed term which incorporates self-consciousness together with the identity this logically presupposes. If Kant's point sounds tautological, this is because it is so, as Kant himself admitted. But it is a significant tautology. All my experiences as a subject can, according to Kant, be prefixed by the words "ich denke..." or "I think..." (as it is *me* doing the experiencing here), which means above all that I am conscious of my unity and have the faculty of connecting my diverse experiences *as mine*. This pure, impersonal self-consciousness is not to be confused with our empirical self-consciousness, which it underlies as a necessary (though not sufficient) condition. Any *empirical* application of the concept of a numerically identical subject of experiences persisting in time requires – logically enough – empirically applicable criteria as opposed to the formal connectedness of the transcendental unity of apperception.

Kant's reasoning was a response to the scepticism of Hume, for whom the identity of the self was a fiction derived from the causally connected concatenation of perceptions of which we consist: "our notions of personal identity," wrote Hume, "proceed entirely from the smooth and uninterrupted progress of the thought along a train of connected ideas, according to the principles of resemblance, contiguity and causation."[41] The self is a batch of perceptions characterized by certain continuities of content and the constant operation of the uniting principles of resemblance and causality. Yet the two theories are not so widely divergent as has often been assumed: Kant's assertion is primarily that this concatenation presupposes its own identity for its constituent perceptions to be anything more than a meaningless jumble. Without the ability to say "I think..." on different occasions and refer to the same thinking subject (me), the idea of me thinking would be incoherent.[42]

Hume's ideas stress that as a subject – a temporal sequence of perceptions or thoughts – the self is dependent upon the causal relationship holding between the experiences in question. (Indeed both Hume and Kant attributed the category of causality to the knowing subject, the former conceiving of it as a product of mental habit, the latter as an *a priori* condition of thought.) That the need for a sense of causal continuity is essential to our sense of coherent selfhood is borne out in practice by cases of hypnosis, where the victim may be induced to behave like a gibbering fool under the influence of the hypnotic suggestion, yet will afterwards produce spectacular rationalizations and excuses to play down the seeming breach in his or her personal continuity. The subject must protect itself from the inner disorder implied by perceptions which defy causal explanation and which rupture the reassuring causal integration governing "normal" experience. The sight of flying pigs thus prompts us to ask such unnerving questions as "Am I hallucinating or dreaming?" or "Are my senses playing tricks with me?" and is correspondingly unsettling unless we are able to place it safely in an explicatory context, such as a comedy. The fourth chapter of this essay is concerned with comedy as a means of allowing its onlookers to distance themselves from the sight of potentially disconcerting disorder and to overcome the fearsomeness of the inexplicable. German romantics such as A. W. Schlegel even came to see such fantastical or grotesque comedy as a triumph of subjectivity over and against the world. The converse of this latently unsettling comedy is the reassuring predictability afforded by comic repetition, which gives a welcome boost to the spectator's sense of cognitive continuity and generates the pleasures of anticipation and recognition.

Laying the emphasis on the self as a thinking and experiencing subject, it becomes possible to equate personal identity not with physical continuity (of body or brain) but with psychological continuity. This may consist in the continued existence of a purely mental entity, commonly known as a soul, or it may involve the existence of connections or continuity in the *memory*. John Locke saw in memory the essential criterion of personal identity:

> It is plain, consciousness, as far as ever it can be extended, should it be to ages past, unites existences and actions, very remote in time, into the same person, as well as it does the existence and actions of the immediately preceding moment: so that whatever has the consciousness of present and past actions is the same person to whom they both belong. Had I the same consciousness that I saw the ark and Noah's flood, as that I saw an overflowing of the Thames last Winter, or as that I write now, I could no more doubt that I who write this now, that saw the Thames overflowed last winter, and that viewed the flood at the general deluge, was the same self, place that self in what substance you please, than that I who write this am the same myself now whilst I write ... that I was yesterday. [43]

The notion of a self whose identity consists in its consciousness of this identity has not been to every philosopher's taste. As Bishop Butler contended, it is "self-evident that consciousness of personal identity presupposes, and therefore cannot constitute, personal identity, any more than knowledge, in any other case, can constitute truth, which it presupposes." [44] If Butler is right that consciousness of personal identity presupposes personal identity (and this seems at least plausible), then Locke's equation of identity with consciousness takes us on a circular route to the conclusion that consciousness of identity presupposes identity of consciousness or that personal identity is its own presupposition. But again, perhaps such circularity is not inappropriate for so reflexive an entity as self-awareness.

To be sure, Locke's personal identity does fail to give us a criterion for distinguishing true from false memories, as his own thought experiments suggest, nor does it allow for me to be the same person who had experiences I have now forgotten about. And it does seem more in

line with common sense to regard memory as *discovering* rather than
constituting the chain of successive experiences of which our life has
consisted. Yet memory nonetheless appears so vital to our sense of self
that it can perhaps be said – notwithstanding Butler's objection to Locke
– in some way both to discover and to constitute our identity, made up
as this is of a distortive, stylized and embellished narrative which we tell
ourselves (and others) about ourselves and which is notably lacking in
any *inner* criteria for the truth or falsity of its plot. The place of memory
in identity is illustrated most graphically by the effects of Korsakov's
syndrome, a memory disorder reducing its victims to a disconnected
jumble of incoherent experiences. Oliver Sacks gives a moving account
of a certain Mr Thompson:[45]

> Mr Thompson would identify me – misidentify, pseudo-identify me – as
> a dozen different people in the course of five minutes. He would whirl,
> fluently, from one guess, one hypothesis, one belief, to the next, without
> any appearance of uncertainty at any point – he never knew who I was,
> or what and where *he* was, an ex-grocer, with severe Korsakov's, in a
> neurological institution.
>   He remembered nothing for more than a few seconds. He was
> continually disoriented. Abysses of amnesia continually opened beneath
> him, but he would bridge them, nimbly, by fluent confabulations and
> fictions of all kinds. For him they were not fictions, but how he suddenly
> saw, or interpreted, the world.

Yet Mr Thompson is not *aware* of his mythomanic excesses, any more
than of the superficially comic effect his perpetual plot-spinning tends to
have on the people around him. For him, there is nothing the matter.
Less blatantly fictive our memories may be, but most of the rest of us
too remain blithely oblivious to the selective and distortive powers of
our own memory. In itself – as an abstract entity – the subject *must* be
in this position of epistemological invulnerability; it is only through
external criteria, contact with the world and other people, and awareness
of the bounds of possibility, that faulty memories can be modified and
corrected at all.

The reduction of the self to a self-conscious subject of experiences is
a reduction of the self to a punctual core which abstracts from the
spatiality of the body and the structuredness of the social being alike.
Moreover, if the subject is understood merely as one half of the
subject/object opposition, then it is defined by its negative status as *not*
an object and by its exclusion from the order of the objectively
knowable: in other words, the "I" is what refuses to be grasped by
objectivating knowledge, such as that of the natural sciences.
Wittgenstein's assertion that the subject is not a part but a boundary to
the world, as well as his comparison of the "I" with an eye which cannot
see itself but just the field of its vision, likewise conjure the image of a

no-dimensional peeping Tom observing the world through an infinitesimal crack in the partition between the conceivable and the inconceivable, sense and nonsense.

This punctuality or no-dimensionality has additionally contributed to the delusion that there exists a perfectly detachable entity,[46] a soul, that can be distinguished from its embodiment and constitutes a deep further fact about personal identity. The subject's detachment from objective materiality has fostered the picture of an autonomous, rational agency standing in opposition to and in control of physical nature. Criticizing just such a conception of the soul as an individual, non-material, thinking subject, Kant attributes this illusion to a confusion of the necessary unity of experiences (the transcendental unity of apperception) with experience of an immaterial entity which is the unitary subject of all these experiences.[47] Led astray by the former, we wrongly infer that we must each possess a unique, individual soul grounding the unity of our experiences.

While the metaphor of punctuality suggests a no-dimensional or extensionless subject, this subject – as a *succession* of experiences – has also been frequently regarded as one-dimensional, based, that is, in the dimension of *time*. Indeed, one of the traditional Cartesian distinctions between minds and bodies was that whereas physical objects exist both in time and space, minds have no spatial characteristics but exist only in time. Though starting from distinctly un-Cartesian premises, the existentialists Heidegger, Sartre and Merleau-Ponty all emphasize this foundation of subjectivity in "temporality," the latter phrasing it most trenchantly as "I am myself time."[48] All three, moreover, ground this temporality on a conception of the subject as something which is by definition *ecstatic*, in the sense of being "outside itself." Characterized by negativity and lack, the subject is necessarily projected towards what it is not, impelled out of itself towards its other. As consciousness, it is essentially a gap or emptiness, requiring something – an object of thought – for it to come into existence; as volition, it is pre-reflectively oriented towards its future possibilities of action. Again in the words of Merleau-Ponty, "subjectivity is not immobile self-identity: to be subjectivity, it is essential for it, as for time, to open up towards an Other and to go out of itself."[49] So understood, however, "subjectivity" shows constitutional similarities not just in general to those self-organizing, far-from-equilibrium cognitive systems which can only exist in dynamic interaction with the flux of their environment, but to the particular autopoietic system – the brain – in which it is usually understood to be "housed." The transformation of a punctual into a linear self and the introduction of temporality into the picture may cause a marked shift in emphasis from statically tautological self-identity to dynamic imbalance, flow and self-difference.

The Subject in Question

The above-mentioned considerations of temporal flux and dynamic interaction betray once more that the boundary between being and not being oneself may be more problematic than is generally assumed. The following chapter analyzes some of the stumbling blocks encountered at the extremities separating self and other, before moving on to the many sources of division *within* the self, potential fissures between the self and an internalized "other."

Disputed boundaries. The alleged punctuality or linearity of the knowing subject typify the difficulties in question. If I am not spatial, it may be asked, then where am I? One relatively useless answer is that I am here. The truistic unhelpfulness of this response comes from the fact that the word "I" – like the words "here," "this" and "now" – is what is termed a deictic, and its reference thus varies according to context. Just as the place denoted by "here" is a function of *where* the word is used, and the time denoted by "now" depends on *when* it is used, so the person denoted by "I" is contingent on *who* uses it. As a result of their context-dependence, deictics escape translation into objective terms, and a tenseless, fully objective description of the world from no particular point of view must necessarily fail to identify which time is the present and where – among all the people in the world – *I* happen to be. Statements such as "I am R. G." or "It is now 1992" simply do not find a place in such a description. Nonetheless, "being here now" is an absolutely fundamental aspect of our experience of self and world, essential to being an "I" in the most tautologically self-evident sense. This is the way we use the words: the place where I am is always here (i.e. where I am), and the time is always now. As a subject situated in time and space, my inexorably egocentric perspective is a sequence of heres and nows: now I am here, now I am here, now here (yawn)...

Yet not only are such deictics inherently flexible in their reference (meaning that from our own privileged point of view we are all "I"'s), they are also utterly flexible as regards the boundaries of what they denote.[50] Just as the word "here" can refer to anything from this (tummy-) button I am pointing at to this chair, this room, this house, city, county, country, world or solar system, so "now" can refer to this second, this minute, this hour, season, year or millenium. Worse still, our awareness of a "now" is never one of some punctual instant, but of a passage from past to future. As A. N. Whitehead puts it, the instantaneous present is a "non-entity": "What is immediate to self-awareness is a duration. Now a duration has within itself a past and a future."[51] "Now" contains "then" at its margins, and as a duration its bounds are purely arbitrary. "I" is similarly vague in its limits.

The deictics "here" and "now" can arguably both be reduced to an underlying "this," be it "this place" or "this time." As such they are basically demonstrative. Perhaps "I" is demonstrative in the same way. But then the question becomes "This *what*?" What am I demonstrating? This person? This subject? This body? This part of this body? The producer of this token or word ("I")? Again, it is probably irrelevant, as an example may show. When two people grope about in the dark trying to orient themselves and find one another, they might well say "I'm here." In this case, they are not asserting a facetious tautology, nor identifying and naming a place, nor are they even giving information about themselves. The proposition is purely performative; the gropers are drawing attention to themselves. What selves is beside the point. Just as they do not need to know *where* they are to say it, they do not strictly speaking even need to know *who* they are. It is not necessary for us to know what we are referring to for us to be able meaningfully to employ the word "I." [52]

If, therefore, the word is demonstrative in function, then it is primarily an instrument of social interaction. In this case, its use in soliloquy – and consequently in the internalized soliloquies of reflective thought and introspection – can only be secondary or derivative in relation to its use in practical social communication. As a rhetorical flourish to our inward-looking broodings, it has indeed been essential in fostering the fiction of an inner self, the illusion of a stable subject of experience which I can always pinpoint using "I" and which therefore appears to transcend any *particular* context in which I might apply it. The inner self is infinitely huge and infinitely small, punctual and all-encompassing, everywhere and nowhere. It is this ambivalence which led the early Wittgenstein to the conclusion that solipsism, the belief that only the subject exists, in fact coincides with realism, the belief that only the objective world exists. On the one hand "I am my world," [53] while on the other "the I of solipsism shrinks to an extensionless point." [54] Merleau-Ponty writes: "The interior and the exterior are inseparable. The world is all within and I am all without myself." [55] Such lines of thought, though characteristic of the derivative or parasitic use of "I" in philosophically introverted soliloquies, do graphically bring to light the hurdles to be negotiated in demarcating self and other, where the two elements of the opposition are both prone to envelop one another. If taken as meaningful, it is an ambivalence which is bound to remain unresolved; while my mind may encompass the extremities of the cosmos, I will always remain a mere dot in a world that is not me.

At a more earthy level, even the borderlines of my body are condemned to be fudged. I am an *open* system in permanent interaction with my environment, an interaction which is absolutely compulsory for my continued existence as a living organism. My life is an unceasing process of eating, drinking, breathing, sweating, farting, belching, pissing, shitting, nose-picking and sneezing, bleeding, spitting, vomiting, secreting smells and juices, and getting the sleep out of the corners of my eyes. So is yours, dear reader. Ludwig Feuerbach's robust nineteenth-century materialism cheerfully deflates more idealistic views of the subject by recognizing, for example, "that air is an essential part of our self," and punning that "der Mensch ist, was er ißt"; you are what you eat (are).[56] Human identity is a product of what we consume, where consumption comes to stand for other forms of "intake" as well as the gastronomical, such as respiration and even perception. Once again, the crux of the matter is the human openness to the environment, and their incessant exchange. The human body, writes Feuerbach, is "nothing other than the porous I."[57] We are thoroughly perforated, waterlogged organisms, perpetually leaking, dripping and overflowing. Our sense of self thus has its hands full patching us up and making of us an integrated entity, whence the fear or disgust we might feel in the face of certain of our marginal protuberances and discharges. Whence, also, the huge potential for comedy and laughter to overcome this fear.

The arbitrariness of our boundaries is not just spatial. The frontiers between life and death are every bit as open. Even as we live, our bodies are in dynamic interchange with the "dead" matter of which they are ultimately made up and engaged in unremitting war against the onslaught of entropy, our tendency simply to fall back to pieces. As Schopenhauer puts it, approvingly citing the mystic Böhme, all human bodies – like all other organic bodies – are in fact always half dead.[58] Our life is generally understood as beginning at one clear point and terminating at another later on, and forming an unbroken continuity in between. But this too is an oversimplification. The abortion issue betrays more than anything else that the question of when a foetus becomes a "person" can only ever have an arbitrary resolution. From conception to birth, development is so gradual that the idea of an instantaneous change in kind seems incoherent. Nor need death be conceived as such a clear-cut frontier. If my identity as an entity persisting in time is taken as consisting in the psychological continuity or connectedness of my experiences, then there may come a point – given the fading of my memories and the changes in my beliefs – when the question whether I am the same person I was at an earlier point simply knows of no determinate answer. The philosopher Derek Parfit argues for this position.

Parfit offers a reductionist view of the self, claiming that a person's existence consists solely in the existence of a brain and a body, and in the occurrence of a sequence of interrelated physical and psychological events. Two general psychological relations are here of relevance: a) psychological connectedness, exemplified by memories, persistent beliefs and desires, or such relationships as that between intention and execution; b) psychological continuity, which consists in overlapping chains of connectedness. As a reductionist, Parfit rejects the idea of a

deep further fact underlying this continuity. Though persons exist, they
are merely a particular brain and body, and a particular series of interrelated physical and mental occurrences. They are nothing over and
above this, just another way of describing the same thing. Parfit writes:
"It is not true that our identity is always determinate. I can always ask,
'Am I about to die?' But it is not true that, in every case, this question
must have an answer, which must be either Yes or No. In some cases this
would be an empty question." [59] To illustrate the point, he uses the
analogy of a club, whose members disband, and then later reform, with
the same name and the same rules. Is it the same club? The question is
also empty. Unless arbitrarily determined, the claim that it is or is not the
same is neither true nor false, for the existence of a club is no separate
fact beyond the existence of its members behaving in certain ways.
Suppose, by the same token, that personal identity over time can be
reduced to various kinds of psychological connection or continuity and
that there may be cases where the continuity between me now and some
future person will be only limited in extent. In such cases, argues Parfit,
I can always ask whether I am about to die and whether the resulting
person will be me, but there will not always be an answer. The question
may be empty: "If I know the facts about both physical continuity and
psychological connectedness, I know everything there is to know." [60]
Persons exist, Parfit claims, but only in the way that nations do. Their
boundaries are correspondingly contentious.

Parfit considers the hypothetical example of a bisected brain
transplant, in which a person's brain is divided (by severing the corpus
callosum linking the left and right hemispheres, as in some epilepsy
treatment) and each half then successfully transplanted into the body of
one of the person's two twin siblings. Each of the two resulting people
shows signs of being in every way psychologically continuous with the
person whose brain it was. They think they are him, they remember
events from his life, they share his characteristics and convictions, and
even have a very similar outward appearance. In such a situation, Parfit
contends, personal identity is not what matters. There are two people,
each of whom is fully psychologically continuous with the person to
whom the brain belonged, even though they each have the body of one
of his brothers. The question whether the original person *is* now one of
these two people, or the other, or neither, or both, is empty. It can be
compared to the question whether the French Socialist Party – which
split in 1881 – ceased to exist after the split, or continued to exist as one
or both of the two new parties. [61]

Parfit is aware of the counter-intuitive status of this view: "We are
inclined to believe that, to the question 'Am I about to die?', there must
always be an answer, which must be either Yes or No. We are inclined
to believe that our identity must be determinate... This cannot be true
unless we are separately existing entities, such as Cartesian Egos." [62]

For the non-reductionist, for whom personal identity involves a deep further fact beyond our physical and psychological connectedness and continuity, our existence is all-or-nothing, and the borderlines between life and death, between being me and ceasing to be me, are absolute. For Parfit, this need not be the case. The reactions provoked by his argument are telling. One writer claims that, if he were to accept the reductionist view, he would have no reason to continue living.[63] And indeed, to undermine our sense of personal identity may well be to undermine the basis for our rationality. For me to behave in the interests of a future me presupposes an underlying unity which reductionism may call into question. It is not surprising – as an evolutionary measure at least – that we construct definite borderlines in order to know where we stand.

Not only is our sense of ourselves as a unilinear subject with a definitive beginning and end open to doubt. Our autonomy as individuals existing in a moral and social framework is equally shaky, for our very individuality emerges from an ongoing process of social, communicative interaction which brings us up to view ourselves from the perspectives of others, or rather from the perspectives we see others seeing us from. Mead writes: "Selves can only exist in definite relationships to other selves. No hard-and-fast line can be drawn between our own selves and the selves of others, since our own selves exist and enter as such into our experience only in so far as the selves of others exist and enter as such into our experience also."[64] My social identity is a function of my mimetic adoption of the roles, postures and attitudes of others, and this in turn implies an absorption in other people and a tendency to lose any possibility of autonomy by simply playing the social part I expect others to expect of me. As a socially conditioned cipher, I lose all sense of being an independent – and in some way significantly unique – individual. I fail to be the author of my actions but am reduced to a mere plaything in the grip of supra-individual forces. Just as my life is nothing but a configuration of dead matter, so my particularity becomes no more than a node of intersecting economic, historical, social and ideological forces, anonymous forces *over which I have no control*. Fortunately, this debilitatingly one-sided perspective can be countered by a complementary awareness of my bodily existence as a separable and self-moving organism with a capacity to transcend the system and effect changes.

Inner disunity. This duality can also be conceived as internalized *within* the individual human self, taking the form of an inner division or dissonance between subsystems. The fuzziness of our frontiers means that as subjects we "contain" the objects of our thought, as bodies we "contain" the offal and yuckiness which belong outside us, and as living animals we "contain" death. Likewise, as socially structured beings we "contain" the disorder that may threaten the system: one part of me is socially oriented, it might seem, while another part is vigorously anti-social, a diabolical homunculus itching to break out and be *bad*. The remainder of this section will turn to some of the ways in which the identity of the self may be felt to be threatened or impaired from within. In such instances, the self *embraces* its own other. The borders separating me from what is not me run through rather than around me, undermining instead of protecting my unity. Maintaining an integrated self consequently involves asserting myself at the expense of the "other" within me.

This self-division may be seen, for example, as involving a sub-self concerned with the immediate gratification of short-term self-interest (a hedonistic subsystem, rather like Freud's *id*) and a rational sub-self governed by social norms and long-term interests (a prudential subsystem, rather like Freud's *ego*). Here the conflict is between a conformer and a non-conformer, between an orderly and responsible personality and a mutinous spirit aspiring to escape from the chains imposed by sense and conscience. At the same time, it may be a question of temporal priorities, involving a feud between short-term and long-term benefits. The *id*, it would appear, is unable to represent the future or calculate utility, instead merely striving for the maximization of pleasure in the here-and-now; the *ego* by contrast scans the potential as well as the actual alternatives, and its long-term good sense impels us towards morality and socially responsible conduct.

Freudian subsystems are psychological rather than physiological, and only vaguely related to any neurology of the brain. Need we then posit such fixed boundaries and such apparently stable sub-units? In 1924 the celebrated hypnotic therapist Morton Prince wrote of "the composite nature of man, and ... the many little selves of which the mind is composed," suggesting that all of us in fact have "as many selves as we have moods, or contrasting traits, or sides to our personalities." [65] In this case, we are *all* multiple in nature, pathological dualisms being but more extreme expressions of a general condition of inner disunity. For Mead, multiple personality is a perfectly natural consequence of the multiplicity of roles and functions we adopt as we are integrated into the social system. It is in a sense normal, given the variety of different relationships we necessarily maintain with different people. Less normal, by contrast, is the phenomenon of personality-dissociation, caused "by a breaking up of the complete, unitary self into the component selves of which it is composed." [66] And it is when the discontinuity becomes radical enough to threaten our sense of unity that selective amnesia may step in and facilitate the creation of two distinct "selves." The multiple self, that is, is always latently present (as the existential condition of actors who are perpetually swapping parts), but we normally manage to integrate it within a unified whole.

Instead of visualizing the divided self as a temporal discontinuity or as a psychological tension between short-term and long-term considerations, it may just as feasibly be seen as a physiological phenomenon. Work on epileptic patients has demonstrated that severance of the corpus callosum, the bundle of nerve fibres connecting the left and the right brain hemispheres, produces two semi-autonomous functional systems. Various distinctions between the two hemispheres have been formulated. The earliest ones suggested that whereas the left half controls speech, the right is responsible for visual and spatial processes; later studies differentiated between an analytical left hemisphere and a holistic right hemisphere or a left side which processes its information sequentially and a right half based on simultaneous processing. Typically, the right hemisphere, though less advanced in terms of linguistic and mathematical abilities, has greater mastery of skills involved in pattern recognition and musicality. The effects of a commissurotomy (the operation cutting the commissures that link the two hemispheres) have been startling: it is possible for psychologists to present the person operated on with two different written questions in the two halves of his or her field of vision and to get two different answers, one written by each hand.

Such experiments have suggested to some that the operation leads to two separate minds or consciousnesses running in parallel within the same brain, each with its own set of cognitive processes and experiences.[67] This is corroborated by reports of more open discord between the hemispheres, coming to the surface as hand-to-hand conflict between the activities of left and right, often with deeply distressing consequences for the person concerned (as when the left hand beckons to husband or wife, while the right hand pushes him or her away).[68] These cases certainly imply that commissurotomy results in people who have two distinct and unitary streams of consciousness. Yet it is possible to go even further, arguing that consciousness is *permanently* divided in this way. A person can have a complete hemisphere removed and still remain a person (be it left or right half that is removed), intimating to some that even before the operation there does not exist a unitary self: "He or she was a compound of two persons who functioned in concert by trans-commissural exchange. What has survived is one of two very similar persons." Given the respective traits of the two persons within me, however, I ought perhaps to feel sorry for "the untalkative right brain-based person I have been verbosely overruling most of our lives."[69] Indeed, it is tempting here to picture a talented, laid-back, flute-playing, hash-smoking minor hemisphere hippy into T'ai Chi and group sex, while the logically-minded left-hand side bores it senseless with perpetual reasoning and verbal analysis.

It is not necessary to go quite so far, however. Normally there does not seem to be any difference in goal or motivation between the two halves, and the integrated behaviour of the brain as a whole argues against permanent self-division, it being more appropriate to speak of a *potential* for self-division. It is most likely that the two hemispheres in fact follow a "division of labour"[70] as they develop in the growing individual, each specializing in certain skills but remaining interdependent and mutually co-ordinated as an integrated whole. Yet dis-integration is always a possibility. Severance of the corpus callosum means that each half has to de-specialize and re-activate some of its latent powers. In such instances even the right hemisphere can learn to speak.

Perhaps the most fundamental category of self-division is that between mind and body. The theory known as dualism, holding that the mind is a thing or entity separate and distinct from the body, has had an extraordinary purchase on our self-understanding ever since Socrates "proved" that human beings comprise both perishable bodies and immortal souls. The unitary self has in this way been cleaved into a non-material or spiritual "substance" on the one hand and a material, spatially extended one on the other. As a theory, dualism is hugely problematic. It does not follow from the fact that the essence of body is one thing (spatiality) and the essence of mind another (consciousness) that mind and body are two separate entities: there is nothing to stop thinking and spatiality being two attributes of one and the same thing. It does not follow from the fact that we have one set of words to describe the physical and one to describe the mental that we are referring to radically different substances. Indeed the onus is on the dualist to prove that in addition to the physical objects with which we are familiar there also exists a completely distinct class of entities private to the individual and unextended in space. It is likewise for the dualist to explain how mind and body, being so different in nature, can possibly interact with one another (which they must do if they are not simply to proceed in parallel).

In spite of the problems associated with it, dualism – like its opposite, monism – resists definitive refutation, and many would argue that claims concerning the unity or duality of mind and body are accordingly meaningless or nonsensical. For such a reflexive entity as the self, however, where identity and consciousness of identity seem to be perpetually feeding back into one another, there is a sense in which if we understand ourselves in terms of duality, then this dualism may come to structure what we *are*. While identity theorists can thus plausibly contend that mental phenomena (such as thoughts, perceptions, intentions and memories) are identical with processes in the human body or in the nervous system or brain, our self-understanding may still remain staunchly dualistic. It is in the end a question of words: the physicalistic and the mentalistic terminologies create a conceptual rift even while referring to a single set of phenomena. It is a dualism of language (whence its importance to our self-understanding), not an ontological dualism.

It is a dualism that is echoed, moreover, in my sense of myself as both a free agent and a physical body subject to the sway of causal necessity. Bound by physical law and freed by my possibilities for rational choice, my self is *in* the world and yet also *above* the world, immanent and yet somehow transcendent. It is created and creative, dependent and independent, finite and infinite. The natural sceptical response here is to counter that the second elements in the preceding series of oppositions – freedom, transcendence and creativity – are but the fictive concoctions of anthropocentric arrogance. But this is to ignore the holistic, relational side of human beings, who exist in relation to and in interaction with their human and non-human surroundings and who cannot be fully understood as static, atomic entities but are dynamic organisms rooted in temporality and impelled towards their own future possibilities. Seen in these terms, the body-subject is inherently ambiguous: it is both a product of deterministic forces and an agent of freedom. While we may not be able to throw off the influence of the social and historical conditions into which we are born, our very existence requires us to interact with these conditions in ways that will leave neither them nor us the same afterwards. To reason that we are never *fully* free because – even when we are at liberty to implement our wants and desires – we can never choose what these wants and desires are is both to deprive the word "free" of most of its practical significance and to disregard the factor of self-creation. As an autopoietic system, the self produces *itself* (with the help of feedback from the non-self) as much as being just another link in a chain of causation starting and finishing outside the self. So while our interpretation of self and world is on the one hand something we pick up from external sources (from a history of communicative interactions with other people), our capacity to learn (to modify this interpretation of self and world) is on the other hand always inseparable from a pervasive structure of our already existing cognitive assumptions. In this sense, what we learn is a function of what we already know, our development a function of what we already are. What we now believe determines our capacity for future modification of those very beliefs. Again, dependence on externalities and environment is complemented by a self-sufficient circularity.

While these linguistic doublings need not in themselves entail any disunity, their components have regularly been prized apart in human thought systems and thereby gained a potential for inner disruption. Above all ideological and political considerations have wrenched mind and body apart in such a way as to incite man's rational autonomy to wage war against a recalcitrant body in the grip of blind nature: philosophy and theology through the ages have supported this mechanism of political control, but in so doing have perpetuated a deeply schizoid condition. R. D. Laing comments on the pervasiveness of such division at the outset of his study of schizophrenia: "Unless we

begin with the concept of man in relation to other men and from the
beginning 'in' a world, and unless we realize that man does not exist
without 'his' world nor can his world exist without him, we are
condemned to start our study of schizoid and schizophrenic people with
a verbal and conceptual splitting that matches the split up of the totality
of the schizoid being-in-the-world." [71] Philosophy that dissociates man's
mind from his bodily situation is itself schizophrenic.

The mind/body split at the heart of schizophrenia is often
underpinned by an opposition between a true and a false self, a genuine
inner core and a histrionic outer persona. Experiencing his self as more
or less divorced from his body, the individual feels his body to be but
one object among others in an alien world: "Instead of being the core of
his true self, the body is felt as the core of a false self, which a detached,
disembodied, 'inner,' 'true' self looks on at with tenderness, amusement
or hatred as the case may be." [72] Not only does the schizoid see himself
as an actor, playing the parts he believes to be demanded of him, but he
dissociates from these roles, concomitantly protecting his inner, "real"
self (his mind) from the scrutiny of the outside world. The condition
may become chronic, however, when this inviolate inner self – divorced
from its body – reveals itself as utterly empty. As a sanctum of infinite
possibility and boundless freedom, it can do anything, become anyone,
be anywhere in fantasy, but in reality it is nothing. Psychosis steps in
when the veil of the false self is removed to reveal the negativity of the
disembodied self beneath. Pure possibility and absolute freedom turn
into pure nothingness, leaving the person above all with a sense of his
own unreality. Uninhibited self-creation flips over into a sort of death,
indeed often resulting in the "feigned" death of catatonia.

Misrepresentation. There is a further facet of the human self's
ambivalence which does seem to pose particular problems as regards the
matter of unity. This is the so-called subject/object dichotomy, by which
is meant an unbridgeable gap or cleft between the self as something
which "knows" (cognitive subject) and the self as something "known"
(object of knowledge). As a subject and as an object, it is claimed, the
self is two different things, or at best a thing with two radically divergent
aspects. This gap entails the impossibility of absolute self-presence or
self-knowledge and turns the Delphic command "Know thyself" into a
regulative ideal rather than a genuinely practicable imperative. In this
sense, we are *all* comic insofar as we can never completely know
ourselves. Granted, moreover, that all consciousness is also *self*-
consciousness, this self-ignorance is not just a sporadic lapse but
something that shadows us around the whole time. Out of regard for the
Socratic association of the ridiculous with lack of self-knowledge, the
following section will devote a few pages of attention to the nature of
this epistemological split between self and self.

The position in question has been founded above all on a traditional understanding of knowledge as a *representation* of its object, and self-knowledge as essentially *reflective* (and thus a sort of representation of a representation). It is a position that has received recent support from work on artificial intelligence. Consciousness is here frequently equated with the development of an introspective self-image, some of the symbols – or even a whole subsystem – within the intelligent system being taken not as referring to the outer world but as monitoring the operations within the system itself. The brain structures are understood to represent or mirror the real world, and in the case of self-awareness to represent or mirror the brain, in such a way that there is a structural correspondence or "isomorphism"[73] between the representation and what is being represented. In other words, the two structures can be "mapped" onto one another.

While this self-representation has been seen by some as a form of pure self-reference prior to empirical, material or linguistic distractions and thus as the immediate self-presence of a transcendental ego, the metaphor of reflection is more frequently taken to signal a radical split, as between an onlooker and his mirror image. This poses a troublesome epistemological problem regarding the subject's self-identification. In terms of the mirror metaphor, there is no way of guaranteeing that the observer and the mirror image are the same: "Nothing about the mirror betrays that it is really a mirror. I could only testify to the sameness of my mirror image and myself if I were to have at my disposal a pre-reflective knowledge of myself."[74] The reflection model of self-consciousness means (once more) that self-consciousness involves a circular motion: I can only recognize myself as myself if I already know myself. This circularity no more entails the wrongness of the reflection model than it invalidates the concepts of self-organization or autopoiesis, but it does suggest that it is not the whole story in the matter of self-knowledge. More of this presently.

The metaphor of *representation* points up further hitches for self-consciousness. The fact that the German word for representation *(Vorstellung)* also means "theatrical performance" hints at the nature of this division, implying that the self-conscious subject leads a double life as both actor and spectator. As Schopenhauer expresses it, "in his withdrawal into reflection [the human being] resembles an actor who, having played his scene, takes his seat among the audience until he has to go back on stage."[75] Schopenhauer's imagery intimates the *fictive* quality of what is experienced. This does not entail that it is an illusion, nor that it is merely the product of human fantasy. What it does entail is that it is a specifically human construction and that we have no way of definitively ascertaining how close is its correspondence to what it represents.

Not being identical with its object, a representation indeed by definition betokens a relationship of simplification or selective distortion to what is represented. In the case of human consciousness, it is language that contributes to this distortive streamlining as much as anything. Whereas some have understood self-consciousness to consist in a process of pure self-communication unadulterated by the materiality of language, in a sort of idealized inner voice, this ignores that thought itself must be dependent upon a system of differentiated signs for it to have the possibility of signifying anything. Were our "inner voice" no more than an undifferentiated blur, it could be referred to neither as consciousness nor as thought. And if thought is merely internalized speech, or speech merely enunciated thought, then there can clearly be no thoughts without words, nor consequently any form of transparent, prelinguistic self-representation.[76]

One rather counter-intuitive conclusion that has been drawn from this is that the subject does not have any privileged knowledge of his own conscious experiences. Gilbert Ryle in particular has argued for the evolutionary and developmental primacy of (social) speech over (private) reflective thought: "Keeping our thoughts to ourselves is a sophisticated accomplishment. It was not until the Middle Ages that people learned to read without reading aloud. Similarly a boy has to learn to read aloud before he learns to read under his breath, and to prattle aloud before he prattles to himself." [77] Refuting the notion that our emotions are internal or private occurrences and that mind is an occult phenomenon concealed from external witnesses (i.e. all other people), Ryle contends that a person's evaluations of his own actions are not different in kind from his evaluations of the performances of others. For self and other alike the criteria for acquaintanceship with a mind are what is said and what is done:

> Liking and disliking, joy and grief, desire and aversion are, then, not "internal" episodes which their owner witnesses, but his associates do not witness. ... Certainly a person can usually, but not always, tell without research whether he enjoys something or not, and what his present mood is. But so can his associates, provided that he is conversationally open with them and does not wear a mask. If he is conversationally open neither with them nor with himself, both will have to do some research to find out these things, and they are more likely to succeed than he.[78]

In a sense, therefore, the possibility of self-deception makes self-knowledge even *more* problematic than knowledge of others, for self-deception may well offer me fewer opportunities to un-deceive myself than if I am being deceived by others. Ryle persuasively dismantles the illusion that our minds are able to apprehend their own workings any better or more reliably than they can apprehend facts concerning the external world: there is no reason why I should be blessed with some sort of privileged and unfailing access to my own cognitive operations. Knowledge of self and knowledge of others are restored to an equal epistemological footing. The inextricability of self-reflection and language may furthermore constitute a breach in the individual's self-presence in another important sense. To the extent that language always precedes and pre-exists the individual subject, my self can be understood as grounded in something that is not myself. My understanding of myself, as of my world, has evolved as a consequence of continuing activities of interpretation based on assumptions and presuppositions implicit in our very language, and the "pre-understanding" or prejudice that structure our world are obstacles to full self-understanding. Our cultural background determines what we are and how we understand what we are in ways that can never be made wholly explicit: we lack the capacity to transcend the circumstances that have formed us, and our existence in a historical situation means that self-knowledge can never be complete.[79] Seen as social actors in perpetual performance, moreover, we lapse into self-deception whenever we allow ourselves to become thoroughly absorbed in our roles, slipping unthinkingly into prescribed postures and attitudes towards self and other. We delude ourselves whenever we forget the theatricality of social conduct, whenever we ignore the dramatics inherent even in the structure of self-observation. Self-awareness turns the self into the star of a one-man show, enticing him to play to the (one-man) crowd.

Yet human subjectivity is not just rooted in language. It is also characterized by what Heidegger called "being-in-a-world": I am from the outset *thrown* into a concrete life-world with which I am intimately bound up, "projecting" myself forward towards my future possibilities within this world. For both Heidegger and Merleau-Ponty, my being-in-a-world is inextricably connected to my ecstatic nature as a being constantly "outside" itself: it is as a body among bodies that I first come to know myself as I interact with my world, and the self-knowledge of this body-subject is of an opacity in stark contrast to the pure self-presence of a disembodied or transcendental ego: "If we are in a situation, we are circumvented, we cannot be transparent for ourselves, and our contact with ourselves can only happen in equivocacy."[80] As a body-subject acting *as* a body and *in* a world, my own functioning remains largely beyond my conscious grasp: I remain a mystery to myself. The loss of transparency entailed by the body has been crucial especially to Freudian theory, with its accent upon the origins of the mind in bodily drives and the unknowability of the unconscious. The Freudian unconscious has generated infinite potential for (comic) self-ignorance, as we hopelessly fail to identify or acknowledge our bodily motivations. Rooted as it is in the flesh, self-deception may even be felt to signal our moral fallenness; as with Augustine, self-knowledge thus becomes a step towards God.

To the extent that human intelligence is taken to be a necessarily embodied phenomenon, it is also open to a whole hierarchy of levels of description. Human beings can be understood not only in terms of macroscopic behaviour, traits and attributes, but equally in terms of the DNA molecules that determine our constitution, or the neural firings that determine our actions. These conceptual systems are handily compartmentalized, with the result in particular that we tend not to think of ourselves as neurons or genes. We regard our macroscopic selves as the fundamental unit rather than merely as relatively short-lived vehicles for complex configurations of genes which will themselves survive us. We flatter ourselves with our sense of mental autonomy (I am the master in *my* mind), ignoring or ignorant of the chemical cracklings and fizzings carrying on inside our crania. But the pretensions of mental autonomy can soon be put in perspective by such paradoxical commands as "Don't think of sex!" This does not mean that mental autonomy is an utter chimera: while I cannot cause my neurons to behave in a manner that defies the laws of physics, even at a neural level there is a sense in which it is *my* constellation of neural activity at one moment (i.e. me) which – as a self-organizing system – is setting up and determining its (and my) future development.

It can be countered here that our oblivion to our neuro-physiological make-up is a completely uninteresting limitation on our self-knowledge. Our significance as intelligent beings is all a product of "higher" levels of description. Yet the metaphor of *representation* may also have effects on our capacity for self-knowledge only incidentally connected to our material embodiment. If, as the proponents of artificial intelligence maintain, mental activity is basically algorithmic (consisting in the execution of well-defined sequences of computational procedures), then for human as for artificial intelligence it is the formal organization of the system that counts, not its material constituents. It is irrelevant whether the algorithm is effected by a human brain, an electronic computer or a sophisticated mechanical contraption. But if this really is the case, then the human mind is prey to the very limitations which beset any sufficiently powerful formal system: put in a nutshell, it is vulnerable to Gödel's Second Incompleteness Theorem, which demonstrates that any consistent mathematical system sufficiently powerful to perform elementary mathematics can never prove its own consistency.

The logician and mathematician Kurt Gödel showed that in any such formal system there will always be statements about numbers that are *undecidable* on the basis of the axioms of the system in question. These are statements that can never, even in principle, be proven true or false. Gödel's insight in proving his theorem consisted in the use of mathematics to codify statements about mathematics, allowing a statement of number theory to be both a statement of number theory and a statement about a statement of number theory. The Gödelian proposition that causes the incompleteness is "This statement of number theory does not have any proof" or, strictly speaking, "This statement of number theory cannot be demonstrated within this fixed system of propositions" – self-referential statements rather like the claim made by Epimenides the Cretan that all Cretans are liars, and the related "This sentence is not true." If the Gödelian proposition is indeed a theorem of number theory (if, that is, there exists within the system a decision procedure terminating in a finite time which produces or derives the proposition from the system's axioms), then it must assert a truth. But it asserts its own nontheoremhood. Thus if it is a theorem, it is a nontheorem, which means that the system contains a contradiction and is therefore inconsistent. If it is not a theorem, by contrast, there is no contradiction. But the proposition's nontheoremhood is what it asserts. Thus it asserts a truth. As Gödel's proposition is not a theorem, there exists (at least) one truth which is not contained by number theory.[81] It is the existence of this truth in fact that Penrose takes as evidence that there is more to human intelligence than mere algorithmic computability: namely insight.

The vulnerability exposed by Gödel arises because the formal system of number theory – following Gödel's trick – is powerful enough to express statements *about itself.* Before a system contains this capacity for self-reference, there is no problem; once this critical point is attained, however, the system has dug its own grave. Henceforth it is doomed to incompleteness. Gödel's proposition thus incorporates a fundamental duality as both a proposition in its own right and the referent of a proposition: it is a representation which refers to a (coded) representation of itself. As such it serves as a compelling metaphor for mind, intimating that we too may be ultimately incapable, even in principle, of completely fathoming our own mind. A full comprehension would require a view from *outside* our mind, a view from a meta-level. Douglas Hofstadter writes: "All the limitative Theorems of metamathematics and the theory of computation suggest that once the ability to represent your own structure has reached a certain critical point, that is the kiss of death: it guarantees that you can never represent yourself totally." The message of Gödel's Incompleteness Theorem seems to be that to "seek self-knowledge is to embark on a journey which ... will always be incomplete, cannot be charted on any map, will never halt, cannot be described."[82] The philosopher Thomas Nagel expands on the idea of this necessary incompleteness in our self- knowledge without recourse to the terminology of formal systems and mathematical theorems, making the point that "however much we expand our objective view of ourselves, something will remain beyond the possibility of explicit acceptance or rejection, because we cannot get entirely outside ourselves, even though we know that there is an outside."[83]

A comparable scenario occurs if – as Hofstadter imagines – we picture ourselves reading an absolutely gigantic book containing *all* the information inherent in the current neural configuration of our brain, a humdinger of a tome with a hundred billion pages, one for each neuron, crammed with the relevant facts concerning what incoming electro-chemical current would be required to cause it to "fire," what other neurons it is connected to, and a whole assortment of further details. Suppose that we are phenomenally fast readers who do not allow ourselves to be daunted by the mind-blowing boredom of the whole project. Suppose that we do manage to plough through the entire volume before nodding off. By the time we have finished it, it is in effect a history book, a book about how we were before we started reading it: "The fact that I *read* the book makes the book obsolete. The very attempt to learn about myself changes me from what I was." [84] My efforts at encompassing all the information in my brain were a dead duck from the word go. Underlying both these illustrations of incompleteness are forms of logical "feedback." Just as Gödel's proposition presupposes the self-reference through which a proposition is as it were fed back into itself (and is therefore its own "object"), so Hofstadter's book can never be completely perused (in its up-to-date edition at least) because I am both the reader (the subject) and the book being read (the object), and my act of reading the book alters the book that I am.

Gilbert Ryle too recognized that introspection must necessarily be retrospection; the glance inwards is always also a glance backwards. While this is particularly evident for states of mental agitation, such as convulsive merriment, panic or fury, which are in themselves incompatible with introspective self-scrutiny, it applies to all states of mind, according to Ryle, because a thought cannot simultaneously be its own object. Ryle sees this as implied by the popular phrase "to catch oneself doing something": "We catch, as we pursue and overtake, what is already running away from us. I catch myself daydreaming about a mountain walk after, perhaps very shortly after, I have begun the daydream." [85] If this is the case, then introspection – being retrospection – resembles a dipping into our own autobiography, and is as such by no means always reliable, for we may easily misinterpret ourselves. The division separating self from self is here a temporal gap, a split condemning our self-commentary to "eternal penultimacy." [86] Attempts to catch up with ourselves are doomed to failure: as we strive to put our fingers on what "I" stands for, all we ever manage to grasp is the coat-tails of the object of our pursuit.

Time's subjects. So far, the issue has been deliberately simplified by assuming that all self-knowledge is a matter of self-reflection, introspection or self-thematization. Many would argue that this is misleading. Unhappy with the reflection model of self-knowledge (and its tendency to cleave the subject into a duality with no absolute criterion for self-identification), a number of philosophers have proposed that self-reflection presupposes an *immediate* form of self-acquaintance. Reflection, they contend, is a matter of self-*re*cognition, and assumes that I must in some sense already "know" myself. If reflective self-consciousness fails to guarantee the identity of subject and object, then this must be founded upon a direct or prereflective self-knowledge.[87] Yet such a notion of immediate self-consciousness leaves many questions unanswered. Terms like self-consciousness (entailing consciousness *of* self *by* self) are difficult to conceive except as relational.

What is brought to light, however, is that reflective, introspective thought is a derivative category of mental activity. When we think of thinking, we tend ourselves to be sitting reflecting, perhaps at a desk, in a field or in a comfy chair by the fire. We tend correspondingly to characterize thought as a process of *detached* reflection involving mental images, representations, ideas and concepts. This is certainly an important aspect of thinking, but it is a great mistake to take this sort of theorizing as a standard manifestation of cognition in general. Consciousness need not be detached and reflective, and it usually is not. Cognition is the activity of a living organism, one which involves both interaction with the world and self-maintenance or self-preservation against the world, and above all one which does not leave us the same afterwards. A cognitive system is intricately modified by its interaction with the world and with itself. As essentially "plastic" entities, we thus "internalize" what we cognize. Learning is best regarded not as a process of storing structurally invariant "representations" of the environment for use on different occasions but, in Maturana's words, as "the transformation through experience of the behaviour of an organism in a manner that is directly or indirectly subservient to the maintenance of its basic circularity."[88] The plasticity which is so crucial to our capacity to learn and remember means that we are engaged in an incessant process of self-modification.[89] It is in this sense that we are all inevitably time's subjects.

While the term "plasticity" implies change and flux, however, it is only because there is unity underlying the mutability, and there are continuities within the flux, that acts of memory – be this procedural (remembering how to...) or declarative (remembering that...) – are possible at all. The biochemist Steven Rose accordingly speaks of the "specificity" that must complement the organism's plasticity:

> To function effectively – that is, to respond appropriately to their environment – all living organisms must show two contradictory properties. They must retain stability – *specificity* – during development and into adult life, resisting the pressures of the endless buffeting of environmental contingency, both day-to-day and over a lifetime. And they must show plasticity – that is, the ability to adapt and modify this specificity in the face of repeated experience.

It is specificity that "confers on brains the ability to make sense of their environment, to recognize invariance and to respond in an orderly way to regularities in the external world." Without it, and without the inductive learning made possible by it, the survival of the living system as an autopoietic unit would be ruled out. Ordered and restrained variance, as Rose puts it, "can only make sense against a largely invariant background." [90]

The self-knowledge of memory, therefore, is not a contingent relationship between present and past mental states. It is a present mental state, and as such a function of the continuity of a living organism. As a cognitive system with a memory, I am an embodiment of my past, and my memory amounts to a programme for responding to an already encountered situation when something similar recurs in the future. My memory is the effect of my past upon my present, a consequence of the fact that I incorporate my past, albeit in ways of which I may have no conscious inkling. What it entails, understood thus, is not any additional prereflective self-consciousness, but simply the unity and continuity underlying the plasticity of the cognitive system. But in these terms, "recognition" and the problem of self-identification prove superfluous, and the question whether any particular memory I have is mine or not is as absurd as the question whether the hopes and intentions I harbour are yours or mine. This applies not just to my nonreflective or procedural memory – my dispositional ability to make a tasty cup of instant coffee – but equally to the declarative memory I have of my own adventures, my retrospective "visualization" of past events, and my ability to tell myself and others a coherent narrative about my life-history. Of course, I may misremember the past, just as I may misperceive what is present to me. But at least I can always be sure that it is *my* past that I am misremembering. [91]

Given that we are in a manner of speaking constituted by our memories on the one hand and our intentions and hopes on the other, our identities are inextricably bound up with the temporal dimension. This emerges in particular from the philosophies of Sartre and Merleau-Ponty, which star an essentially temporal "prereflective cogito." For Sartre, human consciousness must always be directed upon some object, but – as well as being aware of the object – it will also be aware of itself being aware. Put in this form, Sartre's thesis appears to entail an infinite regression leading to an awareness of ourselves being aware of ourselves being aware, and to an awareness of ourselves being aware of ourselves being aware of ourselves being aware, and so on. Sartre's attempt to forestall this objection was to deny that this "conscience (de) soi" or self-consciousness is knowledge. It is an immediate, prereflective, nonpositional, "a-thetic" self-relationship (and the bracketed "de" shows Sartre's desire to obliterate any relationality), but as such it is the very condition for the possibility of reflection.

His description of it pinpoints its mode of being as one of "flight" and "escape": it is "a being which escapes from knowledge and founds it"; the consciousness it underlies is "a double flight from the world; it escapes its own being-in-the-midst-of-the-world as a presence to a world which it is fleeing. The possible is the free end of the flight." [92] Often taken as wishy-washy wordiness or wilful obscurity, such metaphors nonetheless convey that the prereflective consciousness – being grounded in lack or imbalance – is fundamentally ecstatic, oriented towards its future possibilities: "a being which constitutes itself as lack can determine itself only ... by a perpetual wrenching away from self toward the self which it has to be." [93]

Our immediate self-awareness is not, therefore, a matter of static self-identity. As conscious beings, we are constantly beyond ourselves, dynamically open towards our possibilities of interaction with the world. Clearly this is a different category of self-difference from what is entailed by the reflection model of self-knowledge. It is the self-difference generated by our temporality. Importantly, however, it is a self-difference which Sartre too sees as sustained by an underlying unity; we *are* our past, our present and our future, Sartre would assert, but we are them in the mode of not being them. At the heart of the Sartrean subject is not only temporality but a concomitant negativity: "Consciousness confronts its past and its future as facing a self which it is in the mode of not-being. This refers us to a nihilating structure of temporality." [94] Sartre's jargon recalls to mind the Hegelian notion that negativity (or contradiction) is the source of all self-movement, "the principle indeed of all natural and spiritual vitality." [95]

In the notion of time, another threat to our self-identity has been unearthed. This threat may take the form of the ecstatic self-difference described by the existentialists. The plasticity of the cognitive organism may be taken as signalling that even our brains are in permanent structural flux, and any sense of identity can only be provisional and precarious. (Conversely, the very notions of *self*-organization or of *self*-creation imply a unity grounding the fluidity.) In any case, the self seems to be a process, not a state, a becoming rather than a being. Time surreptitiously undermines the unity of our very bodies. The inanimate matter of which we are composed has been entirely replaced several times since birth, and even the atoms making up my brain cells seven years ago have all taken to their heels.[96] Although an overweight materialism might ignore that the configuration of our constituent matter, our "form," shows a certain limited constancy even as our "individual" atoms go mooning off, the capacity of time to subvert identity is evident: I am simply not the same person I was a year ago, or yesterday, or a minute ago, or at the beginning of this sentence, or word.

Or am I? It is important here not to confuse qualitative and numerical identity. While I may have changed in "quality," surely I am still the same me insofar as there exist physical and psychological continuities and connections between me now and me two minutes ago, and between me two minutes ago and me two minutes before that. It is my sameness over time which is the basis for any sort of moral and legal responsibility, and which is taken for granted by the judicial convention making my present self accountable and punishable for the transgressions of a past me. In *One Way Pendulum*, N. F. Simpson subjects this conception of identity to comic scrutiny. Mr. Groomkirby claims to have interviewed a certain Myra Gantry a few months ago, but cross-examination of the most rigorous stamp exposes his uncertainties:

Prosecuting Counsel:	It is a good many months since all this happened, is it not, Mr. Groomkirby?
Mr. Groomkirby:	Several months, yes, sir.
Pros. Coun.:	You have no doubt in your mind, all the same, that this person who interviewed Myra Gantry last August was the person I am addressing now?
Mr. G.:	It was me, sir.
Pros. Coun.:	It was you. (*Pause*). Mr. Groomkirby – do you know what happens to the body in sleep?
Mr. G.:	It recuperates its energies, sir.
Pros. Coun.:	Certain chemical and other changes take place, do they not?
Mr. G.:	I understand they sometimes do, yes, sir.
Pros. Coun.:	You must have spent a good many hours in sleep since last August?
Mr. G.:	I dare say that would be true, sir. *The Judge begins to look at Mr. Groomkirby with suspicion and curiosity from time to time.*
Pros. Coun.:	You must have eaten a good many meals, and absorbed a fair amount of food?
Mr. G.:	Yes, sir.
Pros. Coun.:	It would be true to say, would it not, that the normal processes of what is known sometimes as metabolism, whereby body tissue is constantly being built up or broken down, have been going on unceasingly since the twenty-third of August last year?
Mr. G.:	I couldn't say, sir. *The Judge looks up and continues to stare intently at Mr. Groomkirby with the same curiosity and suspicion as before.*
Pros. Coun.:	I suggest to you, Mr. Groomkirby, that in view of these changes the man you say was in Chester-le-Street last year is not the man who is standing in the witness box at this moment.
Judge:	(*Intervening*) Are you suggesting he's someone else?

Pros. Coun.:	It is the contention of the prosecution, m'lord, that he has been gradually replaced in the intervening period by the man who is now before the court.
Judge:	(*To Mr. Groomkirby, accusingly*) Is this so?
Mr. G.:	It's difficult to say, sir. (Act 2)

Consciousness especially is in unremitting flow, a river – as Heraclitus the Obscure is reputed to have said – into which we can never step twice. Metaphors of flow, of unending chase or of quest have indeed often structured our self-understanding as human individuals, again implying restive imbalance or lost self-presence. While Ryle refers to the "systematic elusiveness of the 'I'," that enigmatic, momentary me that I never quite manage to catch up with, for Taylor our self-interpretation is more of a *narrative* quest. Our identity is a tale we tell ourselves about ourselves, a story that we extrapolate into the future in such a way as to provide us with inner coherence and moral orientation. "And as I project my life forward and endorse the existing direction or give it a new one," writes Taylor, "I project a future story, not just a state of the momentary future but a bent for my whole life to come." [97] This movement towards our future possibilities is a sort of self-perpetuating narrative self-pursuit. [98]

Just as Ryle portrays our vain snatching at the coat-tails of an elusive "I" always one pace ahead of us, the distinction drawn by Mead between the socially constructed "me" and the individual "I" whose conduct is a *response* to the social environment is likewise elaborated in terms of temporal tardiness. Our immediate bodily reaction is something we can only ever grasp after it has happened:

> The "I" of this moment is present in the "me" of the next moment. There again I cannot turn around quick enough to catch myself. I become a "me" in so far as I remember what I said [i.e. how I reacted].... It is because of the "I" that we say that we are never fully aware of what we are, that we surprise ourselves by our own action. [99]

Even as a social actor trapped in an unceasing sequence of roles and performances, there remains a sense in which – as a subject – I always escape the social system of which I am a part. It is the "I" that manages to elude the objective structure and transcend my series of roles. Insofar as it eludes the system, however, it remains beyond even its own grasp.

The End of the Subject?

Embracing this "contradiction" within itself, the subject is equated by Hegel with "pure, simple negativity," and accordingly with movement, process, becoming and time. Time, for Hegel, is man's fate until he catches up and coincides with himself in static self-identity.[100] Such a conceptual framework was deeply influential upon Sartre's understanding of the human self, structured as this is by a fundamental negativity. The human consciousness is in Sartre's eyes always characterized by not being what it is or by failing to coincide with itself. What is more, this inability to constitute ourselves as being what we are means that "as soon as we posit ourselves as a certain being, by a legitimate judgment, based on inner experience or correctly deduced from a priori or empirical premises, then by that very positing we surpass this being."[101] Such negativity lies at the heart of being a human subject, but it is not simply a traumatic lack of self-identity, for at the same time it represents our very freedom. It denotes not a condition (that we are not ourselves) so much as an activity, that of a knowing subject who can never quite be objectified. It is our facility as subjects to query and deny, to conceive what is not the case, that enables us to change what is. Even while undermining our self-identity, time constitutes the basis for freedom and possibility. Change is a deliverance, not a threat.

Sartre visualizes this freedom as resulting from the capacity of consciousness to "withdraw" from the world of objects. Defined by its difference from the objective realm, however, consciousness may thereby become utterly empty. The subject thus incorporates negativity not just in the sense of contradiction and lack but also insofar as it is something which by definition *is not*, at least not in the world as it is and can be known to us. As a pure subject of experiences it shrinks to an extensionless dot, a purely punctual entity detachable from the external world (including our body), free from material causality and as such an agent of radical self-mastery. It is a synthesizing activity which founds the possibility of ordered representation by combining and structuring the jumbled data of sensory perception, but as a transcendental *creator* of meaning it eludes representation itself. Just as my eye is not something in my own field of vision, neither can my "I" – my metaphysical self – be something in my experience. The subject, as Wittgenstein remarked, could not be mentioned in an account of the world as I found it.

Not surprisingly, the notion of the subject as something which isn't, a thing which is nothing, may easily flip over into the correlative claim that there is no such thing as a subject. This claim has assumed a number of guises, depending on how the word "subject" has been taken. Kant devoted a great deal of energy to denying that there is any such thing as a "soul," where this is assumed to denote some sort of immaterial, non-composite, detachable subject of thoughts and experiences. He argued that it is an illusion to which we are disposed by mistaking the transcendental unity of apperception – the necessary unity of our conscious experiences – for an awareness of a unitary subject who somehow "owns" or has the experiences. The unity of apperception, by contrast, is above all a *formal* condition for our experience. As such, it cannot be directly intuited as an object of experience: it is the basic ground underlying the fact that a subject of experiences can ascribe states of consciousness to himself without having to employ any criteria of identification; it is the foundation of the coherence of our consciousness of self and other; but it can only be thought, not experienced.[102]

Before Kant, Hume had combed the depths of his philosophical mind in search of a subject or identity on which the flux of our conscious experiences could be grounded, but Hume's quest discovered even the continuity of our experiential chain to be fictive. He describes his exploration in the following terms: "For my part, when I enter most intimately into what I call *myself*, I always stumble on some particular perception or other, of heat or cold, light or shade, love or hatred, pain or pleasure. I never can catch *myself* at any time without a perception, and never can observe anything but the perception."[103] The point, for Hume, is not that there is no subject, but that the subject consists simply in a causally connected chain of experiences and is not an additional entity upon which this chain is based.

Lichtenberg responded to the Cartesian belief in an autonomous thinking substance ontologically independent of any material embodiment by querying in particular Descartes's *cogito* or "I think": "We know only the existence of our sensations, presentations, and thoughts. We should say 'it thinks' (*es denkt*), just as we say 'it lightens.' It is going too far to say *cogito*, if we translate *cogito* by 'I think.'"[104] Nietzsche made the related point that "a thought comes when 'it' wants, not when 'I' want."[105] Yet these assertions are not unproblematic. They seem, for example, to allow for the possibility that a thought or an experience may exist even though no one is having it, rather like the Cheshire Cat's grin, which continues even after the cat has disappeared, or the bad temper that stays put though the dog to whom it belonged has wandered off in pursuit of his bone. But it is hard to grasp the idea of a disembodied experience flitting about the world, nor can an experience or stream of experiences be identifyingly referred to except insofar as they are had by some identifiable person. We cannot coherently refer to Mrs. Brown's pain and permit the possibility that Mrs. Brown's pain could be somewhere inside Mr. Brown's or their pet gerbil's body.

On the other hand, although an experience is necessarily embodied, and the identity of the body is always relevant for the identification of the experience, it is arguable that a series of thoughts, and the relations linking them, *could* be impersonally described without being ascribed to specifically identified thinkers. Such an impersonal description, though a woefully unwieldy abstraction, is at least conceivable. Accordingly, Lichtenberg's suggested substitute for the Cartesian *cogito* comes close to the Humean stand that there is no subject over and above the concatenation of lived experiences. Parfit's gloss on Lichtenberg's formulation makes this clear:

> Because we ascribe thoughts to thinkers, we can truly claim that thinkers exist. But we cannot deduce, from the content of our experiences, that a thinker is a separately existing entity. And, as Lichtenberg suggests, because we are not separately existing entities, we could fully describe our thoughts without claiming that they have thinkers. We could fully describe our experiences, and the connections between them, without claiming that they are had by a subject of experiences.[106]

Lichtenberg's *es denkt* can also be taken to draw attention to the origins of thought in the body, or the fact that my thoughts could in theory at least be redescribed in terms of the activity of my body or the functioning of my brain. In opposition to Descartes, materialists thus feel it superfluous to postulate the existence of minds in addition to bodies, for the activities of the former can be attributed without remainder to the latter. Others even deny the existence of an entity called "consciousness": what does exist are only experiences, relations between which constitute knowing. Believers in consciousness, it is claimed, are the victims of a philosophical delusion.[107]

The non-subject has further reared its absent head in poststructuralist and related modes of thinking, which have sought the system behind the individual act and stressed the constitutive structures which determine what we say and think. The human self here ceases to be regarded as an autonomous centre of creative mental activity and intention, turning into the mere function of a structure of meaning which pre-dates and transcends it. This rejection of the subject is often linked to an anti-individualistic tendency, a line of thought which – following in Marx's footsteps – has emphasized that the individual is the product of a network of social determinants and demoted the notion of autonomous individuality to a fiction of bourgeois ideology. Although we may like to see ourselves as free, coherent, self-generating individuals, this is allegedly but a reassuring illusion created by "ideology": in fact we are essentially split, a composite function of a multitude of contradictory forces. In this sense, the intellectual assault on the "subject" is really an assault on the human being as a unitary individual.

These diverse formulations of the idea that the human subject is an illusion and that there is in fact no such thing are all the product of highly abstract philosophical introspection and speculation. The only time I feel like a nobody in practice, it might be countered, is when the stroppy girl at the local bakery skips me in the queue or when I nosedive into a party conversation with somebody whose glances keep straying over my shoulder. Such experiences do indeed remind us of our own relative insignificance and dispensability, a truth we may prefer to hide from ourselves. But this is very different from the armchair acrobatics of subtle hyperintellectuals willing to philosophize themselves out of existence, which has little to do with the way most people actually see themselves, at least in a non-philosophical mood. The confusions are the consequence of a one-sided approach to a phenomenon which has many aspects. If we see the subject as merely a function of structural forces which operate through it, then, yes, the traditional, autonomous individual is an illusion; if we see the subject as an entity underlying or perhaps "owning" a chain of conscious experience, then, yes, it can easily shrivel to a no-dimensional speck, a mere nothing. To privilege this aspect of the self is to engender an uneasy amalgam of omnipotence and impotence.

The second part of this essay assumes, therefore, that it is misleading to regard the human subject as purely negative. Such a claim ignores that the subject is a body-subject and that the body-subject is also a positive phenomenon. While there may not be a timeless subject who "owns" our experiences, what remains is the human being as a living, cognitive system equipped with a facility to reflect on its experiences and to articulate these reflections, an organism whose (limited) identity consists in the continuity within a perpetual process of self-modification. Though not an illusion, however, the self is understood to be a fiction, to the extent that its defining boundaries are arbitrarily demarcated. In this sense a person is comparable to a nation. Like a nation, its borders can prove embarrassingly controversial, and although it usually exists as a conglomerate of well-integrated subdivisions, there may be occasions when inner conflict results in more problematic divisions and rifts.

A sense of self is vital to the continued functioning of an individuated organism. Although it need not be reflective or verbally expressible, *some* distinction between self and other is a prerequisite for the possibility of self-preserving cognitive activity, and at the very lowest level, self-consciousness coincides with a disposition to survive. It is conscious reflection, however, which fosters definitive and persisting frontiers between self and other, our use of the words "I", "myself" or of our names tending to imply a relatively stable and non-composite self being denoted. To this extent we paste over the fissures and cracks in our unity, the blurs in our boundaries, the leaks at our limits. It is primarily when we indulge in a certain sort of critical, philosophical introspection that the disunity within and the disputed borders leap into the spotlight, revealing the schisms from which we are usually protected by the fixed conceptuality of "ordinary" consciousness. Like philosophy, festivity and comedy may fulfil a similar role in throwing our unitary identity into doubt. The second part of this essay will look at some of the ways in which this may happen.

PART TWO:
OF LAUGHTER

Chapter 2

Self as Structure

Victimization

Our sense of self, it has been argued, emerges gradually from the process of social interaction in which we participate. As such it is intimately bound up with the system of values and meanings structuring the organized community as a whole. Our self-awareness is to this extent the function of a complex of social institutions and couched in terms of a framework of values and commitments which may include both our moral and spiritual allegiances (embodied in statements to the effect that I am a Christian, a Buddhist, a working man, a Sheffield United supporter, a terrorist, a true sportsman, an ecologist, a die-hard communist, a cool dude, a dope-head, an old-fashioned kinda guy, a nihilist, a hedonist, an intellectual, the sort of person who minds his own business and never does anyone any harm, an artist, a piss-artist, a hippy, yuppy, sloane or scally) *and* our national, ethnic or sexual identity (I am a white British male, an Indian woman). Our sense of self is inseparable from what we find *good* and thus from our opposition to those with contrary commitments or allegiances, different communal identities. Not that this opposition need entail hostility. But even if we understand ourselves as liberal, latitudinarian or just easy-going (and therefore perhaps welcome a plurality of ethnic, religious or ideological allegiances), then our self-definition still necessarily implies some sort of an opposition, namely to tyrants, bigots and racists (see also pages 3-5).

While our self-understanding may be purely in terms of universal ethical issues, such as a commitment to alleviate suffering and maximize happiness or to save the planet, this seems to be an idealization: in practice, some form of *tribalism* – some (possibly tacit) adherence to a non-universal or localized, "group" identity – is always copresent, if not prevalent. Identification with a group or community plays such a key role in the structuring of individual identity that (as psychological studies show) even when a group of people is *randomly* split into two or more sub-units they tend to develop a bias towards members of their own one, creating a positive stereotype of themselves while prejudging the "others" in terms of less favourable collective stereotypes.[1]

Given this seemingly "natural" tendency towards group identity, what follows will be concerned with laughter-situations firstly as contexts of communal assertion. Not surprisingly, laughter does not always appear in a particularly flattering light. Psychologists have long since recognized the aggression inherent in laughter, and noted its similarity to the rhythmic cries with which many primates (monkeys and apes) collectively threaten an intruder, a gesture of group hostility which reinforces social cohesion by uniting its participants in their opposition to the outsider.[2] Even the well-meaning human smile involves what in all primates is a patently threatening signal: exposure of the teeth. This image of laughter as vocalized belligerence is supported by speculations that satire, at least in its Gaelic manifestation, may have originated as a war-weapon believed to undermine the enemy's strength through its magical powers and capable indeed of causing disfiguration and death.[3] Traditional ritual festivity has likewise tended to counter its capacity to swallow up the individual within the collective and to revitalize feelings of communal solidarity and togetherness with its habit of flipping over into acts of brutality directed at scapegoats, outsiders and underdogs. Group identity is all well and good, but to the extent that collective self-assertion means self-assertion *at the expense of somebody else* laughter proves rather a dubious phenomenon, either proclaiming or seeking to establish a sense of superiority in the person lucky enough to be laughing.

Perhaps the most obvious example of collective animosity is in racist humour, which may of course range from the fairly harmless to the thoroughly malicious. Most Western societies possess a stock butt whose dimwittedness compounds their own sense of superiority: while the English laugh at the Irish (Heard about the Irish lamp-post? Pissed on a dog. The Irish cargo ship carrying yoyos? Sank forty-four times. The Irish waterpolo team? Drowned twelve horses. The IRA man who tried to blow up the QE2? Couldn't get his mouth round the funnel.[4]), the French make fun of the Belgians, the Brazilians make jokes about the Portuguese, and the Americans deride (amongst others) the Poles in the same way. Such jokes implicitly say: "I have such-and-such an identity and am therefore no fool. But look at those idiots!" Interesting, however, are the different uses to which such jokes are put. Whereas Western society tends to aim them at a peripheral ethnic group, the countries of the former communist bloc in Eastern Europe generally directed them at groups exercizing political power, such as leaders of the communist party and members of the militia: Why do Polish militiamen have a stripe round their elbows? So that they can remember where to bend their arms. Why do Czech militiamen go round in groups of three? One can read, one can write, and the other is keeping an eye on the two intellectuals.[5] In Italy too the stock dimwit is the *carabiniere*, a member of one of the country's police forces.

Disrespectful and rude though "stupidity" jokes may be, there are also more malign varieties which prosper for example in the sexist and racist ambience of some working men's clubs. These jokes either present the racial minority in question as socially inferior (greasy, mean, humourless, mendacious or in some way less than human) and thus to be scoffed at, or portray them in situations of misfortune, embarrassment or pain. The successful Mancunian stand-up comic Bernard Manning thus tells jokes about Pakistanis dressed up in white at night (to be on the safe side) who get run over by snow ploughs, justifying himself with arguments like "This is my home" and "I'm just giving people what they want." In one interview Manning makes the perspicacious point: "comedy's all about laughing. If we're telling jokes we're not fighting, are we? I don't believe in rules and theories. You can't say *this* should be funny, *that* can't be." [6] A joke, he would say, is a joke.

The claim that a joke is a joke is a tautology, and in this it is like the empty assertion that play is play: it is almost wholly uninformative. What it means, perhaps, is that a joke is *only* a joke and nothing else (just as play is not serious). This, however, is not quite true, for just as play is a *part* of the serious world to which it is by definition opposed, imitating it, reflecting it, and in turn pervading and affecting it, so a joke is a point of social interaction and exchange and as such it has repercussions. Most immediately, it may offend and hurt those attacked, undermining their identity, threatening their security and in general lowering the quality of their lives. But it may also insidiously foster and propagate harmful stereotypes and prejudices which then become a pretext for actual aggression. The stooge is dehumanized by being caricatured. Of course, there is something to Manning's self-justification: vicious jokes doubtless do serve as a ventilation for "nasty" impulses which we normally have to suppress, an articulation of the social frustrations and tensions we are not usually allowed to express, a safety valve for our insecurities, fears and anxieties. As such they indeed corroborate the Hobbesian point that the laugh of superiority is a sign of weakness. Recent research in the USA, where Blacks, Jews, Puerto Ricans and Italians have been the butt of denigrating stereotypes, shows that these ethnic groups have all represented both an economic and a phallic threat to the white middle classes.[7] As much as anything racist humour is impotence masquerading as power.

While verbal animosity may be a necessary outlet for our residual bestiality, the *universalized* abuse from the mouth of a comedian like Gerry Sadowitz has the great advantage of avoiding the complacency of self-flattering tribalism. Sadowitz hates everybody, including "white people, black people, women, yellow people, old age pensioners, young people ... students." While serving as a letting off of steam, his indiscriminate slaggings off and almost utter disregard for taboo mean that no one in particular is being singled out for dehumanization by his tirades. Like a court fool, moreover, *he* is part of the joke, and so are we: "assassinations and disasters are fair game, in his book, for jokes, so are old age pensioners, right wingers, left wingers, Irish, Pakistanis, Arab hijackings, miners ('I won't support anyone going down a mine ... it's a stupid fucking job'), TV charity, ugly women, feminists, royalty and himself." [8] Offending everyone, however, he may simply get on people's nerves.

As a jovial white male, I may wish to assert myself not only at the expense of those ethnic "outsiders" I regard as encroaching on *my* territory, but also as a signal of my power with respect to the weaker sex. As Freud points out, one of my traditional weapons here has been my ability *as a male* to embarrass the female, verbally denuding her by being "obscene" when I don't succeed in actually getting her in the sack. More generally, I may endorse the image of desirable young women as dumb and gagging for it (i.e. for me), while unavailable, married women and mothers-in-law are dismissed as shrews and witches. And although women are in essence laughable, they are not to take it into their heads to make people laugh on purpose. As Christine Brooke-Rose has put it, women are told: "You are my laughter, but don't you dare provoke laughter in others." Or: "Laugh at my jokes but don't produce any." [9] Male reluctance to grant women intellectual autonomy has thus coincided with a suppression or at least regulation of female humour (women *may* be witty, but never gross or vulgar) that helps account for the near-absence of women from the traditional comic canon of playwrights and novelists. The (male) philosopher Kant made the claim that "laughter is manly, weeping by contrast womanly (womanish in a man)." [10] Laughter is too potent a weapon to be given willy-nilly to that Other in relation to whom men feel such a mixture of dependence, insecurity and contempt.

Officially, of course, this traditional picture is in the process of changing. Comedians such as Victoria Wood or French and Saunders, as well as female joke-tellers in general, are encroaching into what was formerly a bastion of male domination, and man-bashing jokes can now do the rounds with impunity: Why are women bad at parking? Because men keep telling them that this (joker indicates an inch) is eight inches. In this instance the disparaging male stereotype concerning female incompetence at the wheel rebounds with a vengeance on those who *fancy themselves* in the driving seat, and men end up being hoist by their own rather unimpressive petards.[11] Not that this signals the end of the male sexist joke, which can after all always be modified or diluted (for example) with a touch of regionalism: What do Essex girls put behind their ears to make themselves attractive to men? Their legs. But it does at least suggest that the battle of the sexes may be becoming a slightly fairer fight.

Yet women have not been the only victims of sexual self-assertion: derision has provided an outlet for male homophobia ever since Aristophanes's day, and when the festival revelries of the Middle Ages turned sour it was often homosexuals – along with bawds, punks and panders – who were the most immediate targets for verbal and physical belligerence. The polemical point that homophobia is in fact a symptom of *repressed* or *latent* homosexuality hints at the element of fear or anxiety which may be at play in the sphere. Laughing at gays would thus be a way of differentiating oneself from something which presents a (perhaps subconscious) threat to one's own identity, a menace from within.

Communal self-assertion resorts, therefore, not just to factors of ethnicity, geography or gender in its understanding of difference but to more general notions of both moral and physical deviance or norm-infringement. While bodily deformity was a common quarry for ridicule up to and beyond the Middle Ages (holding down the number one spot in the English philosopher Francis Bacon's list of laughable objects)[12] and even now nervousness and fear with regard to the physically and mentally handicapped are channelled into sick humour, moral "aberrancy" has given us perennial pretext for upholding our identity insofar as this consists of a structure of values. Viewing ourselves as *good*, we lose no opportunity to distance ourselves from badness, disparaging those who fail to embody our standards or who do not share our commitments. The racist humourist, therefore, frequently operates by incorporating the absence or negatives of these values in the stereotypical caricature of his target, producing a reassuring equation of racial and moral otherness. As sociologists have pointed out, two particularly prevalent cross-cultural categories of moral or behavioural insufficiency are stupidity and stinginess (or craftiness), both of which have been (though need not be) interpreted in terms of a defective differentiation between self and other:

> *Stupid* acts are often naive, or unselfconscious, and fail to observe differentiations between both the self and the world, and meanings and contrasts which are clear to the average member of the group. *Crafty* or *stingy* acts take such differentiations to extremes, digitally defining a world without licence, ambiguity or "lubrication" in meaning, and are extremely self-conscious in constructing social relations.[13]

While the "stupid" jokes proclaim "They are stupid. We are intelligent," the "stingy/crafty" ones say something like "They are abnormal. We are normal" or "They are immoral (selfish). We are moral." Once again, the tension between fear and its overcoming is reflected in our disposition to laugh both at those who are less clever than we are (the stupid) and at those who are cleverer (the crafty). This tension is indeed internalized within the individual victim himself, who must be both powerful enough to antagonize or to pose some sort of threat and weak enough not to be able to resist degradation.[14]

This brand of humour is essentially *normative* in nature and in the world of theatrical comedy and satire coincides with a marked propensity towards *normalization*, operating both at a fictive level and in its didactic effect upon the spectator. This is comedy in its corrective guise, pillorying the follies and vices of the time, humbling and humiliating the fool or knave, be this a well-known public personality or a more abstract, symbolic representative of some negatively evaluated character trait. Misers, hypocrites, swindlers, cowards, killjoys and braggarts have traditionally all been fodder for stage ridicule, frequently taking a beating for their pains.

One of the nastiest examples of this normalizing tendency occurs in Plautus's *Miles Gloriosus* (*The Swaggering Soldier*), where poor old Pyrgopolynices – loudmouth and lecher as he is – is not only beaten up, but also threatened with the gelding knife. This vindictively moralistic finale is clearly meant to appeal to a scornful sense of moral superiority, reinforcing our ideas of what is right and what is wrong. More to most modern taste is when the knave or fool acknowledges his error, apologizes and promises to be better in future, the comedy culminating in the learning of a lesson rather than the thrashing of a recalcitrant pupil. Society in this case incorporates the deviant (but now reformed) individual as opposed to isolating him, a conciliatory or integrative gesture more characteristic of romantic comedy than of satire. More progressive still is comedy of the sort provided by Nestroy's *Der Talisman*, which questions and challenges the existing physical and moral stereotypes. Dealing with prejudice against redheads, this comedy mocks the exclusive or excluding society as much as those who are excluded, and Nestroy adapts the traditional happy ending to remedy the social injustice. The marginalization suffered by a minority at the hands of the majority turns into a pretext for the two redheads, Salome and Titus, to get down to some serious breeding as soon as the final curtain has dropped, and Titus is only too happy to do his bit for the multiplication of redheads in the world (so at last everyone will get used to the sight of them). Utopian as it is, the happy ending ingeniously combines a promise of the pleasures of procreation with an overcoming of bigotry and the forces of normalization.

Whether leaning towards overt castigation or more gentle

reconciliation, the less progressive varieties of comedy in particular are clearly bound up with either a maintenance or a creation of consensus. The fool or knave needs to be *recognized* as a fool or knave in order to be found funny, and the laughter implies a *shared* judgement (which may veer either towards condemnation of sinful aberration or a cathartic celebration of foolish fun). The "safety valve" theory of popular festivity and Carnival release likewise lays stress on the moment of licensed reversal and madness as a reinforcement of social order and stability, the infringements of the moral and cultural structure clarifying these structures and giving vent to tensions without ultimately calling the system into question. The symbolic folly thus operates as a form of negative feedback.

Humour in general has been understood as an act of social communion, a mode of "tension management" (at the workplace, for example) whose function is above all to promote consensus and unity. As a negotiation of taboo areas, joke-telling especially serves to mark out boundaries of tolerance, demarcating and maintaining the limits of acceptable behaviour. The possibility of retrospectively defining risky actions or speech as "only joking" allows sensitive issues and new ideas to be explored in a particularly flexible way,[15] while even something as simple as a repeated joke or catchphrase may take on a ritual status essential to the identity of the subgroup in question. And like the "joking relationships" of certain tribal societies – ritualized and playful antagonism which licenses not only teasing but also mock-obscenity between in-laws – the humour of industrial societies is invaluable as a means of coping with the pressures and anxieties of communal life. In traditional British stand-up comedy too, perhaps the most typical metonym for the pressures and anxieties of communal life is the mother-in-law. Les Dawson's deadpan disparagements presumably had some sort of nationwide therapeutic effect: "She tries to improve her appearance, but it's all to no avail. In fact, she's had her face lifted so many times that in future they'll have to lower her body."[16]

Recognition

Essential to laughter as an agent of social unity is the element of recognition. Cohesive norm-sharing implies common notions of norm-infringement and an ability to *identify* acts of deviation, which means that to the sense of social or moral self-affirmation is wedded an ego-boosting dose of intellectual self-congratulation. Commenting on the laughter provoked by the contrast between a norm and its infringement, Hegel's *Ästhetik* accordingly depicts it as "just an expression of complacent cleverness, a sign that they too [those laughing] are wise enough to recognize such a contrast and know themselves above it."[17]

At the same time, however, the apparently unambiguous derision of satire may be compounded not only by the communal recognition of behavioural aberrancy but also by a sort of intellectual applause for the skill of the theatrical or fictional representation ("Yes, I can see the likeness there..."), an acknowledgement of the appositeness of the portrayal.

Dependent as it is upon caricature and selective distortion, racist and sexist humour works by creating or perpetuating stereotypes, which – regardless of appropriateness – end up blinding the jokers to the possibility of individual characteristics in their victims. Recognition tags are developed in accordance with popular prejudice, that is, and these recur as permanent features of the racist/sexist humorous discourse, allowing reassuringly reliable pleasures of recognition. This sinister essentialism *defines*, and therefore delimits and in a sense contains or controls, the menacing Other, reducing Blacks to their big lips (or penises), Jews to their noses, or cripples to their infirmity. Once we "recognize" them, we "know" them, and once we "know" them, we have them – conceptually at least – in our grasp.

This applies equally to the timeless theatrical comedy of stock types: here the butt of our derision is reduced to a single dominant trait (of course taken to excess), laughable not simply for its norm-infringement but also for the repetitiveness which structures its conduct and makes it so obtrusively recognizable. The Miser, the Hypochondriac, the Hypocrite, the Bawd, the Braggart, the Parasite, the Pedant, the Lecher and the Spoilsport are all more or less ageless stereotypical abstractions, whose essence is to be predictable. As with the famous *fort-da* game played by Freud's grandson, who was observed to throw one of his toys out of his pram with the exclamation "fort!" (gone away) and then haul it back in by its string to the cry "da!" (here), the repeated return of something we recognize seems to be a source of extremely satisfying feelings of mastery. Indeed, the recognition of patterns is absolutely fundamental to our ability to order and make sense of the world at all.

The element of recognition and the accompanying intellectual pat on the back may take any number of forms. Not only do satire, caricature, racist or sexist humour, and the comedy of character depend upon it (as a picking out of stereotypical human essences), but parody, burlesque and travesty require a prior knowledge of what is being parodied, burlesqued and travestied (and what for), incongruity presupposes an awareness of the disparity (as well as a possible latent similarity) between things that do not "belong" together, and even jokes need to be "got." In the case of jokes in particular, an extraordinarily complex network of social factors contributes to the competence necessary for understanding them. The smallest degree of unshared knowledge or the least discrepancy in assumptions or values can so easily lead to blank faces and all-round embarrassment. Take the sequence of jokes at the expense of Essex girls (and men) which circulated in the early nineties:

e.g. What's the difference between an Essex girl and a supermarket trolley? A supermarket trolley has got a mind of its own. In its full force, this joke will not simply bolster our regionalistic identity by feeding our prejudices. To be effective it also entails an awareness of the whole joke-tradition (Essex girl equals full-time airhead), the joke-technique (the positive statement about trolleys implying a negative statement about Essex girls which *we have to provide*), as well as a recognition of the appropriateness of bringing together the notions of supermarket trolleys and Essex girls (which in turn presupposes both prior experience of disobedient or wilful trolleys and the linguistic versatility to understand a fairly subtle metaphorical use of the term "having a mind of one's own").

Part of the pleasure afforded by a joke, therefore, is the pleasure of a challenge met. Arthur Koestler writes: "the listener must fill in the gaps, complete the hints, trace the hidden analogies. Every good joke contains an element of the riddle – it may be childishly simple, or subtle and challenging – which the listener must solve. By doing so, he is lifted out of his passive role and compelled to co-operate, to repeat to some extent the process of inventing the joke."[18] Elsewhere Koestler distinguishes the "HAHA" reaction of aggressive, self-assertive laughter from the "AHA" of intellectual discovery, where the humour is subtler, more cryptic and more sophisticated.[19] Indeed, he speaks of a continuum stretching toward the "AH" reaction of integrative and self-transcending artistic contemplation, as though the element of self-assertion were diminished in the sphere of intellectual recognition. This does not seem justified. The intelligence test implied by the joke can be every bit as viciously exclusive as more direct verbal belligerence and need not always be separable from it, as where the recognition of social or moral deviance coincides with knowing oneself above it.

Failure to recognize folly may itself thus constitute a type of folly. As George Meredith put it in his *Essay on Comedy* of 1877, if you are not struck by the contrasts illuminated by the Comic Spirit, you will yourself "be standing in that peculiar oblique beam of light, yourself illuminated to the general eye as the very object of chase and doomed quarry of the thing obscure to you. But to feel its presence, and to see it, is your assurance that many sane and solid minds are with you in what you are experiencing."[20] Failing to mock norm-infringement, in other words, is itself a form of norm-infringement. In a slightly different context, not perceiving the particular literary allusion necessary for the understanding of a witticism may be taken as exposing some gap in our education or upbringing, while not getting a dirty joke may betray an embarrassing hole in our sexual knowledge or experience (something Everybody Else has been doing and enjoying since they were knee-high to a short- horned grasshopper). The bawdy pun and the saucy innuendo even go to the trouble of verbally "masking" the naughtiness we are supposed to recognize, making themselves still more inaccessible to the ingenuous.

The exclusiveness of humour simultaneously produces a sense of collusion or complicity among those who are "in" on it. Jonathan Miller has accordingly perceived in jokes a trace of something akin to social sycophancy, describing them as part of a (frequently male) ritual of conviviality which serves as a means of ingratiating those concerned into a social group. Jokes remind him of rental cars: "I don't like them at all. They are mechanized, common property. Other people have driven the joke before; it has cigarettes in its ashtray. ... It's been rather badly Hoovered before you get it." [21] Mind you, this is something which at a certain level could be claimed of *all* language. Bergson too was aware how much laughter hides a secret desire to be on the same wavelength as the rest of our social group: "We would not have a sense of the comic if we felt ourselves isolated from others. Laughter seems to need an echo. Listen to it carefully: it is not an articulate, clear, well-defined sound: it is something which yearns for prolongation by reverberating from one person to the next, something which – beginning with a bang – rumbles on like thunder in the mountains. And yet this reverberation cannot go on for ever. It can make its way through as wide a circle as you please: the circle will still remain closed." [22]

This aspiration for complicity explains the significance of dialect in regional humour, as well as the importance of topicality and local or contemporary relevance. Part of the secret for the success of the Italian *commedia dell'arte*, for example, lay in their knack of incorporating the events of the day into the performance, in this way establishing a dialogue with the spectators and creating a spirit of festive unity. Pulcinella was described by Goethe as a "living newspaper." [23] The catchphrase embodies a similar fusion of exclusiveness and collusion, exemplified in modern times by the code-words of *Private Eye* (tincture, Ugandan discussions, tired and emotional) or the hip nonsense of Vic Reeves, which leave the uninitiated feeling either disconcertingly dull, out of it, or bored.

As much as any comic form, irony testifies to the pleasures of complicity. Depending upon a recognition of the disparity between what is said and what is meant, verbal irony – to take but one category – assumes some degree of collaboration between narrator and reader, speaker and listener. In Wayne Booth's words: "Whenever an author conveys to his reader an unspoken point, he creates a sense of collusion against all those, whether in the story or out of it, who do not get that point. Irony is thus always in part a device for excluding as well as including." [24] This tacit concord may be facilitated by signals either within the content of what is said (such as exaggerations or contradictions) or accompanying it (in the form of winks, nudges, smiles or other twitchings),[25] but more generally it requires a shared system of values between the two parties. Indeed, even lumberingly telegraphed irony-signals rely upon a *receptiveness* to signals, a receptiveness which may be absent in those who, as they say, "only see (or hear) what they want to see (or hear)."

In the world of comic theatre, it is the omniscience tending to accompany the audience perspective – by contrast with the limited viewpoint of all but the most perceptive of fictive figures – which most frequently serves to flatter the spectator's intellectual self-esteem: the Olympian overview characteristic of ironic distance permits the onlooker to see through disguises and deceptions played out on stage and to revel in the privilege of knowing better than the deceived. Here it is the fictive gull or fool who is "excluded" by his or her oblivion to the gulf between appearance and reality, the spoken word and the underlying intention. *We* share the outlook of the cunning, streetwise (and often lovable) rogue or trickster, whose asides in particular let us in on his secrets and make us a party to his machinations.

Given the evident significance of collusion and cohesion, it is not surprising that some commentators have been prone – slightly one-sidedly – to stress this aspect of comedy to the detriment of its opposite, excluding exclusion from the comic moment. Visions of laughter as basically sociable and good-natured are in many cases applicable and informative, but clearly beg the question regarding what is good; a racist or sectarian is likely to have ideas of goodness and of what is funny which themselves could be targeted for derision by more progressive or conciliatory manifestations of the comic impulse. Nonetheless, the "normal" (just to beg the question again) understanding of laughter's good-natured side – voiced, for example, by the eighteenth-century British benevolist Hutcheson in opposition to Hobbes's more pessimistic view[26] – sees in it an expression of fellow-feeling and empathy.

Laughter directed at a victim (at someone, say, in an excruciatingly embarrassing situation) need not therefore simply be a signal of scornful superiority, but may incorporate sentiments like "I know how that must feel (shudder)" or "yes, equally nightmarish things have happened to me": whence much of the comic potential inherent in someone caught short, or trying in vain to stifle a burp, smother a fart, placate an untimely erection or keep on a wayward piece of underwear. Laughter at gaffes and blunders may contain a covert rapport or warmth ("finally! someone as clumsy as me!"), an understanding recognition of the mechanisms by which the gaffe came to pass, or a recollection of situations in which *we* wished the earth would swallow us whole. The sort of affection built up for comic heroes during the course of a narrative or through repeated performances, moreover, is also likely to mean that we end up laughing *with* as much as *at* them: Don Quixote is perhaps the most celebrated example of a fool whose folly infects and wins us over by the novel's conclusion. By the same token, people *love* Laurel and Hardy.

The empathetic laughter of recognition may coincide both with an unmasking of unacknowledged or semi-private aspects of ourselves and with intellectual applause for the narrator's or author's insight or perceptiveness ("I wish I'd noticed or formulated or thought of that"). Don DeLillo's novel *White Noise* affords masterly examples of both. One of DeLillo's skills lies in his ability to pick out the type of minor absurdities and inconsistencies that are encountered in daily life perhaps without ever being consciously registered or put into words. His description of a supermarket shopping experience is typically observant:

> ... we walked past the fruit bins, an area that extended about forty-five yards along one wall. The bins were arranged diagonally and backed by mirrors that people accidentally punched when reaching for fruit in the upper rows. A voice on the loudspeaker said: "Kleenex Softique, your truck's blocking the entrance." Apples and lemons tumbled in twos and threes to the floor when someone took a fruit from certain places in the stacked array. There were six kinds of apples, there were exotic melons in several pastels. Everything seemed to be in season, sprayed, burnished, bright. People tore filmy bags off racks and tried to figure out which end opened.[27]

DeLillo's characters Grappa and Lasher have a comic habit of unmasking some of each other's, and perhaps the reader's, more confidential or personal experiences with their direct questioning: "Did you ever brush your teeth with your finger?"; "Did you ever crap in a toilet bowl that had no seat?"; and later "Did you ever spit in your soda bottle so you wouldn't have to share your drink with the other kids?"; "Did you ever get an erection from a dental hygienist rubbing against your arm while she cleaned your teeth?"; "When you bite dead skin off your thumb, do you eat it or spit it out?"[28] Their answers are equally direct.

Exorcism

The ironic perspective which theatre grants its spectators puts human observers in a position of godlike transcendence. This highly favoured position has been described by D.C.Muecke: "The ironic observer's awareness of himself as observer tends to enhance his feeling of freedom and induce a mood of satisfaction, serenity, joyfulness, or even exultation. His awareness of the victim's unawareness leads him to see the victim as bound or trapped where he feels free; committed where he feels disengaged; swayed by emotions, harassed, or miserable, where he is dispassionate, serene, or even moved to laughter; trustful, credulous, or naive, where he is critical, sceptical, or content to suspend judgement.

Where his own attitude is that of a man whose world appears real and meaningful, he will see the victim's world as illusory or absurd." [29] Theatrical comedy in this case comes to satisfy voyeuristic or even sadistic impulses, for knowledge implies power. Like Jeremy Bentham's *Panopticon* (an eighteenth-century carceral design allowing permanent surveillance of delinquants or madmen),[30] theatre – in its bourgeois or boulevard forms at least – dissolves the dyad of seeing and being seen that characterizes outside life: the audience enjoys the unilateral power to look, while the actor can only ever be the one being looked at, the object of a prying gaze. Like the *Panopticon*, moreover, theatre – in its bourgeois or boulevard forms at least – can be quite aggressively reformative, although the process of normalization may surreptitiously work in both directions (as both fictional fool and real-life spectator learn what is to be scoffed at or expelled from the social community).

If theatre at times seems rather like a reformatory institution, then the sense of superiority in evidence in so much theatrical laughter can be understood to be at the expense of the comic actor inside that institution. Jean-Paul Sartre suggests that, forced as we normally are in daily life to suppress our propensity to purely derisive laughter, theatre gives us an excuse to shelve sympathy and give vent to feelings of mastery, the actor himself becoming the butt. The actor provokes mirth by "wallowing in subhumanity in order to smear his own self with the stains that might tarnish the 'human personage' and to display them as the taints of an inferior race vainly trying to approximate to ours." [31] The actor, writes Sartre, is a "helot," a slave to *our* need for laughter. The search for a scapegoat or victim or outsider is channelled into scorn for the person who spends his life making a joke of himself.

The idea of the actor as an outsider goes back at least to Plato, who in the *Laws* decreed that it should be left to "slaves and hired strangers" to represent the laughable on stage. Nor is comedy to be permitted in his utopian Republic, for the comic actor – through his mastery of mimicry – constitutes a menace to the well-being of the city-state:

> Suppose, then, that an individual clever enough to assume any character and give imitations of anything and everything should visit our country and offer to perform his compositions, we shall bow down before a being with such miraculous powers of giving pleasure; but we shall tell him that we are not allowed to have any such person in our commonwealth; we shall crown him with fillets of wool, anoint his head with myrrh, and conduct him to the borders of some other country.[32]

As a representative of non-identity (not being oneself), the comic actor poses a threat from within to the order of the *polis* and so must be reverentially expelled for the good of all. The comic poet too faces expulsion: if there is to be poetic mimesis at all, it must at least express

nobility rather than licence, lubricity or the ludicrous, for these jeopardize
the sovereignty of reason. The problem with comedy is its infectiousness. You are allowing your character to be undermined "if in listening
at a comic performance or in ordinary life to buffooneries which you
would be ashamed to indulge in yourself, you thoroughly enjoy them
instead of being disgusted with their ribaldry. There is in you an impulse
to play the clown, which you have held in restraint from a reasonable
fear of being set down as a buffoon; but now you have given it rein, and
by encouraging its impudence at the theatre you may be unconsciously
carried away into playing the comedian in your private life." [33] Clearly
an orderly state must be protected from such subversive forces.

As such a contagious enemy of order, laughter came to be viewed by
many in the Middle Ages as diabolical in nature. The Platonic
association of laughter and disorder was perpetuated in Christian terms
by Augustine, an association reinforced by the contention in certain
quarters that Christ never laughed. Laughter – as later with Baudelaire –
was regarded as a result of man's Fall, for in our original perfection our
lofty joys could be voiced in less carnal manner.[34] According to a figure
in the prose of Bonaventura (the German romantic, not the Saint), the
devil "sent laughter down in order to get his own back on the master
builder: without being noticed this was skilfully able to worm its way
into a mask of joyfulness, and people readily accepted it – until it finally
tore off its mask and stared at them with its evil face of satire." [35]
Fortunately, the medieval doctrine of rigorous rejection was countered
by a more tolerant lineage stemming from the Aristotelian recognition of
laughter as something quintessentially *human*, while several Christian
authorities – including Julian of Norwich, Luther and Sir Thomas More
– went so far as to see laughter as a weapon *against* Satan.[36]

If the Platonic-Sartrean viewpoint on the actor is to be accepted, it is
the player-cum-scapegoat who seems to constitute the most palpable
human embodiment of the diabolical. Imperilling the stability of
identity, the actor – with his capacity to be somebody other than himself
– incarnates the subversive possibility of dissolution from within. The
other side of the coin is that the Devil is an actor. As God's double, he is
the archetypal mimic, a parody of God's self-identity ("I am that I am").
The four surviving English medieval Corpus Christi cycles depict him
accordingly: after his Fall, Lucifer turns into a grotesque caricature of
his former archangelic splendour, his feet becoming cloven hooves, his
teeth fangs, his smooth skin and wings changing into a tangled
hotchpotch of fur and feathers. In the Temptation of Eve of the York and
Chester plays, moreover, Satan dons a squeaky falsetto, as well as a
woman's face-mask, gloves, a snakeskin and a pair of falsies in his
efforts to entice his victim into his snare. Again, he is the prototypical
impostor, the original (comic) actor, and the originator of laughter and
the laughable.

In the diabolic form of the actor, the comic victim assumes a guise more general than any representative of *specific* ethnic, sexual, moral or intellectual otherness. In this case it is a question less of self-assertion at the expense of other identities than at the expense of symbolic incarnations of *non-identity*. In laughing at the actor (if Sartre is correct to claim that this is what we do), we are laughing not at someone who is not us, but at someone who is no-one at all (for being anybody, he is nobody); in deriding the devil we are deriding not someone who negates our values, but someone who negates Value. Clearly such distinctions are clumsy oversimplifications: the ethnic or ethical outsider, for example, may be turned into and serve the function of a more abstract representative of disorder. The point, perhaps, is that as such the outsider takes on a symbolic significance which goes beyond any specific rivalry or antagonism and reflects a deep-seated human fear of disorder.

In *The Origin of Attic Comedy* (1914), F. M. Cornford thus traces the roots of Ancient Greek comedy back to festive religious *sacrifice*, prehistoric death-and-resurrection rituals involving the killing of the old year (the aged king or god) followed by the birth or accession of the new. Related to this was the ancient rite of purifying the tribe by the expulsion of a scapegoat felt to embody the evils and debilities of the community as a whole. These fertility rites seem to have had a number of layers of signification, saving the community from the sterility of (its king's or god's) old age, expelling the tribe's evils or devils, and thus redeeming the whole group by the sacrifice of a single victim. The Cambridge anthropologist Sir James George Frazer understands this as explaining the ambiguity of the protocomic ritual of "Carrying out Death": having originally been a spirit of vegetation or tree-spirit who was annually slain in spring in order to return to life invigorated, the dying god of vegetation gradually turned into a scapegoat, a figure evoking fear and abhorrence as a bearer of all the evils that had visited the community during the past year. René Girard by contrast refuses to see the origins of the scapegoat in rituals of seasonal change and the "death" and "resurrection" of nature. For Girard, who regards *violence* as the latent origin of all religious celebration and indeed of all social organization, festive sacrifice is a ritual re-enactment of a historically specific occasion on which a substitute victim was killed in order to avert a more general descent into indiscriminate violence, disorder and non-differentiation within the community. The sacrificial process is cathartic in function, purging the social unit of its innate tendency to self-destruction and thus re-establishing order: "the antagonism of everyone against everyone else yields to the union of all against one."[37] Where the chaos of violent non- differentiation threatened, unanimity is brought to prevail.

The scapegoat, contends Girard, must be a marginal figure, both internal and external to the community, both similar and different (slaves, prisoners of war, beggars, children, and vagrants all fitting the bill here).[38] His or her sacrificeability consists furthermore in a complete dispensability, by which is meant that the victim will neither strike back nor be avenged: the sacrifice must be the act of violence to end all acts of violence. Girard's account makes it clear how absolutely essential the margin or borderline (the scapegoat) is for maintaining the structures of identity within: in its absence indeed, it seems the ordered system would rapidly crumble into a free-for-all internecine bloodbath. The ritual repetitions in fact *re-enact* the crisis – the moment of identity-loss and structural disintegration – immediately preceding the original sacrifice, and the periodic scapegoating is frequently associated with a spell of general licence, in which ordinary social and moral restraints are cast aside and anything goes.[39] In many cases the ritual scapegoat in particular is permitted to speak the unspeakable, perform the impermissible.

If it is the case that comedy descends from this sacrificial festivity, then clearly its murderousness is well and truly diluted or displaced. Comedy is, superficially at least, a polite or civilized re-re-enactment of the eruption of disruptive forces and the return to unanimity. Even so, in the words of Wylie Sypher, "one of the strongest impulses comedy can discharge from the depths of the social self is our hatred of the 'alien', especially when the stranger who is 'different' stirs any unconscious doubt about our own beliefs. Then the comedian unerringly finds his audience, the solid majority, itself a silent prey to unrecognized fears. He can point out our victim, isolate him from sympathy, and cruelly expose him to the penalty of our ridicule." The comic mechanism is to this extent a reactionary mechanism, protecting us from self-doubt or moral questioning. As a symptom of fear, writes Sypher, "our mirth indicates the zeal with which we are maltreating our scapegoat." [40] In the Christian comic canon the archetypal scapegoat – armed with unpalatable denials of what all Christians know to be true – is the Devil. Speaking the unspeakable, the fool Satan denies God and would have us do likewise. Negating the Truth, he is the symbolic representative of duplicity and disorder.

Medieval mockery of Lucifer is typified in the Corpus Christi or mystery plays. What in the Scriptures had been a dark, deadly earnest threat rarely appearing in physical form, is metamorphosed into an extravagantly posturing grotesquery. For those who see themselves as Christians, he is *the* Other, the embodiment of their spiritual anxieties, but this Other and the anxieties he embodies are overcome by being lowered to the level of the ludicrous. That a fiend should be presented, for example, as farting "for fere of fyre" – besides being a satisfying alliterative onomatopoeia – reduces him to a cowardly clown in the grip of rather unimpressive bodily disorders. Not that such deep-seated apprehensions can be easily vanquished. The overcoming of fear is as ever only partial. By the same token, the Devil can vary in his capacity to frighten. Sometimes the comic Satan is relegated to being but the minister of another more powerful but absent fiend (Lucifer or Beelzebub); on other occasions, audience scorn is directed instead at minor devils and demons, evil but fundamentally stupid and incompetent creatures. Such are the devils in the inferno of Dante's *Divina Commedia*, grotesque flatulent monsters who quarrel among themselves and two of whom topple into the boiling pitch intended for the sinners in their custody.

In the morality plays written between the fourteenth and sixteenth centuries, the Devil is generally superseded by the Vice, who – though acknowledged to be distinct from the Devil – performs the same diabolical role as Tempter. Yet devilry bounces back to something like its old form in Marlowe's *Doctor Faustus*. The complexity of the matter is indicated by the hierarchy of devilry which appears in this play: while Lucifer and Beelzebub cut imposing figures, Mephostophilis is a somewhat subordinate Tempter, and a whole array of lesser devils are responsible above all for physical horseplay, chasings, manhandlings and fireworks. When Faustus asks for a wife, Mephostophilis even resorts to the stage tradition of devilry in drag (plus the obligatory fireworks), to which Faustus testily responds with "A plague on her for a hot whore" (1.5). Diabolical magic is never particularly awesome, but more of a theatrical antic or practical joke, and even after he has taken a pummelling at the hands of two devils summoned by Wagner, the Clown withholds any sign of respect ("A vengeance on them!" he fumes, "They have vile long nails!" 1.4). As Bristol explains, "Hell is only a 'cautionary fable,' the devil is a bogeyman contrived to compel obedience and subordination; devilish manifestations are mainly noise, firecrackers, and scary masks." [41]

By the time of Grabbe's *Scherz, Satire, Ironie und tiefere Bedeutung* (1822), the Enlightenment has further weakened the grasp of the Devil on the popular imagination. The equivocality of the Devil's status now comes to light above all in the contradictions in his character. Grabbe's *Teufel* is a curious hybrid of grotesque bodily trickery (as when he pulls off his arm and uses it to beat one of the tiresome natural historians) and impotence and vulnerability (manifest in his compulsion to sit in the fire to keep from freezing, his discomfort when his horseshoe is loose, his susceptibility to the bait of sixteen condoms laid for him, and the ensuing ignominious captivity together with the humiliation of having his rather sexy grandmother come and pick him up to take him back to a freshly spring-cleaned Hell). And all this is coupled with the superiority of perspective that has enabled him to write a tragedy in fourteen years entitled *The French Revolution* (though it was given the chop by the critics). What is being derided in Grabbe's play, therefore, is less the traditional incarnation of evil itself than the lingering popular conception of evil insofar as it is embodied in such a pathetic semi-anthropomorphic aberration. Grabbe's Devil is a parody of the Devil, and so a parody of a parody.

Many other comic rogues and heroes are less obtrusively derived from the Devil. Kleist's lecherous and thoroughly corrupt judge Adam – armed with clubfoot and a hellish case of B. O. – is distinctly diabolical in nature, while Shakespeare's Falstaff, who in a sense acts as a "Tempter" in relation to Prince Hal, is clearly a descendent of the morality Vice. Arlecchino, or Harlequin, of the *commedia dell'arte* can likewise be traced back to the clown-devils of the early Middle Ages. His demoniacal half-mask and remnant of a horn testify to his origins in Hell (one of Dante's devils also having the name Alichino), as does a characteristic combination of muddle-minded stupidity and acrobatic dexterity. He is, moreover, a natural actor, prepared to impersonate anything, disguise himself as anybody, male or female. As a perpetual performer he perhaps exemplifies Sartre's point about the laughter we aim at people who spend their lives not being themselves. In this capacity Harlequin is a symbol of the non-identity we both fear and despise.

Yet this is evidently not the whole truth: Harlequin is a lovable comic hero as much as a victim or a butt, and the laughter he provokes is sympathetic as much as castigatory. The same has applied to so much of what is diabolical or infernal. In the case of *Doctor Faustus*, there can be little doubt that Marlowe's contemporaries would have at least partially identified with the farcical pyrotechnics accompanying the devilry, particularly (for example) with the anti-papist dig implicit in Faustus's and Mephostophilis's exuberant friar-bashing. In such scenes of devilment and physically retributive horseplay, writes Bristol, Faustus is "no longer a character in a theological *mise-en-scène*, but the ringleader of a Carnivalesque disturbance. Faustus the damned magician has become Faustus the low-life, hanging about in taverns and living by his wits. In this world of ordinary vulgar entertainment the only devils are manmade, funny monsters, animated spooks used to frighten the credulous."[42] The Renaissance devils of Rabelais's *Gargantua* and *Pantagruel* sequence of books are by and large a jolly set of fellows, and Pantagruel himself – before his humane and thoroughly humanistic Rabelaisian incarnation – was already renowned as a mystery-play devil with a habit of throwing salt into revellers' mouths in order to keep them supping. Devilry in this guise is clearly associated with the festive folly of popular celebration, i.e. with having a Good Time. The *diableries* which accompanied the French mystery plays often spilled over the footlights in the most riotous manner. On such occasions the devils were frequently allowed to run loose around town for a matter of days prior to a performance, their diabolical disguises giving them an infectious feeling of carnivalesque liberty and immunity from the law (which they often exploited for their own illicit ends).[43] And even within their role on stage they were allowed to indulge in abuse, oaths and obscenities. The Lord of Misrule who presided over English festive ceremonials was equated by the Puritan Phillip Stubbes with Satan.[44]

In such cases our fear of the diabolical may yield to a (more or less) empathetic or identificatory recognition and release of the diabolical within ourselves. Festive devilry asserts the necessity of disorder for the maintenance of order, the dependence of our identity upon the normally excluded Other. The German theorist Joachim Ritter accordingly argues that laughter's function is to spotlight "what is not accessible to seriousness – the affiliation of the Other to the existential reality which excludes it."[45] But this also explains our deep-seated ambivalence towards otherness: schematically put, to the extent that we are different from it, it is something to be laughingly expelled; to the extent that – at our logical or physical margins – we ourselves internalize it or are "infected" by it, it becomes something with which we may identify, something which needs to be acknowledged and allowed out to play. Seen in this way, the contradiction we display in our response to the demonic Other (celebration *and* scorn) is a reflection of the contradiction we contain at our own "margins," where self embodies other (I = not-I). The philosophical anthropologist Plessner, aware of the ambivalence of laughter as both self-affirmation and self-exposure, understands the laughing response as the signal of a failure to cope (*nicht-fertig-werden*) with an ambivalence or contradiction.[46] In a certain sense, it is perhaps a failure to cope with the contradiction within ourselves.

As a playground for acting out this inner contradiction, an opportunity for the diabolical or disorderly impulses inside us to go on a licensed bender, Carnival revelries and popular festivity partake of a like ambivalence. Consequently, although festive observance may consist by and large of anti-social conduct, this transgression as a rule takes place against a background of social oneness and jovial togetherness: "Paradoxically, a ritual that stages or mimics the community's conflictual dissolution appears to be an act of social collaboration. Or, ... during carnival, the height of holism and the height of individualism appear to coincide."[47] At the same time, the unity of the celebrating masses has shown itself (in medieval revelry, for example) liable to snap over into acts of sinister scapegoating, the pent-up animosity of one oppressed social group being channelled into the victimization of an even more disadvantaged group, with verbal or physical attacks on Jews or foreigners, actors or homosexuals. Festive fun could transform itself into scornful persecution.

An analogous ambivalence lies at the heart of the traditional ritual scapegoat or *pharmakos*. In Cornford's words, "the *Pharmakos* ... is a representative both of the power of fertility and of the opposite powers

of famine, disease, impurity, death." [48] For René Girard, who interprets
scapegoating as a re-directing of indiscriminate internal violence
towards a single marginal or external figure in order to re-establish
communal unanimity, the sacrificial victim seems to unite the malignant
and the benign aspects of violence: "Religious thought is inevitably
brought to see in the scapegoat ... a supernatural creature who sows
violence in order then to reap peace, a mysterious, awesome saviour
who makes men ill in order then to cure them." The *pharmakos*, in other
words, has "a double connotation; on the one hand, he is seen as a
lamentable, despicable, even guilty personage; he is the butt of all sorts
of mockery, insults and of course violence; he is surrounded, on the
other hand, with an almost religious veneration." [49] The *pharmakos* is
both a poison and a remedy, a much-commented semantic pairing itself
present in the Greek term *pharmakon*, which means both of these things.
One of the maxims of the seventeenth-century French writer La
Rochefoucauld sheds light on the interdependence and inextricability of
cure and poison, self and other: "Vices enter into the composition of
virtues like poisons enter into the composition of remedies. Prudence
assembles and tempers them, and puts them to use against the evils of
life." [50] Violence, diabolical and vicious, lies (normally hidden) at the
core of the social order, like the poisonous ingredients within a life-
saving drug.

In the Athens of four centuries B.C., the fictional-cum-historical
figure of the philosopher Socrates serves as a revealing incarnation of
the ambiguities of the scapegoat. Though not a *pharmakos* in the strict
sense (one of the "useless" and "degraded" beings kept in Athens at the
public expense to be beaten on the genitals and stoned to death in times
of impending catastrophe), Socrates was nonetheless the victim of a
crisis in the Athenian identity, which since the death of Pericles in 429
B.C. had suffered the rigours of defeat in the Peloponnesian War with
Sparta and the re-establishment of an embittered democracy. Socrates's
prosecution was founded upon the charge that he injured the community
by "corrupting the young" and failing to worship the traditional gods.
He was sentenced to death for being "a criminal and a busybody,
investigating the things beneath the earth and in the heavens and making
the weaker argument stronger and teaching others these same things." [51]
Like many of the traditional scapegoat figures, Socrates is an asker of
awkward questions: he queries assumptions normally taken for granted.

In addition to this, however, Socrates had been scapegoated and
pilloried in at least four comedies of the time, of which the only extant
one is Aristophanes's *Clouds*. Written twenty-four years before the
prosecution of Socrates, this (at the time highly unsuccessful) play
ascribes four attributes to him which would have been viewed as
especially dubious by the Athenian philistines and reactionaries of the
420s: like the controversial Sophists of the time, the Aristophanic

Socrates is an atheist, as well as a champion of rhetoric and techniques of persuasion, of speculation and scientific enquiry, and of a new progressive morality questioning paternal authority and social institutions. The fact, in particular, that the Sophists combined philosophical activities with an interest in oratory resulted in a popular association of philosophy with legal and political craftiness (and high fees), an association which finds expression in Aristophanes's portrayal of Socrates as an utterly unattractive rogue and swindler. Yet the comedy ends with the established order carrying the day: Socrates's subversive innovations are heartily condemned, his "Thinkery" is set on fire, and the ugly old con man is stoned out of town. Having had his day and his say, the threat to the communal unanimity and well-being is cruelly but laughingly expelled from the *polis*.

The Socrates of Plato (and of Xenophon) could hardly be more different. As Cornford has argued, the oldest comedy frequently consisted of a contest, or *agon*, caused by the presence of an intruder or impostor (the *alazon*) who defiles the sacred rites and is put to flight either by the young king or a character known as the *eiron*, the ironical man. Where Aristophanes's Socrates had been a boastful *alazon* and as such ultimately identical to the scapegoat, the Platonic Socrates assumed the character of the ironical man, professing ignorance and deflating boasters and impostors by showing that they in fact know less than they had thought.[52] The non-Aristophanic tradition indeed presents a Socrates who differs in fundamental ways from the Sophists with whom he is lumped together in the *Clouds*, a Socrates who is openly critical of oratorical techniques (and teaching for money), who is far from atheistic, had little interest in scientific investigation and whose moral enquiries were not aimed at establishing a new morality but at using questions to get to the foundations of the existing one.[53]

It is the Platonic account that has of course had the greater influence on the history of thought, turning Socrates into a secular saint, sublime and benign in the face of his philistine persecutors. Yet – behind the idolatry – even the "philosophical" figure can be seen to have had his dubious characteristics. Underneath the humility of his profession of ignorance lay the self-congratulation of one who still considered himself to excel the rest of humanity (and who had his own private demon, or inner voice, to boot); indeed, irony itself can easily be taken to be a sort of mock-modesty veiling scorn and intellectual contempt. Politically he displayed the anti-democratic aloofness of one who despised the hoi polloi of Athens and derided their democratic leaders, and many of his pupils turned out quite disastrously – witness the repulsive tyrant Critias. As I. F. Stone reports, the speech "Against Timarchus," made by the orator Aeschines fifty years after Socrates's death, testifies to the still popular feeling that "the old 'sophist' got what he deserved" for his part in the education of the hated despot.[54] Socrates is a more ambiguous figure than his reverential philosophical successors have liked to acknowledge.

This ambiguity is expressed in the inner/outer distinction, which either sees Socrates's mock-modesty as masking an overweening arrogance or his outlandish looks as masking a treasure within. He was frequently compared in appearance to the mythical figure of Silenus, chief of the satyrs and foster father to Dionysus, represented as a bald, dissolute old man but also an inspired prophet. In Plato's *Symposium* Alcibiades likens him to one of the carved images of Silenus, a comparison taken up and expounded by Rabelais in the prologue to the first book of *Gargantua*:

> Sileni, in days of old, were little boxes of the sort nowadays seen in apothecaries' shops, painted on the outside with joyful, frivolous figures ... designed to move people to laughter (in the manner of Silenus himself, master of good old Bacchus). But inside these boxes were kept rare drugs such as balm, ambergris, cardamon, musk, civet, as well as precious stones and other things of great value.
>
> Thus, too, was Socrates said to be. For to see him from the outside and judge by his external appearance, you would not have given a shred of onion for him, so ugly was his body and so absurd his mien. He had a pointed nose, the expression of a bull and the countenance of a fool; his manners were coarse, his apparel boorish, his wealth little; he was unlucky in his wives and unfit for any public office. He was always laughing, always carousing with the next man, always playing the fool, always concealing his divine knowledge. Yet had you opened that box, you would have found inside a heavenly and invaluable drug: an understanding surpassing the human, wondrous virtue, invincible courage, unequalled sobriety, unfailing contentment, perfect assurance, and a marvellous disregard for all the things for which men search, rush, work, voyage and struggle.[55]

Socrates's ambivalence also brings to mind that archetypal comic scapegoat and rascal, Falstaff, whose character displays a similar triplicity as a buffoon, an ironist (or *eiron*) and a boastful impostor (or *alazon*).[56] The time has come to turn to Falstaff himself.

Chapter 3

Self as Individual

The complexity and subtlety of the figure of Falstaff is implied by the multiplicity of his origins. Descended from the Vice of the morality play, the Riot of the moral interlude and perhaps even from the Devil of the Corpus Christi play, he also incorporates elements of the jester, the court fool, the stock braggart soldier, the Lord of Misrule, the *senex* or old man, the parasite and the mock-king. We may thus both laugh *at* him as a dishonest old rogue and *with* him as an instigator of Saturnalian revelry and the motor driving the comic action of the *Henry IV* plays and *The Merry Wives of Windsor*. Starting out from our identification with (as opposed to our rejection of) Shakespeare's gluttonous, mendacious, impious, bawdy, irreverent old devil, this chapter will focus on comedy – and occasionally other humorous institutions such as jokes and festivities – as outlets for anti-social, unruly impulses we are normally compelled to keep a check on. While popular festivity, for example, is on the one hand an act of social unanimity, it simultaneously functions as a ritual enactment of communal disintegration and every-man-for-himself individualization, allowing its participants a period of paroxysmic release from the tyranny of moral and social constraint. And to the extent that an audience identifies with the invective, obscenities and impieties acted out on the comic stage, theatre is but a watering down of the same tendencies. As these points have been amply made in the past, the sketch here will be limited above all to the one larger-than-life comic figure. The later part of the chapter will turn to the channelling of this generalized disorder into more critically specific attacks on the cultural system in question, as well as other assertions of identity *in opposition to* the social whole. Here the playful assault on Order has been refined into the critique of *an* order. If the preceding chapter were a photograph, this one would in a sense constitute its negative, focusing as it does on the laughter-situation as a mouthpiece for dissent rather than as an agent of unanimity. Comedy's equivocacy as a conjunction of social ("holistic") and anti-social ("individualistic") forces echoes the ambivalence of the laughing subject who is both a social being and an autonomous organism with the inherent capacity to respond *negatively* to the structures that constitute his self-understanding. This chapter is concerned with the anti-social and individualistic half of the equation (see also pages 5-7).

Rather like the diabolical Tempter of the moralities, that quintessential negator who denies God, Falstaff's chaotic folly comes to light primarily in his disrespect for established truths. Most celebrated in this context is his deflation of the abstract military and social ideal by the name of honour ("Can honour set to a leg? No. Or an arm? No. Or take away the grief of a wound? No. Honour hath no skill in surgery, then? No. What is honour? A word." *1. Henry IV*, 5.1), as well as his praise of the wisdom of sherris sack ("skill in the weapon is nothing without sack, for that sets it a-work, and learning a mere hoard of gold kept by a devil, till sack commences it and sets it in act and use..." *2. Henry IV*, 4.3). Yet Falstaff's subversions are not purely negative: the rationalization of cowardice coalesces with anti-militaristic insight, sinful intemperance with festive wit. His parodies highlight his versatility and skill as a performer: he mercilessly mocks the vacuous religious cant of the time, blasphemously misappropriates a text popular among contemporary Puritans (1 Corinthians 7:20) in order to justify his own thieving ("tis no sin for a man to labour in his vocation," *1. Henry IV*, 1.2) and feigns repentance for his transgressions with blatant insincerity ("I must give over this life, and I will give it over. By the Lord, an I do not, I am a villain," *1. Henry IV*, 1.2). The withering blasts of sexual abuse that he directs at the heir to the English throne are part of the performance of a court fool and testify to his prowess in the entertaining art of flyting: "you starveling, you eel-skin, you dried neat's tongue, you bull's pizzle, you stockfish!" he rants, "O for breath to utter what is like thee, you tailor's yard, you sheath, you bow-case, you vile standing tuck..." (*1. Henry IV*, 2.4)

Like the ritual clown who openly utters profanities and blasphemes, Falstaff takes upon himself the taboos of his society, leading Prince Hal through the low-life dissipation of the tavern scenes in order for the future king to exorcize the unruly instincts within himself and so become a good monarch. But Falstaff's status as something akin to a scapegoat-figure also entails his ultimate expulsion:

[Falstaff] has offered Hal various comic stratagems for evading responsibility – the enjoyment of appetite for its own sake, game-playing and parodies of success, carnival escape into holiday – but the Prince must learn to put these games behind him as he casts off the "old man." Falstaff has embodied the mythology of the cycle of the year and its ever-returning fertility, but by so doing he has created for himself the role of one who must be sacrificed to ensure that renewal. We accept the rejection as necessary because it represents a process of death by means of which a diseased land can be restored to health.[1]

Whether "we" really do accept the necessity of this rejection and Hal's apparent heartlessness towards the old scallywag will depend in part on an appraisal of the socio-political circumstances prevalent in Hal's (or in Shakespeare's) time: Barber relates the need for the expulsion of Falstaff to a need to counter the onset of a "dangerously self-sufficient everyday scepticism" felt to be infecting and undermining contemporary culture.[2] Alternatively, or additionally, it will hinge on whether transgression is taken as valuable only insofar as it permits a return to and a strengthening of order or as having value *in itself*. While the historical dramas, which profess to mimic reality, sanction the play-limiting recognition that "If all the year were playing holidays, / To sport would be as tedious as to work" (*1. Henry IV, 1.2*), Shakespeare's festive comedies – with their Toby Belches – tend to celebrate their own playfulness. But these operate outside the realm of concrete political responsibility in a romantic haven where, far from presenting any sort of danger, cakes and ale are *fun*.

The Falstaff who appears in *The Merry Wives of Windsor* has become less of a Vice, Tempter and Lord of Misrule than a dying god of vegetation. Northrop Frye writes of the play: "there is an elaborate ritual of the defeat of winter, known to folklorists as 'carrying out Death,' of which Falstaff is the victim; and Falstaff must have felt that, after being thrown into the water, dressed up as a witch and beaten out of the house with curses, and finally supplied with a beast's head and singed with candles, he had done about all that could reasonably be asked of any fertility spirit."[3] All in all, this Falstaff is a rather less impressive figure than the earlier white-bearded Satan, lacking the foil of Prince Hal to set off his ingenious madness. Whereas the Falstaff of *2. Henry IV* could claim to be both the cause of wit in other men and witty in himself (1.2), the later figure has been widely seen to be reduced to a mere laughing-stock, a fate provoking critical protest a-plenty. Hazlitt laments: "His wit and eloquence have left him. Instead of making a butt of others, he is made a butt of by them. Neither is there a single particle of love in him to excuse his follies: he is merely a designing, bare-faced knave, and an unsuccessful one."[4] A.C. Bradley is even more indignant at Shakespeare's degradation of Falstaff, who, he writes, is "baffled, duped, treated like dirty linen, beaten, burnt, pricked, mocked, insulted, and, worst of all, repentant and didactic. It is horrible." [5]

Yet Falstaff is not quite as pitiful as sensitive critics would make out. What Bradley refers to as "assailing for financial purposes the virtue of two matrons" combines two of what are hardly comedy's most heinous follies – using trickery to get out of a pecuniary pickle, and making a cuckold of a wealthy local. Nor is his verbal vivacity so completely vanquished as some have claimed: his ducking in the Thames, for example, still prompts a curious mix of self-mockery and self-pity: "you may know by my size, that I have a kind of alacrity in sinking: if the bottom were as deep as hell, I should down. I had been drowned, but that the shore was shelvy and shallow; a death that I abhor, for the water swells a man, and what a thing should I have been, when I had been swelled! I should have been a mountain of mummy" (3.5). Even his repentance is only ever conditional ("if my wind were but long enough to say my prayers, I would repent," 4.5), suggesting perhaps that his moral reformation is about as likely as a reformation of his diet. As long as he possesses his paunch, that is, he will be "given to fornications, and to taverns, and sack, and wine, and metheglins, and to drinkings, and swearings, and starings, pribbles and prabbles" (5.5). Yet the ending is conciliatory. Those who sought to deceive Falstaff have themselves been deceived (by the young lovers), and the outcome is a situation of *general* embarrassment which will nonetheless bear repetition as fireside anecdote: "Let us every one go home," says Mistress Page, "And laugh this sport o'er by a country fire, Sir John and all" (5.5).

In short, even the less self-assured Falstaff of *The Merry Wives* shows the ambivalence of the scapegoat as a character we may both identify with and distance ourselves from, as a rogue we may both enjoy (for his schemes) and make fun of (for their failure). The shameless and unprincipled vitality which *could* have emerged merely as sinful abnormality to be chased out of town is encased in a figure of the utmost verbal and intellectual nimbleness and unflagging physical energy: the negative (the Other) is "positivized" by Falstaff's charisma. It would be misleading, of course, to interpret Falstaff as "individualistic" in any modern sense of the word. For all the intricacy of his character, he is not really an individualist. He is never out to explore or express his "true self," to assert his uniqueness in the manner of the romantics, expressionists and hippies of later centuries. Like the playfully chaotic Harlequin, he has his origins in a (diabolical) *mask*, and – again like Harlequin – he is a natural actor. The early Falstaff in particular is a sort of court fool and entertainer whose "true self" consists in his perpetual performance, i.e. in not being himself.

Though not so in the case of Falstaff, who had to be banished from the new king's company and into the realm of comedy, the seeming subversiveness of the traditional court fool could often be ultimately conservative in function, not only having the sort of ventilatory effect we encountered in the last chapter but also giving despots and tyrants the opportunity to display their alleged magnanimity and liberality. In Renaissance France the royal fools championed orthodoxy. And while the French fool-societies of the fifteenth and sixteenth centuries tactically deployed their folly as a mask for critically exposing the universal folly of the world (and especially that of their opponents), English festive folly tended either towards random riot or a much more muted madness. According to Welsford, "our ecclesiastical Feast of Fools succumbed easily to the attacks of reforming bishops, and the Société Joyeuse never flourished at all in our country. The English Lord of Misrule is not the leader of a permanent confraternity of merry young Bohemians pledged to continuous criticism of contemporary society; he is either a temporary court official appointed to provide entertainment for the Christmas holidays, or a leader elected by young students at the Universities or Inns of Court to preside over their rejoicings at Christmas and Shrovetide. ... Our English Lords of Misrule govern a set of very well-behaved fools, who caper beneath the watchful eyes of dons and censors."[6] The temporal delimitation of folly and foolery to a *periodic* celebration, like the vocational restriction of folly and foolery to a single office (or sodality), and its institutional confinement to a theatrical enactment of it, can all be seen as measures of control, keeping disorderly forces benign or harmless or at least contained and thereby defusing the potential explosiveness of riot.

Nevertheless, the universality of folly characteristic of certain sorts of popular festivity and perpetuated in the dramatic activities of French fool-societies, German carnival plays, Tudor city comedies and Shakespeare's celebratory comedy permits an implicit relativization of folly which undermines the very boundary between order and disorderliness. Like the late medieval *topos* which helped make this relativization possible through its recognition of man's natural imperfection, the portrayal of ubiquitous folly – forcing or at least encouraging us to acknowledge the folly within ourselves – deprives us of an identificatory pole (a "wise" or "good" perspective) from which we can unequivocally *look down on* all the rest of the fools. If laughter is provoked by a deviation from the normal, by infringements of a socially accepted norm, then our view of what is funny will be a direct function of our view of what is normal. But if *nobody* is normal, then the notion of a norm goes down the drain. A profligate is ludicrous to a miser, but a miser is likely to be equally ludicrous to a profligate, and while a rumbustious rogue (a Toby Belch) may be laughable to a Puritan killjoy (a Malvolio), the killjoy may be every bit as much a joke to the rogue. A knave may scoff at his gull, but who will have the last laugh?

The German comic theorist Wolfgang Iser indeed regards this relationship of reciprocated negativity as essential to the comic contrast,

producing what he terms a "see-saw phenomenon"[7]: one (moral or
social) position negates its opposite but without being able to form a
stable opposition, instead being in turn negated by the contrary position.
Our laughter, Iser writes, is a symptom of a cognitive or emotive failure
to cope with this fluid negativity. In these terms it represents an inability
to grasp the kind of stable conceptual opposition upon which our moral
and social self-understanding (our ideas of what is of value or good) is
based. It is a response to the type of situation that undermines our sense
of self.

Yet festive folly, whether carnivalistic or theatrical, need not be quite
so relativistic as this might imply. Even where everyone is insane, goofy
or foolish, as in Shakespeare's *Twelfth Night*, the celebratory context has
a habit of creating an order of its own. An audience is likely, for
example, to identify and laugh *with* a charming and ingenious Italian
beffatore or prankster, while directing more derisive mirth *at* the self-
important idiots he outwits. Even though both are in a sense norm-
infringing rogues, the spectator cannot help but drag along a deep-seated
hierarchy of emotional values which means we are never completely
stranded on Iser's see-saw. In the midst of the madness of Shakespeare's
play in particular, there is one fool who comes closer to being
"victimized' than all the others. While the fatuous fop Sir Andrew
Aguecheek and the unruly rake Sir Toby Belch both end up with bloody
coxcombs, it is the killjoy Malvolio who is most unambiguously
exposed to the scorn both of the spectator and the rest of the fictive
figures. Made laughable by his self-love (which is what renders him so
vulnerable to the trick played on him by the others), Malvolio's real
comic crime is his hostility to holiday, his rejection of revelry. In this he
is a caricatural portrayal of the Puritan spirit, the spirit which would seek
to banish disorder out of existence but which in so doing becomes
ridiculous by failing to recognize the disorder (the *hubris* and the self-
love) within itself. Having been treated as a madman by the more
convivial fools, Malvolio makes a final irate exit (muttering vague
threats of revenge) which amounts to a sort of *self*-expulsion from the
fraternity of merry-makers. In spite of the Duke's words of conciliation
("Pursue him, and entreat him to a peace", 5.1), Malvolio's absence is
crucial to the happy ending, for his presence would have spoiled the
party.

A possible predecessor of Malvolio in his role as spoilsport or
agroikos is the figure of Mercy in the medieval morality play *Mankind*.
In a context of universal folly Mercy represents the variety known as
Christian folly, a motif which has its roots in Paul's two letters to
Corinthians and the idea that in the eyes of a scornful world the
Christian – with his belief in the Incarnation, the Crucifixion and the
Resurrection of the body, and his renunciation of secular values – must
appear thoroughly deranged. As such Mercy takes on a redemptive

stature, saving Mankind from the excesses of sinful folly and securing the happy ending. Yet there is something ambiguous about him: in spite of embodying the metaphysical wisdom which rescues Mankind (and by implication the medieval spectator too), he is a pompous fool whose speeches are tedious and stuffed with latinisms and who is easy prey to the jibes of the more sinfully foolish Vice Nowadays:

> "I haue etun a dyschfull of curdys,
> Ande I haue schetun yowr mowth full of turdys."
> Now opyn yowr sachell wyth Laten wordys
> Ande sey me this in clerycall manere!   (lines 131-4)

He is chaffed by Mischief for his dullness ("Yowur wytt ys lytyll") and generally buffeted for refusing to join in the dancing with the boisterously roistering Vices. Manifesting the paradox of wise folly, the character of Mercy was at the same time performing the equally paradoxical function of "playfully" bringing festival/theatrical play to a close for the period of Lent.[8] But in this capacity he is a deeply anti-comic persona, and one who must be mocked for his attempts to delimit and contain the comic or disorderly spirit. Mockery of Mercy is a vicarious release for the inherently self-perpetuating unruliness which Lent – and normal life – will require to be curbed.

As an incarnation of wise folly, the figure of Mercy is at a certain level analogous to that of Christ himself. Revolving as it does around the themes of death and resurrection, the story of Christ is indeed the story of an archetypal scapegoat, comparable as well to Socrates in his awkward questioning of accepted doctrines and truths. Sypher asks: "Should we say that the drama of the struggle, death, and rising – Gethsemane, Calvary, and Easter – actually belongs in the comic rather than the tragic domain? The figure of Christ as god-man is surely the archetypal hero-victim. He is mocked, reviled, crowned with thorns – a scapegoat King."[9] Girard goes as far as to suggest that Christ is the *final* scapegoat, the scapegoat to end all scapegoats. Christ, he argues, *exposes* the scapegoat-mechanism by declaring himself one: in so doing, he renders it obsolete, announcing instead that there is another way to expel violence – his way.

Dramatic representations of Christ in the medieval Corpus Christi cycles display the equivocacy characteristic of the scapegoat figure. While most scholars claim that all the laughter on these occasions was directed solely at the evil and demonic and stupid, others have argued that the cycle-plays involve a mockery of sacred personages, a ritual degradation of what is normally inviolate.[10] In this case, the laughter of the audience – as with the jeering at Malvolio and Mercy – would be an anti-authoritarian eruption, an outburst of resistance to Order (here the metaphysical order as a symbol of the social and moral one). While this is plausible, it is of course impossible to reconstruct the precise nature of the compound of fear, awe and reverence lugged about by a medieval audience. Given the ascetic hostility to laughter, however, it seems likely that the presence of even a moderate and didactic measure of mirth in the context of a story concerning the fate of man's eternal soul could have a certain subversive force.

For all their symbolic significance, the farcical episodes of marital disharmony involving Noah and his cantankerous Uxor function as comic relief from the more serious business. The same can be said of the festive treatment of the shepherds. Even the grotesque appearances of Lucifer offer a form of comic release, as a deprecation and overcoming of the potentially fearsome. In a mood of overriding veneration, moments of light-heartedness or incongruity provide a comic defusion of tension, allowing those with baited breath to breathe again (for a while). The scenes concerning the torture and death of Christ, by contrast, are more difficult to assess. Kolve writes: "The *tortores* find for themselves a great deal of amusement in the torturing of Christ; they make jokes, they think each other very funny. But we are separate from them. These dramatists presented the death of Christ as a thing of consummate horror and shame, clearly intending that the violence and laughter on stage should be answered by silence and awe in the audience."[11] If Kolve is right, the ambivalence in the responses provoked by the scapegoat can here be split into the derision of the ignorant (the fictive characters) and the reverence of the wise (the audience). The duality of the scapegoat is as it were cleanly cleft in two by the footlights. And indeed, perhaps "we" are separate from "them." But just *how* separate are we, and, more to the point, how separate were the spectators of the day?

The issue is complicated in particular because the play/reality distinction proves not to be as watertight as the clean-cut cleavage between fictive "them" and real "us" requires. The *tortores* themselves transpose the killing of Christ into a game, a jolly jape or jest. In the York cycle, for example, his claim to prophetic powers prompts them to blindfold him and take turns beating him with sticks: Christ's part is to tell which one of them it was. They dress him in a white fool's tunic and put him on public display, present him with a sceptre in order to treat him with mock-reverence, and at times even regard him as a joker: "The medieval dramatists show Christ killed as a figure in a series of such games; only a few times do the *tortores* define Him in their action as a man who claims to be the son of God, and never is He defined *as* the Son of God. The *tortores* can be said to kill only what they understand. ... From the very beginning we can see two kinds of 'substitution' shaping the action: these men decide in advance that Jesus is a joker, a trickster, an absurd impostor, and never properly see Him or hear Him as a result; and they constantly substitute games and jokes for the serious religious and legal examination that it is their proper duty to conduct." [12] In a sense, therefore, the *tortores* are punishing Jesus for being a braggart, an *alazon*, a comic fool. And though the wider perspective complements this view with an awareness that he is ultimately an *eiron* just *seeming* to lose a game that he is bound to win in the long run, it is too late – Iser's see-saw has been set swinging. While the *tortores'* games may be understood to dramatize Christ's statement of forgiveness ("They know not what they do," Luke 23:24), there is also a sense in which the cruelty of their playfulness reflects a certain cruelty inherent within the theatrical play, a voyeuristic enjoyment which, for all the well-meaning didacticism of the event, either presupposes or creates a distance between the spectator and Christ's suffering. To this extent, we – the audience – know not what we do. It can only be speculated whether or not a superstitious, hell-fearing medieval holiday crowd – kitted out with a distinctly hard-boiled attitude to physical pain and punishment – would be moved by such distancing to overcome its fear and awe in laughter. And if it was, it can only be speculated whether or not this was intended by performers or playwright.

While the amusement of the *tortores* consisted in the laughing humiliation of a wretched victim, that of the spectator (if such there was) possibly contained more anti-authoritarian impulses. Yet again, the ambiguity of the scapegoat-figure as a god-man comes to light. What on the one hand is a man claiming to be divine, who is thus a sort of *alazon* or impostor and (like the Devil) an imitator of God, on the other hand *is* God. As such he is an incarnation of Order, the metaphysical origin of moral and social structure. As the examples of Malvolio, Mercy and arguably Christ demonstrate, therefore, the disorderly tendencies which come bubbling up in festive *diableries* or in laughing association with diabolical characters like Falstaff can alternatively be channelled into mockery of symbolic representations of order. Bakhtin's description of medieval laughter sheds light on its irreverent tendencies: "It was the victory of laughter over fear that most impressed medieval man. It was not only a victory over mystic terror of God, but also a victory over the awe inspired by the forces of nature, and most of all over the oppression and guilt related to all that was consecrated and forbidden ('mana' and 'taboo'). It was the defeat of divine and human power, of authoritarian commandments and prohibitions, of death and punishment after death, hell and all that is more terrifying than the earth itself." [13] Like the ritual mockery of the sun, this laughter is playful impudence, an act of self-assertion in the face of the divine Other we can never fully grasp.

Without ever being deeply subversive, Aristophanic mockery of the Greek gods is likewise a gesture of Saturnalian disrespect, a release from the cosmic hierarchy. Portraying the lower gods (such as Dionysus) as rather unimpressive cowards with only limited bowel control drags them

down to (and below) "our" level, deflating their superhuman pretensions
by making them seem graspably human. While Zeus himself is spared
concrete humiliation in person, Peisthetaerus in *The Birds* treats him
with remarkable flippancy and cheek, threatening both to burn down his
palace and to rape his daughter Iris. Yet the contradiction between a
belief in superhuman agents (upon whom the communal well-being
depends) and a comic impiety allowing these agents to be humbled and
derided and manhandled on stage is only apparent, developing gradually from festive traditions which do not deny Zeus's existence but
reinvigorate his power by playfully calling this power into question. It
seems unlikely that traditional Greek religion – being ceremonial rather
than theological in nature[14] – was felt by most to be contradictory until
the appearance of those troublemaking Sophists who were so repulsive
to Aristophanes.

This seditious impulse – whether regarded as ventilatory or as potentially subversive in nature – is not restricted to the mockery of divine
authorities. The whole genre of New Comedy is based upon the youthful
use of wit and wile to overcome a *senex* figure, an angry old man or
parent who constitutes an obstacle to the course of Young Love. This
figure of parental authority thus presents a special subcategory of
agroikos or killjoy. Northrop Frye has indeed perceived an essential
comic opposition in the contest between the buffoon and the killjoy,
an opposition which goes back to Aristotle's distinction between the
bomolochos and the *agroikos*.[15] While, as Frye suggests, the category
of the churlish *agroikos* tends to combine with the impostor and to
incorporate the *senex*, the *bomolochos* by contrast includes all those
parasites, benevolent tricksters and rogues who seek to outwit the aged
fool, bring about a happy ending and generate a mood of celebration.
Even the relatively norm-affirmative New Comedy, that is, comprises a
victory over a representative of authority, who is mocked insofar as he
stands in the way of the good of the community (i.e. young people
getting together and breeding). If such comedy is anti-authoritarian, it is
the *excesses* of paternal power which are the butt, comedy here serving
as a form of social self-regulation.

The standard outcome of the generation conflict has led to an
understanding of comedy as a reversal of the Oedipal pattern frequently
found in tragedy, the guilt being displaced from son to father;
psychoanalysis, meanwhile, has rather dramatically speculated that the
laughter provoked by New Comedy is the aggressive laughter
accompanying a fantasized patricide.[16] Jokes too can be interpreted in
Oedipal terms. In his explanation of what he terms "tendentious" jokes,
Freud describes a joker-protagonist surmounting a series of social
obstacles in procuring for himself a surrogate happy ending: jokes
permit "the satisfaction of a drive (the lustful or the hostile drive) in the
face of an obstacle which stands in the way. [They] circumvent this

obstacle and thereby draw pleasure from a source rendered inaccessible by the obstacle." [17] Unable – due to cultural/authoritarian/paternal constraints – to gain *immediate* satisfaction for our aggressive or sexual drives, a manner of happy ending is attained instead in the playful form of a narrative/verbal substitute. Although such Oedipal analogies are interesting and provocative, however, the restriction of laughter's anti-authoritarian energies to a patricidal origin does seem unnecessary and counter-intuitive, as well as being purely speculative.

What is less contentious is that obscene and offensive jokes provide an outlet for drives and impulses not normally tolerated in social interaction. This applies to sick humour as much as to racist jokes, to personal satire as much as to "dirty" jokes. If this anti-social tendency seems to contradict the essentially collusive force of laughter pinpointed in the last chapter, the contradiction is only superficial. The controlled tension-release (limited to a play/joke context) is itself a mode of tension management: the ventilatory mechanism lets out society's foul or anti-social winds and replaces them, so to speak, with the fresh air that makes continued co-existence possible. Or, at least, this is part of the story. The complete equation of tension-release with tension-management presupposes an idealization of the play context, which must be airtight or "sealed off" from the rest of life so as not to "infect" it: in practice, of course, jokes can never be isolated or insulated in this way (in the way implied by the claim "a joke's a joke"), for they penetrate and permeate our outlook and can have far-reaching effects, just as Carnival and plebeian festivity can spill over into actual riot and rebellion. There is always the danger, in other words, that the safety valve proves inadequate for coping with society's subversive energies. The unresolvable opposition of social and anti-social moments which is at play in comedy and humour-situations is underlined by the hostility latent in norm-assertive jokes at the expense of people felt to be deviant and the whiplash malice of corrective lampoon. Anti-social forces lie at the very heart of the social structure.

The anti-authoritarian vigour that is harnessed into mockery of the *senex*, the spoilsport or the gods can equally be directed at the symbolic (and professional) representatives of the *law*. The youthful revellers of medieval popular festivity, for example, would often – when not aiming at some more abject social group – take especial pleasure in bashing and baffling the local constables, "an expression of resentment of and resistance to the official surveillance of desire and its satisfaction." [18] Likewise, when it was not subjecting the *senex* Pantaloon to comic rough-and-tumble for thwarting the union of Columbine and Harlequin, the pursuit or harlequinade of nineteenth-century English pantomime was meting out a buffeting either to the corrupt and incompetent London constabulary (before 1829) or to the newly-formed Metropolitan Police (after 1829). In the fourth book of Rabelais's *Gargantua* and

Pantagruel, the anti-authoritarian violence is related with particularly Rabelaisian enthusiasm. Arriving at the island of the Chiquanous (or bailiffs), a curious race who allow themselves to be thrashed for money, Frère Jan is only too willing to put their services to the test, singling out one called Rednose for this purpose. As the narrator recounts: "Frère Jan thwacked and cracked Rednose so lustily with his staff, on back and belly, arms and legs, head and all, that, as he slumped to the ground, I feared for his life." [19] But Rednose gets up, as pleased as Punch. This is very much a Carnival beating, accompanied as it is by laughter and carousal, and for all the exuberant anatomical precision with which the manhandling of the bailiffs is narrated, they remain as resiliently indestructible as puppets. But despite the mood of ritual and jocular conviviality, the Chiquanous are *also* schemers and slanderers, irksome upholders of established order and officialdom whose fate doubtless afforded a sweetly retributive comic pleasure for those contemporaries of Rabelais themselves plagued and pestered by money-grabbing bailiffs.

In the case of bailiffs, constables and policemen, the object of derision is a *symbolic* incarnation of the social order. But this is not all it is: mockery of people symbolizing the system may frequently merge with or incorporate elements of protest, dissent or dissatisfaction. In nineteenth-century England, to take one example, the ineffectiveness and dishonesty of the constabulary before Sir Robert Peel's reformation of the police in 1829 led to a widespread disaffection with law enforcement which fuelled the need for comic redress in pantomime. And as popular festivity develops in "self-awareness," it has been argued, it becomes more and more likely to combine or overlap with definite political points of view. As Victor Turner puts it, "the inversions characteristic of industrial leisure do not have the comprehensive, pansocietal, obligatory qualities of tribal and agrarian ritual and are not rooted in a commonly shared, relatively systematic world view. Rather are they piecemeal, sporadic, and concerned with the setting of one segment of society, one product of the division of labor, against another." [20] Of course, social dissatisfaction may vary in its manifestations from vague, inarticulate feelings of injustice, coupled with a retaliatory desire to misbehave and cause commotion, to fully thought-out ideologies or explicitly formulated grievances, expressible in the form of parody, satire, caricature and joke. Nowhere has the latter been more clearly exemplified than in the former communist bloc (as in Italy), where frustration with the corruption and the excesses of the police was funnelled in particular into a speight of jokes at the expense of the militia or the *carabinieri*, jokes which in their own way make their butt seem every bit as brainless as the moronic constables whizzing round in the English harlequinade.

What is in evidence in such cases is not some form of impulsively anti-social release but the assertion of a rationally justifiable point of view; it is not a negation of order or value in itself, but a critique of the specific order and system of values in which the dissenting individual or sub-cultural group finds itself. This is typified in Carl Zuckmayer's *Der Hauptmann von Köpenick*, a turn-of-the-century comedy set in Berlin and based on the real-life episode in which the unemployed cobbler Wilhelm Voigt used a second-hand military uniform to take command of the local watch, assume control of Köpenick Town Hall, arrest the Mayor and impound the treasury funds. This incident, restricted in Zuckmayer's play to the last of the three acts, has something of the festive world-upside-down about it (with the little man enjoying life on top), but more than this it offers a critique of Prussia's obsessive militarism. Apart from a few other sympathetically portrayed down-and-outs and losers, almost all the characters are either brashly authoritarian or meekly submissive. The leitmotif of the uniform brings to light the rigidity of an order which has inflated itself to the *parody* of an order, functioning in comic terms as a mask which both turns the Prussian citizens into predictable automatons or puppets and blinds them to Voigt's (mis-)use of it to lead them up the garden path. But not only are the excesses of order amusingly repetitive, they can also prove deeply and self-perpetuatingly harmful, trapping outsiders in a vicious circle which keeps them wandering around despondently at society's margins: Voigt, whom Zuckmayer takes great pains to present as the most human and humane of the figures (even to the point of sentimentalization), cannot work without a residence permit, but cannot get a residence permit unless he is employed. The following snippet of dialogue between Voigt and the well-meaning but rather spineless Hoprecht (minus Berlin accents) testifies to Voigt's dissatisfactions:

Hoprecht: You're only a *human* once you're in a human order.
            Even *insects* are alive.
Voigt :   That's right! They're alive, Friedrich! And do you
            know why they're alive? First comes the insect, then
            the insect order. First the human, Friedrich, then the
            human order.
Hoprecht: You just don't know your place, that's your problem.
            If you want to be a human, you've got to know your
            place, right?
Voigt: Know my place. Sure. But my place in what? That's
            what I want to know. The order's got to be right,
            Friedrich, and it's not!   (Act 2, scene 14)

While Zuckmayer's satire is aimed at a mindless surplus of order, others of the same genre have sought to expose the *hollowness* of the order. Gogol's *Government Inspector*, for example, lays bare the crookedness of Tsarist bureaucracy, unmasking the disorder and injustice which exists beneath the surface of the social order. As with Voigt, the point is made comic by presenting the targets of Gogol's ridicule as *gulls*, taken in by an impostor owing to the inflexibility of their vision.

Alternatively, it might be the process of normalization itself that is parodied, society being understood as something which either dehumanizes or brutalizes the individuals who make it up. This is the case with Brecht's *Mann ist Mann*, which depicts the metamorphosis of an easy-going Irish docker called Galy Gay into a human killing-machine (which recalls to mind Bergson's notion that machine-like people are comic). Though intended as an attack on the dehumanizing effects of capitalistic imperialism, Brecht's comedy ironically ends up as much a prognostication of the type of totalitarianism he himself advocated. This raises an important point about such satire: as a primarily *negative* impulse (saying "this will *not* do"), it tends to leave unstated its positive counter-image, and in the absence of a central character with whom we identify (like Voigt), it relies on the moral or political norms of the spectator. While Marxists – implicitly bringing along a positive socialistic yardstick for comparison – might have enjoyed the play for mocking the system in its entirety, non-Marxist liberals could equally justifiably see the satire as targeting the aberrations *within* the system rather than the aberrancy *of* the system.[21] Its reception (the climate in which it is received) will clearly affect whether the play is potentially revolutionary in its message or merely reformative.

Less problematic in this respect is Nestroy's *Lumpazivagabundus*, which, like Zuckmayer's play, provides us with endearing individual "heroes" with whom to empathize. The play – a sort of fairy-tale comedy – combines satire of society's inherent tendency to normalize non-conformists with parody of comedy's inherent tendency to normalize non-conformists (in the traditional happy ending), adding an acerbic dose of the Baroque *theatrum mundi* motif. The inner play, which follows the spiritual development (or rather non-development) of the three protagonists Leim, Zwirn and Knieriem, is watched not without partiality by the fairies of the frame-play, the outcome being that the bibulous Knieriem and the hedonistic Zwirn are sent to Hell for their recalcitrant refusal to be caged in by a comfy bourgeois order. "Fortunately," however, one of the onlooking fairies-cum-deities intervenes on their behalf and gives them another chance; the final scene presents the two debauchees fully reformed, singing the praises of diligence and domesticity in a parodic cloud-cuckoo-land. The loner, social critic and professional pessimist Knieriem, who, in his own words, would have had to turn to the bottle if he weren't able to get pissed to drown his sorrows (1.6), is transformed into a paragon of social orthodoxy. The happy ending is the saddest part of the play.

One way of resisting normalization or homogenization is to use laughter as a means of asserting one's individual, marginal or subcultural identity. Humour and joke-telling thus operate as a particularly effective way for an ethnic or racial minority to maintain and even reinforce its own identity, as is exemplified by the Jewish tradition of humour. This tradition has indeed been absolutely crucial to the development of the modern (Eastern European) political joke as a means of self-protection against discrimination. The joke's most common weapon is its unveiling of the limitations, blindspots and prejudices in the bigot's way of thinking, using insight – as Leo Rosten has written – as "a substitute for weapons: one way to block the bully's wrath is to know him better than he knows himself."[22] The self-protective quality of ethnic humour is augmented, moreover, because it tends to work within and affirm a common cultural background, a shared framework of institutions, beliefs and customs, and as such it will never be fully accessible to the outsider. Obscure idiom and allusion may be used to bolster this cohesive/ exclusive effect. Just as important in the Jewish tradition, however, is the technique of ironically appropriating the negative stereotypes employed by outsiders in their attempts to put an identificatory "tag" on "The Jew." Sandy Cohen quotes the following example:

> This miser is dying and just to make sure his soul makes Heaven, he calls a rabbi, a priest, and a Catholic padre and asks each of them to pray for his soul. If they agree, he will give each of them $20,000.
> They agree, and when the miser says, "Well, it's a deal if you each will agree to put $10,000 in my coffin ... just in case I can take it with me", the three of them still agree.
> Well, the miser dies and at his funeral, the priest steps up to the coffin, makes a cross, says a short prayer, and puts $10,000 in the coffin, keeping the other ten thousand. The padre steps up to the coffin, sprinkles some Holy Water, makes a cross, and puts his $10,000 in the coffin.
> Then the rabbi steps up to the coffin, says a *Va-yisgadah*, puts in his personal check for thirty thousand, and takes out the twenty thousand.[23]

Nor are Jews the only ethnic group or subculture to employ this tactic. Where Jews may make jokes about their financial craftiness or their "big noses," Oriental Americans latch on to the cliché of their own "inscrutability." And there is perhaps a similar element in the Catholic priest's joke about Catholic priests who wear underwear in the shower because "it is a sin to look down on the unemployed."

Although such humour may perpetuate the stereotype in question, Cohen suggests, it may at the same time have a supportive effect, enabling the group's members to consider such stereotypes as a unifying social image, something that is both acknowledged and risen above and that contributes to a collective sense of identity. Accordingly, "it is the perception, the acceptance, of the stereotype, not the truth of it, that becomes the unifying element to the in-group. The group may not want the stereotype, but it has it anyway, and might as well use it for its own purposes. That is why such a story as the one above is humorous to the in-group if one of its members tells it, but offensive if an outsider does." [24] While such self-deprecatory jokes have been understood in terms of self-hatred or masochism, therefore,[25] they seem more like a response to and a mode of vanquishing insecurity: ironic self-disparagement is in fact a way of turning defeat into victory, the converse of Hobbesian pusillanimity. To be able to joke about oneself is ultimately a sign of self-assurance or strength. The identity-*preserving* impulse in Jewish humour is especially evident in the time-honoured stock comic figure of the *geschmat* who converts to Christianity but whose Christianity remains only skin-deep, and in the still popular issues of assimilation and name-changing. Cohen cites the story of Mr Charles Clive-Smythe walking his poodle past the old synagogue. Turning to the dog he says, "You know, I used to be Jewish." "Sure," says the poodle, "And I used to be a dog." [26]

The comedy of recognition encountered in the last chapter may also have its roots in a feeling of shared identity on a subcultural level. Here the complicity is particularly pleasurable for being marginal, or for operating in matters that are generally frowned upon, hushed up or treated as taboo. In Martin Amis's *Money*, for example, John Self laments the "normalizing," domesticating effects of a girlfriend on his slobbishly antisocial bachelor life: "with a chick on the premises you just cannot live the old life. You just cannot live it. I know: I checked. The hungover handjob athwart the unmade bed – you can't do it. Blowing your nose into a coffee filter – there isn't the opportunity. Peeing in the basin – they just won't stand for it. No woman worth the name would let it happen." [27] For Lasher in Don DeLillo's *White Noise*, micturating in basins is bound up with a way of life that incorporates

> Bowls with no seats. Pissing in sinks.The culture of public toilets. All those great diners, movie houses, gas stations. The whole ethos of the road. I've pissed in sinks all through the American West. I've slipped across the border to piss in sinks in Manitoba and Alberta. This is what it's all about. The great western skies. The Best Western motels. The diners and drive-ins. The poetry of the road, the plains, the desert. The filthy stinking toilets. I pissed in a sink in Utah when it was twenty-two below. That's the coldest I've ever pissed in a sink in.[28]

Chapter 4

Self as Subject[1]

As the examples of subversive, anti-authoritarian and socially critical comedy have shown, laughter may signal the self-assertion of an individual in opposition to the social unit of which he or she forms a part. Equally, however, a certain type of laughter has been interpreted as a triumph of the self in the face not just of the human community but the "objective" world in general. Such a distinction is drawn by Baudelaire, who differentiates between what he calls "significative comedy," where the laughter stems from man's superiority over man, and "absolute comedy," where the laughter is an expression of man's ascendancy not over his fellow-men but over nature.[2] While Molière is the French master of the significative variety, it is the creative grotesquery of Rabelais which – in Baudelaire's eyes – furnishes the supreme example of absolute comedy. This chapter will explore both this form of "absolute" comic self-assertion and its less celebratory converse, the anxiety felt by the human subject in relation to the inexplicable object that eludes its grasp. It will be dealing, that is, with comedy's more fantastic manifestations, seen either as the subject's imaginative triumph over the objective world or as a triumph of the unfathomable objective world over the subject (see also pages 22-26).

The Rabelaisian comedy feted by Baudelaire is a unique medley of belief-defying flights of fancy, nonsensical surreality and vigorous bodily grotesquery. It portrays a gargantuan world, where the people are larger than life and the stories even taller than the people. As an irreverent affirmation of such unbridled imaginative fertility it shares the spirit of the boisterous ancient Greek comedies of Aristophanes. The theoretical celebration of such comic fantasy goes back to the German romantics, who see in the genre an assertion of creative subjectivity. For them comedy is "in its essence unleashed subjectivity": in the words of one follower of A. W. Schlegel, "the comedian annihilates the world by releasing it from all necessity and logicality, in order to turn it into a mirror of his own freedom and caprice."[3] This romantic point of view was founded upon Fichte's idealistic radicalization of the Kantian insight into the role of the subject in constituting the world as a phenomenon. Positing the absoluteness of the knowing subject's activity, Fichte conceived *all* objective reality as the product of this subjective creativity, and for the romantics it was but a small step to see comic play in particular as a jubilant demonstration of a godlike subjectivity, a signal of the detached sovereignty of the ego over a world (or non-ego) which *it* has posited. Fantasy is an assertion of the subject's freedom, a negation and an overcoming of the causal and logical necessity characteristic of the world.

It is not surprising, therefore, that romantics such as Friedrich Schlegel viewed Aristophanes as a paragon of the true comic spirit, transcending all the limitations of causal coherence and dramatic unity with his sparklingly inventive brilliance. *The Birds*, produced in 414 B.C., is a case in point. One of the wackiest of Aristophanes's plays, it revolves around the ingenious idea of the disillusioned Athenian citizen Peisthetaerus to found a great Cloud-Cuckoo-City in the sky between mankind and the gods. Effectively blockaded by this new city, the gods – represented by an embassy comprising Poseidon, Heracles and a "barbarian" deity – are compelled to come and negotiate with Peisthetaerus, who has little difficulty in enforcing all his demands, taking Zeus's housekeeper (who looks after the divine thunderbolts) in marriage and becoming the ruler of the universe. The play thus combines a playfully subversive humiliation of the deities with a streak of the sort of fantasy that defies causality by cocking a snook at the law of gravity and the limits of mundane feasibility. In the words of the critic K. J. Dover, *The Birds* combines two typically Aristophanic features: "the fulfilment of a grandiose ambition by a character with whom the average member of the audience can identify himself, and its fulfilment by supernatural means which, although treated almost casually, overturn many of those sequences of cause and effect with which we are familiar in ordinary life."[4]

Human flight is one of the archetypal flights of fancy, bringing together wish-fulfilment and a respite from the exigencies of causation and thus representing an escape from the bounds both of earth and (until recently at least) of possibility. At a relatively modest level, the spectacular acrobatics of *commedia dell'arte* performers like Arlecchino aroused admiring wonder by seeming to flout human bodily limitations, and this tradition was perpetuated in nineteenth-century English pantomime, where Harlequin's natural tumbling agility was compounded by theatrical props and machinery which helped propel him to even more awe-inspiring heights: thanks to his soaring suppleness Harlequin could appear to do the impossible. Of proportions more akin to Aristophanic aeronautics is Ariosto's comic-chivalric epic *Orlando Furioso*, a product of the effervescent Renaissance imagination, in which the English knight Astolfo flies to the moon on the back of a hippogriff, intending to recover the lost wits of his friend Orlando but in fact also stumbling across some of his own wit with which he had parted company when *he* had fallen in love. The thematic link between love and flight (in the sense both of transcendence and of escape or fleeing) has persisted as a popular topos to the present day: people in love still wander around with their head in the clouds.

Narrative in fact offers a slightly different set of possibilities from theatre in the realm of fantasy, for while the latter can simulate causal impossibility through theatrical tricks and delusion, the written word has a greater potential for infringing even logical or conceptual coherence, for articulating the inconceivable. This is demonstrated by the astonishing flights of fancy in Italo Calvino's *Cosmicomics*, a selection of short stories each of which adopts and plays with some particular scientific hypothesis about the origin of the universe. One of the most mind-boggling (and beautiful) stories, "All at One Point," narrates the situation "before" the Big Bang, in which all the matter in the universe was concentrated at a single point. But not only is all the matter reduced to a single point, more to the point – so are all the people. Everyone is packed in there "like sardines," or, more accurately, everyone completely coincides with everyone else. Co-existence is as a rule peaceful enough, but of course when space is so tight that it does not even exist, unwelcome company – such as that of the irritating Mr. Pber^t Pber^d – can prove exceedingly cramping.[5]

Calvino revels in the sheer impossibility of conceiving such a moment (or non-moment) and in the contradictions entailed by having a narrator, old Qfwfq, as well as the subjects of his narration, exist not only before space but before time. "Peopling" this punctual non-space alongside the narrator and the irksome Mr. Pber^t Pber^d are the all-encompassingly beautiful Mrs. Ph(i)Nk$_o$ with her orange dressing-gown, and the cleaning woman, who – not having the most tasking of jobs – spends her time gossiping and complaining. The first punctiform seed of xenophobia has also been sown, targeted at the "immigrant" Z'zu family with all their clobber and their inconvenient habit of hanging their washing-line across the communal point.[6] In particular, the narrator shares with us the blissful serenity of his punctiform love for Mrs. Ph(i)Nk$_o$, a love which knows no jealousy or ill-will despite certain

logistical complications (for if a point is all there is, then it will coincide
not only with any bed there may be but also anyone who happens to be
in it).[7] In these rather cosy circumstances, the notion of having one's
head in the clouds loses its immediacy: there is nowhere where one's
head is not. Nor is it surprising that – now time and space have come
into existence – the narrator yearns for the Big Crunch, that moment of
definitive reunification with The Woman of His Dreams, that final
overcoming of separation and distance.

The act of narration and the events of the narrative scoff at all
conceptual order, juxtaposing seemingly mundane situations, concerns
and occurrences with a "location" outside of space and time which can
be visualized just about as graphically as Nothing. The whole story is
structured around a logical incongruity, the narrator himself as a
narrator-cum-character having a distinct persona yet as a dot in a
punctiform universe being completely indistinguishable from everyone
else. In another story, "How Much Shall We Bet?", old Qfwfq enters into
a wager with Dean (k)yK that there *is going to be* a universe. When he
was a kid, he narrates in another, he used to spend his time playing
games with hydrogen atoms. In yet another, by contrast, he is a mollusc
who has difficulty telling his mouth and his anus apart. Old Qfwfq – for
all his endearing anthropomorphic traits – is a fluid verbal construction,
who pre-exists and transcends logical fixity and conceptual stability. He
exists everywhere and nowhere, i.e. wherever Calvino wants.

While Calvino's imaginative sparkle thus operates in a sort of no-
place sited "outside" the realm of temporal succession, a comic breach
in expectations may also be effected by a *reversal* in the direction of
time: the flight of fancy in this case comes to bear on the flight of time's
arrow. In the ordinary run of things it is patently impossible for a
smashed wine-glass of its own accord to reassemble itself from its
myriad fragments and jump back up onto the table from which it has
fallen. Our intuition tells us so, but, slightly more reliably, so does the
Second Law of Thermodynamics, which says that the disorder or
entropy in an isolated system always increases, or that all isolated
systems tend towards a state of maximal disorder or equilibrium. (Of
course, the wine-glass scenario is far from being an isolated system, but
perfect isolation is an idealization anyway: ceteris paribus, it would take
infinite information from an external source to reverse the fall and
reassemble the broken shards). Without the Second Law, we could have,
for example, a time-reversed cricket match, where every ball ends up
being caught by the bowler with a backwards looping arm motion.[8] Such
a scene, even the sucked in sound wave as the ball leaps from the field
against the bat, is perfectly compatible with Newton's laws of motion,
which are utterly time-symmetric and so reversible. Yet it is infinitely
improbable. Even the marvellously complex workings of the brain are
themselves subject to the law of entropy, constituting a *local* abatement

in disorder which can only be "bought" (through an exchange of energy and matter) at the expense of an *overall* increase. The knowing subject can only ever experience a world relentlessly galloping towards the future and leaving the past standing in its wake, for knowing is itself a function of this gallop.

Yet the preposterous scenario of time-reversal can be, and has been, *imagined*. The philosopher F. H. Bradley, for example, contrasts the appearance of unidirectional temporal succession with the timeless Absolute, which the human subject – being condemned to his own limited perspective – can of course never properly know. According to Bradley,

> we naturally regard the whole world of phenomena as a single time-series; we assume that the successive contents of every other finite being are arranged in this construction, and we take it for granted that their streams all flow in one direction. But our assumption clearly is not defensible. For let us suppose, first, that there are beings who can come in contact in no way with that world which we experience. Is this supposition self-contradictory, or anything but possible? And let us suppose, next, that in the Absolute the direction of these lives runs opposite to our own. I ask again, is such an idea either meaningless or untenable? Of course, *if* in any way *I* could experience *their* world, I should fail to understand it. Death would come before birth, the blow would follow the wound, and all must seem to be irrational. It would seem to me so, but its inconsistency would not exist except for my partial experience.[9]

Although the dependence of cognition upon entropy-increase seems in fact to bind *all* experience (human or not) to a "forward"-flying temporal arrow, fictive fantasy at least can always do the impossible, playfully exempting the physics of its narrator's brain from the time-reversal being narrated.

This is the case in Martin Amis's *Time's Arrow*, which portrays a time-reversed perspective where giving becomes taking, falling is rising and defecation ingestion. From within this perspective killing is life-giving and destruction creation; a meal out finishes with a dogged description of it to the waiter ("with the menu there to jog our memory"), and anger is vented by repairing a dent in the fridge with the skilful kick of an aching foot.[10] In Kurt Vonnegut's blackly comic *Slaughterhouse-Five*, Billy Pilgrim, who has a habit of coming "unstuck" in time, watches a late-night war-movie in reverse mode. He sees damaged American planes full of the dead and wounded taking off backwards from English airfields and then over France having some of the bullets and shell fragments sucked out of them by German fighters, who do the same for other planes that fly up backwards from wreckage on the ground to join the formation. He sees the formation flying backwards over a German city in flames, as if by magnetism drawing up from the city great cylindrical steel containers that miraculously shrink the flames. And he sees a comparatively intact formation returning to base in England.[11] As in *Time's Arrow*, the taking of life is transformed by the reversal of time into the giving of life, and everything ends up "as good as new."

In *Slaughterhouse-Five*, it happens to be Billy Pilgrim, and not the film, that is in reverse mode. But clearly, what philosophical speculation and narrative skill can achieve through the medium of words can – more easily but less inventively – be produced in the cinematic medium simply by playing the film in question backwards. As Auden comments, the film running backwards transforms the action of a man taking off his coat into that of a coat putting itself onto a man, thereby reversing the flow of volition from object to subject. According to Auden, the comic thus arises, broadly speaking, from "a contradiction in the relation of the individual or personal to the universal or impersonal which does not involve the spectator or hearer in suffering or pity, which in practice means that it must not involve the actor in real suffering."[12] Yet in spite of Auden's stipulation about suffering, the idea of a contradiction in the relation between self and non-self implies that the comic effect may be decidedly more unsettling than in the examples of fantastic comedy so far encountered. In the example above, the normally active human subject is reduced to a passive object, while the non-human object is metamorphosed into a subject with a will, a radical undermining of the human agent's tendency to see *himself* as a cause in what goes on around him. Nietzsche indeed regarded this tendency as essential to the development of the idea of causality in general:[13] causation for him is a fiction originating in man's desire to master his surroundings, to control and "know" the world. In these terms, play with causal succession – disrupting the orderly and predictable flow from past to present to future – has the effect of sabotaging the subject's pretensions to mastery. As an indication of weakness, it becomes a source of unease.

Precisely the sort of tinkering with patterns of cause and effect which on the one hand seems to announce a "triumph of subjectivity" in the face of the logical and physical limitations of the objective world can on the other hand come to undercut our very sense of self, confounding and unsettling us with the sight of the inexplicable or the unfathomable, swallowing a powerless subject up in an objectivity which is beyond its grasp. Fantasy may thus be a source equally of exhilaration and of traumatic disconcertment. This tension again reflects the deep-seated ambiguity of the human subject, which is a curious hybrid of omnipotence (insofar as it transcends the objective) and impotence (insofar as it tends towards emptiness and nothingness *without* the objective).[14] If we detach the subject from the chain of objective causality, then it becomes exceedingly difficult to re-attach it to reality at any other point.

As a temporally ordered concatenation of perceptions or thoughts, the subject is thus dependent not only – as Hume recognized – upon the causal relationship obtaining between its constitutive experiences but also – as Kant recognized – upon the causal relationship obtaining between the objects of these constitutive experiences. It is for this reason that breaches in the chain of causality have such a disruptive effect on the human mind. Events (seemingly) without causes lead the observer to *search* for causes, questioning the sequence of occurrences and querying his or her own perceptual faculties: did I really see that pig soaring through the sky? Surely it must have been in some way propelled? Or perhaps my senses or sanity are having me on? An alternative is to attribute the "impossible" event to a cause beyond or outside the "natural" chain of worldly occurrences, inventing a supernatural cause which is perceptually inaccessible to us. There are still any number of people who – unable to *see* why the goblet on the table is nervously rattling or the hands on the grandfather clock are frantically whirling round – would shove their head back under the pillow and attribute the whole thing to ghosts. I certainly would.

Just as the temporal chain leading from cause to effect is one-directional, propelled in the direction of entropy-increase, so time itself is considered to be one-dimensional, comprising a unique linear sequence of contiguous instants or events.[15] And in accordance with time's egocentricity, which always binds "me" to "now," the human subject is equally unilinear in nature, consisting of a single continuous history of spatio-temporal experiences. As Kant argued, this single and connected consciousness is one of the formal preconditions for the production of knowledge. For there to be a series of experiences of an objective world, there can only be *one* consciousness doing the experiencing. The subject must be unitary if it is to be a subject at all. Indeed, for all the multiplicity of conflicting and competing sub-selves and cerebral subsystems ascertained by present-day neurologists and cognitive scientists, this pandemonium of mental activity is always somehow revised and co-ordinated in such a way that we experience a single, coherent stream of consciousness.

The unity underlying my ability to connect my diverse and temporally separated experiences *as mine* presupposes some sort of identity in me (the kind of identity, perhaps, that we ascribe to two points of the same river, or trajectory, as we move along it). It presupposes, in other words, that I am me. But this is not enough. In order to be aware *of myself* as having a particular sequence of experiences over a particular time, I need the idea that these experiences are experiences of things or events partaking of a system of temporal relations over and above the experiences themselves. This in turn depends upon the permanence or re-encounterability of the things or events in question. For any consciousness of myself as having different experiences at different times, that is, I must have an awareness of lasting things distinct from myself.[16] To be able to make a distinction between subject and object, I require empirically applicable criteria of permanence within the flux of perception, change being experienced not as an absolute transformation of something into nothing or nothing into something but as a relative modification of what is. Breaches in this framework of continuity disrupt my sense of self in the same way that events without causes do. And just as the objects of the world cannot coherently be understood as zipping into and out of existence like rabbits conjured from a magician's top hat, so a magician's tricks lead us to question our senses or ask ourselves what really happened. The sight of a living dove "becoming" a crumpled piece of paper thus unsettles us by shattering the comfortingly truistic certainty that a dove is a dove and a piece of paper a piece of paper. In this sense, the comedy of a magician's jiggery-pokery is the converse of that reassuring comedy afforded by repetitions and obtrusive patterns, where the onlooker is allowed to *recognize* what he already knows rather than have the very foundations of cognition turned on their head.

Of course, the magical transformations effected by a trained prestidigitator are never all too disconcerting precisely because the context allows us to ascribe them to the magician's sleight-of-hand. Admiration and wonder prevail over alarm and anxiety. Likewise, the logical and physical impossibilities of the theatre can always be cognitively classified by their occurrence *onstage*, and the unbelievable traced back to a trick of theatrical illusionism. In the pantomime of the last century, Harlequin in particular has a knack of performing magic with the aid of his baton, using it above all to change one object into another, conjuring animals or people out of nowhere, transforming a cow into a milk-maid or a clutter of old women into a gaggle of geese, providing food for Columbine and making it disappear when Clown tries to snatch it. One of the most popular tricks of the day, which was part of Drury Lane's 1816 piece *Harlequin Horner; or, The Christmas Pie* but which could be enjoyed again and again with the most minimal of variations, is described by Mayer: "Harlequin finds Clown in Covent Garden Market stealing produce, hat boxes, and a sedan chair, which he fashions into a watch house or temporary prison for Harlequin. When Clown enters the watch house, Harlequin strikes it with his bat, changing the house into a balloon that carries off a screaming, frightened Clown."[17]

All these "impossibilities" were of course cons and stunts requiring a skilled machinist, gymnastic actors and a whole network of technical devices (such as the "falling flap" or the "rise and sink" apparatuses[18]) and hidden traps and apertures. But the important point is that the play context as it were screens or protects the viewer from the most unnerving effects of the inexplicable and implausible, providing a framework in which the absurd can be both (half-)expected and dealt or coped with. As with narrative fantasies – such as the metamorphoses which take place in Lewis Carroll's Wonderland and through the looking-glass – a certain tension is present, which permits the spectators or readers both to suspend disbelief, fasten their seat-belts and credulously abandon themselves to the flight of fancy *and* to distance themselves from it insofar as it is just pretend, just play, a mere verbal or theatrical fiction. The play context thereby makes possible an *overcoming* of fear.

If aesthetic distance encourages a sense of omnipotence and invulnerability in an audience, the opposite occurs when an onlooker has the sensation of being *swallowed up* in the immediacy of the unfathomable. This is clarified in particular by Albert Camus's description of the absurd. Here it is a question not of immediate causal inexplicability but of the absence of some sort of deeper cause, a reason that might account for why the world is as it is, an underlying coherence to give meaning to it. Camus writes: "what is absurd is the confrontation of the irrational and the wild longing for clarity whose call echoes in the human heart. ... The absurd is born of this confrontation between the human need and the unreasonable silence of the world. ... It is that divorce between the mind that desires and the world that disappoints, my nostalgia for unity, this fragmented universe and the contradiction that binds them together." [19] The absurd, that is, is the product of a showdown between a self which yearns for meaning and order and a non-self which resolutely refuses to yield either. What for Camus is a reason for regret and wistfulness need not, however, be accepted in this light. Nietzsche viewed the causally anarchic comedy of Aristophanes as a release from and a means of *overcoming* absurdity: "the comic as the artistic discharge from the nausea of the absurd." [20] Faced with meaninglessness, Nietzsche's answer is to have a good laugh at it.

The metaphor of unilinearity provides insights into related aspects of comedy, being applicable not just to the temporal succession of our experiences but also to the realm of discourse, in that speech and narration likewise operate *sequentially*. In the terminology of the structural semanticist A.J.Greimas, our ability to identify the meaning of a given text depends on our identification of a so-called "isotopy" running through it, the semantic unity or coherence which results from a repetition of semes (the minimal semantic features of our conceptual map of the world). The isotopy, in other words, consists of a sequence of lexical items connected with one another by the dominant seme they have in common. But, says Greimas, while "serious people always know, or believe they know, what they are talking about; spiritual conversation ... is characterized by the parallel and successive utilization of several isotopies at once." [21] And so too are jokes, toying as they do with the rules of comprehension and communication. Greimas quotes a quip which must have devastated some sophisticated Parisian soiree. One guest remarks to another: "Ah! belle soirée, hein? Repas magnifique, et puis jolies toilettes, hein?" (Isn't it a delightful evening! Magnificent food, and the dresses [toilets] are lovely, aren't they!). The other says: "Ça, je n'en sais rien... je n'y suis pas allé." (Couldn't say, really. I haven't been). The "spiritual" pleasure, claims Greimas, "resides in the discovery of two different isotopies inside a narration presumed homogeneous." [22] Puns rupture the supposed unilinearity of discourse by revealing a latent plurality of meanings within themselves and within the proposition or text as a whole, jerking the listener or reader out of their comfortable cognitive torpor.

If functional, unequivocal, "normal" discourse is conceived as a linear or syntagmatic succession of (smaller or larger) semantic units each of which means *one thing*, then it is not only puns which have this disruptive effect. Irony and ambiguity open up possibilities for a text not to mean (just) what it says, while verbal tropes such as metaphors and metonyms breach the discursive unilinearity that restricts signification to a reassuring one-thing-at-a-time basis. With one word "standing in" for another, metaphors display the plurivalence of language, and although many come to "adopt" their metaphorical meaning and thus cease to be in any way startling (e.g. the heart of the matter), an original, incongruous, mixed or misused metaphor (e.g. I wouldn't like to be sitting in your shoes; the winds of change have opened a whole new can of beans; he strove to keep a stiff upper lip and it came off) is more likely to be ludicrous. The wider the disparity between vehicle and tenor (between the trope and what it "stands for"), the more comically disconcerting the effect.

Infringing the law of contradiction, the metaphor is a miniature verbal enactment of a confusion of identity and difference. The same applies to the grotesque pun-formations which inhabit the surreal worlds explored by Lewis Carroll's Alice, where snap-dragon-flies and rocking-horse-flies defy the laws of contradiction and identity by being both snap-dragons and dragon-flies, rocking-horses and horse-flies. Renaissance portrayals of the devil or the damned frequently resort to a similar sort of surreal grotesquery which throws together an incongruous hotchpotch of bodily members from reptiles, monsters, fish and human beings, producing an ultimately formless "non-thing" that resists all attempts at conceptual classification and lustfully transgresses all categories. This link between verbal or visual playfulness and the diabolical indeed hints at a parallelism between conceptual and moral transgression. The metaphor of unilinearity in this case becomes a symbol of order and control, limiting the potential for meaning to run amok. For any degree of social structure, language must be able to exercize its prerogative of unambiguous functional communication, and the subversive duplicity of not meaning what we say must be stifled or contained. By the same token, linearity may be taken as an instrument of repression, denying playfulness and negativity. One-dimensionality here symbolizes an unquestioning normality which is uncritically "straight" and holds in check all trains of thought which run the risk of going off the rails.

Chapter 5

Self as Living Organism

Being and not Being

So far we have examined the human self in its ambiguous relationship to the social/moral order and the objective world which (fail to) constitute it. As a living being, however, the self also forms an oasis (or is it a mirage?) within an infinite desert of non-existence, a desert which would swallow us up in its quicksands but which we *resist*, battling instinctively against the disorder that gnaws away at our astonishingly complex biochemical and physiological structures. It is through our temporal delimitation that our life is given meaning *as life*, the possibility of not-being "defining" us and granting us a significance which ends up transcending our limited physical existence. Not surprisingly, therefore, the two margins – conception (or sex) and death – which link us to and separate us from the eternities preceding and succeeding our life are constant preoccupations and consequently lie at the heart of comedy. As the gateway we still have to come, death in particular is a timeless source of anxiety, despite all the reassurances of reason (and Epicurus) that when we are, death is not, and when death is, we are not (see also pages 13-17).

Of course, the rational and stable conceptual opposition between being and not-being, self and non-self, is a somewhat arbitrary construct. Not only are there problems in positing the continued existence of a single "self" persisting in time between the two temporal poles demarcating life, but the location of the poles themselves is a matter of controversy. If we intellectually reduce the human being to a

vehicle for a collection of mutually co-operating genes, moreover, what
is generally regarded as curtains for the individual becomes the demise
merely of a particular *combination* of genes, while the genes themselves
have potentially very long lives which go beyond any personal history.
In the form of copies of itself, one molecule of DNA can in fact survive
for millions of years, and there is a sense therefore in which something
about us surpasses our individual biography. At the same time, our own
death is a permanent presence structuring our life. The shadowy threat
of disorder follows us through existence as persistently as the need to
eat, breathe or defecate (i.e. to postpone disorder's inevitable triumph),
and the possibility of not-being is the most fundamental of all human
possibilities. Influenced by the insights of the Danish philosopher
Kierkegaard,[1] Heidegger stresses the centrality of the individual death,
but less as an event, for as an event it is marginal, than as a possibility
(albeit one from which inauthentic existence prefers to hide itself).
Drawing on a romantic view of death as life's crowning achievement, he
lays especial emphasis on what he terms the *Jemeinigkeit* of death, its
deeply personal, seclusive nature. My *own* death is the only one I can
ever directly experience: nor can anyone else help me out by having it
for me. In the words of the *commedia dell'arte* figure Trappola, "only
two days are truly one's own: the day one is born, and the day one
dies."[2] And in spite of the interpenetration of life and death, it tends to
be these two days that are taken as the limits defining the human self.

   The following chapter is concerned with the role of laughter in the
complex relationship of the human self to the margins of its existence
and the non-existence which lies beyond. As blatantly as ever, it is a role
permeated by ambivalence, characterized on the one hand by bravura
and indifference and on the other by nostalgia or sheer knock-kneed
nervousness. Laughter is a manifestation both of our anxiety in the
spheres of reproduction and death and of our (partial) overcoming of this
anxiety, a signal both of self-control and of self-control's ultimate
failure. It may be an affirmation of life (and in this context a dictionary
of German superstition attributes to laughter the power of breaking the
spell of Death and bringing Life about[3]), but it may equally come to
celebrate death, be it as a herald of renewal and symbol of fertility or as
a release from earthly tribulations and a return to grass roots. Most of
what follows focuses on laughter generated in the context of death, and
the mixture of celebration and awe it is called upon to sublimate. The
final subsection of the chapter turns to comedy both as a rejoicing in
procreation and life and as an outlet for fears and apprehensions in the
angst ridden realm of sex.

   Before we get to grips with these themes, however, the rather
awkward notion of my non-being or non-existence poses problems
which cry out for attention. As generations of philosophers have
insisted, the use of the terms "non-being" or "non-existence" as nouns is

treading on treacherous logical ground, implying as it does the existence of something which does not exist and which is therefore characterized by the contradictory status of both being and not being. It has this in common with the equally tricky notion of "nothing," which can easily come to be treated as a sort of something, and in both cases it is language that is the source of the confusion. In fact, my "non-existence" refers to a state (the state of the world without me), not an entity (like a shadow or a photographic negative following me around and waiting to put on my clogs once I have popped them). It is less misleading to regard death not as the fact that I will become nothing but as the simple truth that I will one day cease to exist.

More bewilderment arises because my non-existence – whether a state or an entity – can only ever be conceived from the point of view of a being thinking about or observing it "from the outside": truistically, I cannot give a live, first-person account of it. Or as Kierkegaard put it, death is not "objectively" graspable, "since [the living individual] cannot experimentally come near enough without comically sacrificing himself upon the altar of his own experiment ... and so learns nothing from it, being incapable of taking himself out of the experience so as to profit from it subsequently, but sticks fast in the experience." [4] But while my non-existence may remain inconceivable except as a *gap* framed in by the observatory of my possible or actual existence (just as the nothingness of a vacuum cannot be visualized but as contained within or delimited by, say, a thermos flask), perhaps the problem is really just a pseudo-problem. Perhaps we cannot imagine what it would be like not to exist for the simple reason that – for us at least – it would not be much like anything. Tom Stoppard's *Rosencrantz and Guildenstern are Dead*, a play structured around the thematics of acting and death (and trying to "grasp" death through acting), gives a brilliant demonstration of the comic confusions to which talking about our own non-existence can lead:

Ros.: Do you ever think of yourself as actually *dead*, lying in a box with a lid on it?

Guil.: No.

Ros.: Nor do I, really.... It's silly to be depressed by it. I mean one thinks of it like being *alive* in a box, one keeps forgetting to take into account the fact that one is *dead* ... which should make a difference ... shouldn't it? I mean, you'd never *know* you were in a box, would you? It would be just like being *asleep* in a box. Not that I'd like to sleep in a box, mind you, not without any air - you'd wake up dead, for a start and then where would you be? Apart from inside a box. (Act 2)

In a sense, non-being becomes a sort of pun, on the one hand denoting the possibilities that apply to us during life (if I am here, then I *am not* there or there or there...), while on the other denoting the curious metaphysical gobstopper that we can never properly get our intellectual teeth round. On the boat to England, the two morbid anti-heroes continue their musings on non-existence:

> Ros.:   We might as well be dead. Do you think death could possibly be a boat?
> Guil.: No, no, no.... Death is ... not. Death isn't. You take my meaning. Death is the ultimate negative. Not-being. You can't not-be on a boat.
> Ros.:   I've frequently not been on boats.
> Guil.: No, no, no – what you've been is not on boats.
> Ros.:   I wish I was dead.   (Act 3)

If Rosencrantz and Guildenstern seem a mite melancholy in their conceptual blurring of life and death, a more cheerful variant is provided by the acclaimed Munich comedian Karl Valentin. About to be executed in one sketch, Karl the delinquent has one last wish: to have his eyes unbound, so he can at least watch his execution. But it is Edgar Allan Poe who is the master of such frivolous morbidity, frequently even parodying his own obsession with death. In "The Premature Burial," the narrator alerts the reader to his or her own most harrowing horrors: "To be buried while alive is, beyond question, the most terrific of these extremes which has ever fallen to the lot of mere mortality. That it has frequently, very frequently, so fallen, will scarcely be denied by those who think. The boundaries which divide Life and Death are at best shadowy and vague. Who shall say where the one ends, and where the other begins?"[5] In the episode in question, however, this most spine-chilling of nightmares proves to be a comedy of errors, concluding with the narrator's bathetic but relieving realization that he has just woken up after a rather cramped night's sleep in the berth of a small sloop lying at anchor.

One of Poe's most macabre creations is "A Predicament," a parody of his renowned short story "The Pit and the Pendulum." In this instance the narrator, Signora Psyche Zenobia, is unfortunate enough to get her somewhat vacuous head caught in an aperture in the clock of a church-steeple and ends up being decapitated by the revolving clock-hands. Yet the whole affair is recounted with an air of chirpy nonchalance which – illogically enough – continues both during and after the narrator's loss of her noddle. The departure of her eyes epitomizes the absurdity:

> My eyes, from the cruel pressure of the machine, were absolutely starting from their sockets. While I was thinking how I should possibly manage without them, one actually tumbled out of my head, and, rolling down the steep side of the steeple, lodged in the rain gutter which ran along the eaves of the main building. The loss of the eye was not so

much as the insolent air of independence and contempt with which it regarded me after it was out. There it lay in the gutter just under my nose, and the airs it gave itself would have been ridiculous had they not been disgusting. Such a winking and blinking were never before seen. This behaviour on the part of my eye in the gutter was not only irritating on account of its manifest insolence and shameful ingratitude, but was also exceedingly inconvenient on account of the sympathy which always exists between two eyes of the same head, however far apart. I was forced, in a manner, to wink and to blink, whether I would or not, in exact concert with the scoundrelly thing that lay just under my nose. I was presently relieved, however, by the dropping out of the other eye. In falling it took the same direction (possibly a concerted plot) as its fellow. Both rolled out of the gutter together, and in truth I was very glad to get rid of them.[6]

Merrily disregarding our common-sense assumption that a narrating subject "is" where her eyes are, or at least somewhere causally connected to them, Poe – like his clock-hand – cleaves in two what is normally a unity. Just as the minute-hand separates head from torso, Poe creates a comically unsettling breach or incongruity between the narrating first person as a subject and as an object, between the mind (which continues its narrative oblivious to all) and the body (which is taken apart). In so doing he is both implicitly lampooning his narrator for being a body without (much of) a mind in attendance and producing a grotesque parody of the disembodied subject doing the philosophical rounds in the USA at that time. The result is a characteristically jaunty dismantling of the distinction between life and death, self and non-self. It is at three twenty-five that the Signora's head definitively takes its leave from her trunk:

I was not sorry to see the head which had occasioned me so much embarrassment at length make a final separation from my body. It first rolled down the side of the steeple, then lodged, for a few seconds, in the gutter, and then made its way, with a plunge, into the middle of the street.

I will candidly confess that my feelings were now of the most singular – nay, of the most mysterious, the most perplexing and incomprehensible character. My senses were here and there at one and the same moment. With my head I imagined, at one time, that I, the head, was the real Signora Psyche Zenobia – at another I felt convinced that myself, the body, was the proper identity. To clear my ideas upon this topic I felt in my pocket for my snuff-box, but, upon getting it, and endeavouring to apply a pinch of its grateful contents in the ordinary manner, I became immediately aware of my peculiar deficiency, and threw the box at once down to my head. It took a pinch with great satisfaction, and smiled me an acknowledgment in return.[7]

Grave Levity

As the deep-seated ambivalence of our response to death suggests, laughter and tears are but two sides of the same coin. In the development of the human baby, the laughing response is indeed believed to *evolve from* the crying one, first occurring when the mother does something startling which would have produced tears if performed by a stranger, and there is a much-commented visual similarity between the two phenomena.[8] As a literary theme, their proximity is an age-old commonplace. The French humanist Montaigne observes "how we weep and laugh at the same thing,"[9] the Italian heretic Giordano Bruno precedes his unreservedly raunchy comedy *Candelaio* (1582) with the epigraph "in tristitia hilaris, in hilaritate tristis," and the German wit Lichtenberg remarks that we generally laugh at things we should otherwise want either to cry or to fume about.[10] Beaumarchais's fictive revolutionary Figaro endeavours "to laugh at everything, for fear of otherwise being obliged to cry about it" (*Le Barbier de Seville*, 1.2), a sentiment echoed by the real-life poet-cum-revolutionary Byron. And just as Nietzsche attributes man's "invention" of laughter to his capacity for deep suffering, Kierkegaard in his *Concluding Unscientific Postscript* describes the humorist as having "an essential conception of the suffering in which life is involved." In fact, he continues, "the first thought is the pain in the humoristic consciousness, the second is the jest, and hence it comes about that one is tempted both to weep and to laugh when the humorist speaks."[11] Cheering news indeed for those who thought they were having a good time when they were laughing.

A parallel complementarity to that between the two apparently opposed bodily reactions exists between comedy and tragedy, two apparently opposed literary genres. The *Tractatus Coislinianus*, a Greek manuscript dating from ca. 920 A.D. and believed by some scholars to be a summary of Aristotle's lost *Poetics II* on comedy,[12] makes the claim that comedy, like tragedy, is cathartic in effect, "purging" us of excessive emotions by means of *representations* of real events which bring us to release these emotions in laughter (or tears). The Neoplatonic philosopher Iamblichus (ca. 280-340 A.D.), presumably commenting on Aristotle's lost text, writes: "The potentialities of the human emotions that are in us become more violent if they are hemmed in on every side. But if they are briefly put into activity, and brought to the point of due proportion, they give delight in moderation, are satisfied and, purified by this means, are stopped by persuasion and not by force. For this reason, by observing others' emotions in both comedy and tragedy, we can check our own emotions, make them more moderate and purify them."[13] As Richard Janko comments, "both kinds of catharsis are homoeopathic; both work on the emotions by arousing the emotions, just as we treat a fever by piling on blankets."[14] For Northrop

Frye,"tragedy is really implicit or uncompleted comedy": both derive from a mythic/ritual cycle grounded in patterns of seasonal renewal, he argues, but comedy represents the *resurrection* of the god-man, whereas tragedy stops short after the first half of the death-and-resurrection pattern.[15]

Equally, it has been contended that comedy or humour is but a *mask* to a more serious, if not tragic, vision on the human condition. Schopenhauer distinguished between irony, where a joke (the "intentionally ludicrous") is hidden behind seriousness, and humour, where the joke itself *conceals* the seriousness,[16] while more recently the critic Eric Bentley, regarding happy endings as ironical and misery as the basis of comedy, has asserted: "Comedy is indirect, ironical. It says fun when it means misery. And when it lets the misery show, it is able to transcend it in joy."[17] Comedy is a mode of overcoming problems by shelving them.

Self-evidently enough, the closeness or coincidence of the comic and the tragic comes to the fore most emphatically where playwrights create hybrid genres such as tragicomedy or simply ignore rigid generic distinctions altogether. Traditionally, this mixing of genres has not been uncontroversial. The English courtier and critic Sir Philip Sidney, for example, found fault with *Hamlet* for its unsettling juxtaposition of death scenes and funerals with clownery and low comedy, although two centuries later Coleridge's lectures on *Hamlet* and *King Lear* provide an explanation and a justification which would have perhaps enlightened Sidney. Recognizing that the "laugh is rendered by nature itself the language of extremes, even as tears are," Coleridge sees *Hamlet* as touching "on the verge of the ludicrous" because "laughter is equally the expression of extreme anguish and horror as of joy."[18] Such a blend of tragedy and comedy, so characteristic of the English stage of the period, tends to be permeated by an unruly savagery, as well as an ebullient interplay of tones and styles in stark contrast to the much more restrained and "classically" regulated French tragicomedy of Corneille. More recently, the plays of Brecht, of Beckett and Ionesco, and of Peter Barnes and others, have reinvigorated the hybrid tradition (albeit in an utterly different form), providing twentieth-century visions which refuse to hold the tragic and the comic apart. In the case of Beckett in particular, laughter is a response to the human being's miserable existential condition, a bitter and hollow gesture signalling both defiance and utter impotence. In laughing at the pathetic creatures peopling Beckett's plays, the spectator is – by implication at least – laughing at his own equally unenviable predicament.

The critic Norman Holland has described comedy as tragedy speeded up, pointing out that if a silent movie of *Hamlet* were played at a brisker tempo the result would be "a kind of Keystone Kop comedy (the bumbling pursuit of a criminal)."[19] Pantomime would be tragic if

we had the time to ponder its manic violence. In a sense, comedy thus
becomes a *parody* of tragedy, a caricatural exaggeration of its ferocity
and gore, a burlesque bloodbath. Again, the English Renaissance
tragicomedies provide a remarkable illustration. Marlowe's *Jew of
Malta* (1590) displays the whole range of comic techniques and themes:
intrigue, deception, irony, structural repetition, bawdry, wordplay, as
well as a goodly measure of the most savage farce. Barabas is a parody
of The Baddy, a monomanic murderer who straddles the borderline
between the repulsive and the ridiculous, the serious and the plain silly.
The account he gives of the atrocities he has committed testifies to this
grotesque wickedness:

> As for myself, I walk abroad a-nights,
> And kill sick people groaning under walls.
> Sometimes I go about and poison wells;
> (...)
> Being young, I studied physic, and began
> To practise first upon the Italian;
> There I enrich'd the priests with burials,
> And always kept the sexton's arms in ure
> With digging graves and ringing dead men's knells.
> And, after that, was I an engineer,
> And in the wars 'twixt France and Germany,
> Under the pretence of helping Charles the Fifth,
> Slew friend and enemy with my stratagems.   (Act 2 , scene 3)

The play is peppered with fatally resolved duels, hyperbolic mourning,
poisoning, indeed the massacre of an entire nunnery, and it ends –
suitably enough – with the ironic spectacle of Barabas himself falling
into a cauldron he had devised for someone else.

In the same tone is Cyril Tourneur's *Revenger's Tragedy* (1606).
While Marlowe's play has a rather blackly comic episode in which
Barabas and Ithamore strangle one friar, prop him up with his own staff
and then look on with amusement as a second friar attacks the body he
believes to be purposely blocking his path, the morbid irreverence of
The Revenger's Tragedy culminates in the trickster Vindice stabbing
someone he knows to be already dead. Bereft of their conventional
inviolability, the corpses are in both instances debased to objects of
diversion. Tourneur's astonishingly flippant tragedy is in fact better
termed a tragic burlesque, a bizarre amalgam of macabre slapstick, the
most bitterly sardonic satire, and sombre broodings on death and
dissolution. Farcical misunderstandings and misrecognitions deflate the
more serious impulses in the play, typified when the corrupt Duke's
equally corrupt Younger Son is executed by mistake and his severed
head serves as the focus of a grotesque comedy of confusion. Having
believed that it was their *other* brother who had had his head chopped

off, the scheming Ambitioso and Supervacuo reveal themselves to be
nothing more than farcically bickering fools:

Ambitioso:	Whose head's that, then?
Officer:	(...) Your own brother's.
Ambitioso:	Our brother's? Oh furies!
Supervacuo:	Plagues!
Ambitioso:	Confusions!
Supervacuo:	Darkness!
Ambitioso:	Devils!
Supervacuo:	Fell it out so accursedly?
Ambitioso:	So damnedly?
Supervacuo:	Villain I'll brain thee with it! (Act 3, scene 6)

Vindice himself combines elements of the comic trickster, the moralistic
satirist and the tragic revenger, yet he delights in gruesomely cruel
deceptions and wiles. His revenge on the Duke who has poisoned his
beloved is accomplished by disguising the *skull* of his dead lover as a
living courtesan and applying poison to her lips; his moments of triumph
are always accompanied by gloating barbs which humiliate and deride
his victims as they lie dying. The play climaxes with a typical
combination of revelry and gore, as two sets of revengers exploit the
protection afforded by a masque ("'Tis murder's best face, when a
vizard's on!") to massacre the new Duke and his nobles. As it happens,
Vindice's revengers get there first, and the revengers of the second
masque – finding their intended victims already dead – slaughter one
another instead:

Supervacuo:	Then I proclaim myself. Now I am duke.
Ambitioso:	Thou duke! Brother thou liest. (*stabs Supervacuo*)
Spurio:	Slave! So dost thou. (*stabs Ambitioso*)
4th Lord:	Base villain, hast thou slain my lord and master?
	(*stabs Spurio*) (Act 5, scene 3)

The jocular tone is compounded by the glee of a successful and
thoroughly vindicated revenger/trickster ("'twas somewhat wittily
carried," though he says so himself), a mood which persists even when
Vindice is himself sentenced to death.

In such cases, of course, it is not always possible to draw a watertight line between violence and the parody of violence, between a
sensationalistic satisfaction of our appetite for brutality and a more
critical mockery of this appetite and of theatrical panderings to it. A
similar argument can be applied to the compound of sex and violence in
the "parodic" films of Russ Meyer. Self-mockery is nearly always a
moot point, for it is ultimately a question of that invisible and highly
controversial entity known as an intention. Yet there can be relatively

few doubts about Henry Fielding's parodic intentions in his completely over-the-top burlesque *Tom Thumb*, where the prologue proclaims:

> With Mirth and Laughter to delight the Mind
> The modern Tragedy was first design'd.
> . . .
> Since then, to laugh, to Tragedies you come,
> What Heroe is so proper as Tom Thumb?

The madness comes to a head towards the play's close. Initially seeming to end in a happy spirit of marriage, revelry and dance, the penultimate scene has the King wax magnanimous:

> Open the Prisons, set the Wretched free,
> And bid our Treasurer disburse Six Pounds
> To pay their Debts. – Let no one weep to-day.
> Come, my fair Consort, sit thee down by me.
> Here seated, let us view the Dancers Sport;
> Bid them advance. – This is the Wedding-Day
> Of Princess Huncamunca and Tom Thumb.
>
> (Act 2, scene 11)

But it all goes horribly wrong. Tom Thumb is consumed by a passing cow ("of larger than the usual Size"); Grizzle the homicidal maniac is thus deprived of his chance for vengeance; and the final scene has the King wax tyrannical:

> Shut up again the Prisons, bid my Treasurer
> Not give three Farthings out – hang all the Culprits,
> Guilty or not – no matter. – Ravish Virgins,
> Go bid the School-masters whip all their Boys;
> Let Lawyers, Parsons, and Physicians loose,
> To Rob, impose on, and to kill the World.
>
> (Act 2, scene 12)

This rather excessive reversal proves not to be much of an exaggeration. The final scene is one of hearty comic carnage which out-Tourneurs Tourneur, ending with a heap of bodies and nothing else. Tom Thumb's ghost is the first to give itself up:

Ghost:	Thom Thumb I am – but am not eke alive.
	My Body's in the Cow, my Ghost is here.
Grizzle:	Thanks, O ye Stars, my Vengeance is restor'd,
	Nor shalt thou fly me – for I'll kill thy Ghost.
	(*kills the Ghost*)
Princess:	O barbarous Deed! – I will revenge him so. (*kills Grizzle*)
Doodle:	Ha! Grizzle kill'd – then Murtheress beware. (*kills Princess*)

Queen:	O wretch! – have at thee. (*kills Doodle*)
Noodle:	And have at thee too. (*kills the Queen*)
Cleora:	Thou'st kill'd the Queen. (*kills Noodle*)
Mustacha:	And thou hast kill'd my Lover. (*kills Cleora*)
King:	Ha! Murtheress vile, take that. (*kills Mustacha*)
	And thou take this. (*kills himself, and falls*)

(Act 2, scene 12)

Such grizzly humour is not something restricted to the English stage. Rabelais's comedy in particular seems to revel in its accounts of war and gore. Bold Frère Jan on one occasion slaughters 13,622 of the enemy (not counting women and children) and all in a good cause at that. Yet he does not simply "kill" them, for this would be much too pale a term; he beats their brains out, slits their noses, shatters their heads, knocks their teeth down their throats, rearranges their bowels, whacks them on the ballocks in such a way as to lacerate their bum-gut, and – predictably enough – impales them up the bottom. [20] When, at a later point, Frère Jan skilfully dispatches the archer who is unfortunate enough to be guarding him, this provides Rabelais with yet another excuse to display his not inconsiderable medical learning: "Then, with a single blow, he cleft his head, opening his skull over the temple bone and taking off the two parietal bones and the sagittal suture together with a great part of the frontal bone. In so doing he sliced through the two membranes and made a deep opening in the two posterior lobes of his brain, so that his cranium remained hanging over his shoulders by the skin of his pericranium..." [21] It is in the same robustly medieval spirit when, in Irish legend, the warrior Cuchulain encounters a soldier "with half his head on" in the aftermath of a battle. Human compassion again comes a rather poor second to morbid amusement; Cuchulain's response is not to search around for the other half but playfully to lop the remainder off and use it as the ball in the traditional Irish game of hurling. [22]

More recently, this tradition of the comically gruesome has been perpetuated not only in films like *Man Bites Dog*, *True Romance* and *Pulp Fiction*, but in the grotesque figure of Alfred Jarry's Ubu, who tortures, mutilates and debrains anybody who crosses his path ("Hold on a minute, Père Ubu," his wife cautions him in *Ubu Roi*, "what a king you're proving to be, you're massacring everybody," 3.2). But what is striking in this instance is the resilience of the figures, who can be sliced in two one minute but bounce back right as rain the next. Even after being cleft from head to toe by Mère Ubu in *Ubu Enchaîné*, Pissembock still insists on looking on the bright side of butchery, pointing out to his niece that she now has two uncles instead of one. On the one hand stemming from the origins of Jarry's theatre in *grand guignol* puppetry, such irrepressibility also represents a vicarious triumph over death, a refusal to lie down.

Such narrative and theatrical violence operates at a number of levels at once. On an immediate level, the pleasurable catharsis of our fear of death itself embodies a contradiction or ambivalence, generating both anxiety in the face of brutality and relief that it is not us being mutilated and is only an enactment of death. On a more reflective level, however, it may also involve an ambivalence in our attitudes *to our attitudes* to death: critical condemnation of the macabre fascination it exerts may here come into conflict with the enjoyment gained by a (temporary) emotional anaesthesia in a realm where angst is the norm. Furthermore, parody may aim not just at theatrical, narrative or cinematic models but at more general social or political attitudes, condemning indifference to death and thereby serving as a plea for life. The ferocity of satiric wit may be deployed to attack war and war-mongers, as is most poignantly and angrily the case in Voltaire's *Candide* (1759). In this philosophical *conte*, Voltaire's humanistic anti-militarism creates its disturbing comic/critical effect by bringing together the horrific barbarity of life-negating butchery with the glib justifications and rationalizations of contemporary philosophical optimism: "First of all, the cannons upended round about six thousand men on either side. Then the musketry removed from the best of all worlds approximately nine to ten thousand rascals who had been infecting its surface. The bayonet was also the sufficient reason for the death of several thousand men." [23] Voltaire proceeds to give an account of the injured and mutilated which combines Rabelaisian precision with Enlightenment outrage. More light-hearted and less realistic is the satire in Apollinaire's surrealistic play *Les Mamelles de Tirésias*, where Lacouf and Presto – arguing about whether the play's action is taking place in Zanzibar or Paris – repeatedly "kill" one another in a series of duels and repeatedly come back to life afterwards. As is nonetheless realized by Presto, who is bored with being dead, the whole business is symptomatic of the levity with which people regard death nowadays.

The satire on our attitudes to death may just as easily work in the opposite direction, targeting obsessive morbidity instead of militaristic indifference. In N.F. Simpson's *One Way Pendulum* (1959), for example, with its whimsical mockery of various categories of fixation, Kirby Groomkirby's inordinate attachment to wearing black clothes, developing into a compulsion for mourning, turns him into a mass-murderer, for this at least provides him with somebody to go into mourning for. Yet the theme is an ancient one. Petronius's *Satyricon*, presumed to have been composed in the middle of the first century, makes fun of the vain and self-important social climber Trimalchio, whose insistent preoccupation with his own death prompts him to read his testament to all his "friends" in advance as well as to finalize the most elaborate of details for his monument and tomb. The entire event is nauseously maudlin and succeeds – thanks also to a surfeit of wine, for Trimalchio knows how to throw a good drunken orgy – both in reducing the narrator to tears and in churning his stomach. The culmination of Trimalchio's morbid desire for a prehumous taste of posthumous flattery is his staging of a mock-wake: "Pretend I'm dead and say something nice," he bids his guests, adopting an appropriate position. The whole emetic episode (fortunately) comes to a farcical close with the arrival of the fire brigade, mistakenly alerted by the din of the cornet-players striking up a dead march.

In his short treatise *On Funerals*, the second-century Greek writer Lucian mocks the excesses of the mourners themselves, scoffing at the clichés, the histrionics, the sheer *bad acting* to be observed on such occasions: "Next come cries of distress, wailing of women, tears on all sides, beaten breasts, torn hair, and bloody cheeks. Perhaps, too, clothing is rent and dust sprinkled on the head, and the living are in a plight more pitiable than the dead; for they roll on the ground and dash their heads against the floor..." [24] In the tradition of the Greek Cynics, Lucian pokes fun both at the show and ostentation in public displays of grief and the myths and superstitions in the popular understanding of death (and especially Hades, the underworld), instead espousing a cheerful equanimity in dealings with the Great Leveller. It is in the same spirit when Erasmus, in his *Praise of Folly*, draws attention to the madness inherent in the "comedy of grief"[25] hammed out by over-theatrical mourners.

Perhaps the most subtle of all comic explorations of our macabre obsessions is Don DeLillo's novel *White Noise*. Set against the background of plane disasters, everpresent TV catastrophes, car pile-ups, toxic "events" and glorious post-modern sunsets, the novel is in a sense a polyphonic treatise on death, our fascination with it and our fear of it. Like his family and colleagues, the narrator Jack Gladney – chairman of the department of Hitler studies at the local college – is obsessed by the subject, and much of the comic effect is that of repetition and gently derided monomania. Husband and wife recurrently discuss the question who will die first; they worry that their fourteen-year-old son Heinrich, with his tendency to introspection and his already-receding hairline, will end up running amok with some sort of automatic firearm; and Jack himself – with whom the reader has the direct contact of first-person narrative – constantly broods about deaths and death, scouring obituaries to compare the ages of the deceased with his own and fantasizing about how the great warriors and conquerors of yore coped with their mortality:

> It's hard to imagine these men feeling sad about death. Attila the Hun died young. He was still in his forties. Did he feel sorry for himself, succumb to self-pity and depression? He was the King of the Huns, the Invader of Europe, the Scourge of God. I want to believe he lay in his

tent, wrapped in animal skins, as in some internationally financed movie
epic, and said brave cruel things to his aides and retainers. No weaken-
ing of the spirit. No sense of the irony of human existence, that we are
the highest form of life on earth and yet ineffably sad because we know
what no other animal knows, that we must die. Attila did not look
through the opening in his tent and gesture at some lame dog standing at
the edge of the fire waiting to be thrown a scrap of meat. He did not say,
"That pathetic flee-ridden beast is better off than the greatest ruler of
men. It doesn't know what we know, it doesn't feel what we feel, it can't
be sad as we are sad." [26]

The self-irony running through such passages means that they succeed
in simultaneously expressing Jack's obsession and in making fun of it,
here through the unflattering comparison with death-despising Attila
(though even Attila's bravura can only be visualized as a filmic pose).

Yet Jack's perspective is complemented by a number of other
attitudes which both reinforce and relativize the validity of his
agonizings. During one of his several comically candid exchanges with
Lasher, Grappa reveals a Trimalchio-esque penchant for funereal self-
pity. Asked by Lasher whether, as a child, he ever imagined himself
dead, Grappa bares all:

> Never mind as a kid, ... I still do it all the time. Whenever I'm upset over
> something, I imagine all my friends, relatives and colleagues gathered at
> my bier. They are very, very sorry they weren't nicer to me while I lived.
> Self-pity is something I've worked very hard to maintain. Why abandon
> it just because you grow up? Self-pity is something that children are very
> good at, which must mean it is natural and important. Imagining yourself
> dead is the cheapest, sleaziest, most satisfying form of childish self-pity.
> ... But there is something even more childish and satisfying than self-
> pity, something that explains why I try to see myself dead on a regular
> basis, a great fellow surrounded by sniveling mourners. It is my way of
> punishing people for thinking their own lives are more important than
> mine. [27]

Whereas Trimalchio is simply held up to ridicule for his self-indulgence,
however, Grappa's frank revelation of a daydream he is normally
obliged to keep to himself (for otherwise he would be no less irksomely
self-pitying than Trimalchio) unmasks the reader too. How many people
have *not* wallowed in fantasies about their own funeral?

Jack's colleague Murray, by contrast, currently giving a seminar on
car crashes ("part of a long tradition of American optimism"), justifies
his obsession with a pastiche of second-hand mystical and esoteric
wisdom: "once we stop denying death, we can proceed calmly to die and
then go on to experience uterine rebirth or Judeo-Christian afterlife or
out-of-body experience or a trip on a UFO or whatever we wish to call
it." [28] Heinrich's best friend Orest Mercator, meanwhile, astounds Jack

by attempting to break the world record for sitting in a cage full of deadly snakes. Yet even Orest's fearlessness is alloyed with a form of self-affirmation and self-projection: "There are more people dead today than in the rest of world history put together. What's one extra?" he asks. "I'd just as soon die while I'm trying to put Orest Mercator's name in the record book." [29]

If there is one perspective which transcends and thereby vindicates or legitimizes the whole range of other more quirky or idiosyncratic views, it is the one put forward by the brilliant but elusive research neurochemist Winnie Richards: "I think it's a mistake to lose one's sense of death, even one's fear of death. Isn't death the boundary we need? Doesn't it give a precious texture to life, a sense of definition? You have to ask yourself whether anything you do in this life would have beauty and meaning without the knowledge you carry of a final line, a border or limit." [30] Though not presented as any more or any less valid than what is said by Jack, Grappa, Murray or Orest, Winnie's words account for the fears as well as the reactions to these fears both of the fictive figures and the morbidly fascinated reader.

If a nostalgic compulsion to talk about death is considered to be one pole in a range of possible attitudes on the theme, then its opposite – the more Victorian option – is to turn death into an area of taboo, something to be mentioned, if at all, in hushed and deferential tones. The reverse of the garrulous sentimentality of DeLillo's characters is a muted sentimentality signalling a refusal to speak about anything so painful. It is in such a context that death, and playfulness or openness with regard to it, acquires potential as a means of startling or, more to the point, *shocking* those for whom it is a non-subject.

Nowhere is this more crassly illustrated than by the effect of Joe Orton's irreverently black comedy *Loot*, set in the post-Victorian England of the nineteen-sixties. One of the consequences of a general refusal to talk or think about an issue is the tendency to resort to commonplace, cliché or truism when the theme cannot be avoided. Just as Shakespeare's dimwit Shallow vacuously warns that "Death, as the Psalmist saith, is certain to all, all shall die, ... Death is certain" (*2 Henry IV*, 3.2), Orton's characters regale us with such platitudes as "Death can be very tragic for those who are left" and "The exit of a loved one is always a painful experience," while Orton's (not Shakespeare's) Hal, referring to his deceased mother, provides the obligatory "She was a great lady. Nothing was too good for her." The hollowness of such utterances is symptomatic of an all-round insincerity which is further betrayed by such comments as Fay's "Blow your nose. People expect it," "I'm not in favour of private grief. Show your emotions in public or not at all," or Hal's "The leader of the Mother's Union has given the signal for tears ... We must ride the tide of emotion while it lasts" (act 1). As blatantly as ever, the onlooker is brought face-to-face with Erasmus's comedy of grief. The amateur dramatics is all the more flagrant for being so sporadic, interspersed as it is with naked flippancy, a disregard for any sense of propriety (Dennis sticks his chewing-gum on the underside of the coffin), and much farcical manhandling of the body (which is carelessly tossed to and fro between coffin and cupboard in order to create the necessary space for a hoard of loot just stolen by Hal and Dennis). Nor does Orton shy off from bodily grotesquery, incorporating a repeated measure of comic confusion concerning one of the corpse's eyes that culminates in Hal's suggestion that they bury it separately.

Orton's caricature of the double standards in "decent" British society and the chasm between the appearance of decorum and the irreverent reality shocks our sense of decorum (provided we have one) by exposing our latent irreverence. Though markedly different (more philosophical in tone, and less of a comedy of manners), Tom Stoppard's *Jumpers* exploits similar comic mechanisms, starting with a death on stage and bringing in lots of farcical mucking about with the body. In the original production, the corpse was suspended on the inside of the door of a cupboard adjacent to the heroine's bedroom door, and whenever the latter shut, the former mysteriously opened. This stock device plays a game of hiding and (half-anticipated) revelation with the body which mimics society's antics regarding the theme in general. The fact that the object of taboo (be it a dead body or the subject of death) is normally hidden from view makes its occasional appearance startling and comic, a scream and a hoot.

The disrespectful treatment of stiffs is nothing new in comedy, going back at least to Petronius and frequently featuring in the *commedia dell'arte*, where the *zanni* or servants would play pranks on the corpse of their master. Such behaviour has counterparts in ritual and festivity too: the game of "performing tricks on the corpse" is reputed to have been part of the historic Irish wake,[31] while among the Luguru people of Tanzania the burial of a so-called mtani (a descendent of one of the original inhabitants of the Uluguru area) is traditionally accompanied by jokes and foolery on the part of his fellow watani, who tease the mourning women and sometimes lie down next to the deceased, pretending to be dead.[32] In the early years of the Roman state, the funeral rites of notables comprised simultaneous lamentation *and* derision of the dead. As the ritualization of irreverence implies, the mockery of the departed may be an attempt less to shock or create a comic scandal than simply to *affirm life*, a refusal – in the case of Orton especially – to allow sanctimonious silence to mystify and exalt death when there is living to be done, fun (and sex) to be had.

The power of comic deaths to *jolt* the spectator into laughter depends on a breach in expectations. In the case of Grabbe's *Scherz*, for example, where Baron Mordax goes for a walk and massacres thirteen tailors, this breach operates on two levels at once, being at variance both with social norms (what we expect to encounter in "normal" circumstances) and with theatrical and generic norms (what we expect a play, and in particular a comedy, to contain). Above all, there is a comic contrast between the rather gruesome happenings and the cheery matter-of-factness with which they come to pass. This effect of jarring incongruity is a particularly widespread phenomenon in the humorous handling and manhandling of death. Levity of tone coincides with gravity of theme in a way that Bentley regards as crucial to comedy in general: "The main dynamic contrast ... is between a frivolous manner and a grim meaning. The tone says: life is fun. The undertone suggests that life is a catastrophe." [33] It may take the form of simple understatement, as when Tweedledee – in Alice's world through the looking-glass – soberly points out that "it's one of the most serious things that can possibly happen to one in a battle – to get one's head cut off." [34] More frequently, however, a robust jauntiness seems to serve as a way of coming to terms with what would otherwise be unbearable, as in Morgenstern's bitterly surreal grotesquery *The Knee*, where Poe-esque poetic play with the concept of death merges into play with the bodily boundaries of the human self:

A lonesome knee roams through the world.
It's just a knee, that's all!
It's not a tent, it's not a tree.
It's just a knee, that's all!

There was a man who in the war
Was shot to smithereens.
His knee alone survived the gore,
Inviolate, it seems.

Since then it's wandered through the world.
It's just a knee, that's all!
It's not a tent, it's not a tree.
It's just a knee, that's all! [35]

Just as Signora Psyche Zenobia light-heartedly narrates her own decapitation, looking on with amusement as her bodiless head takes a pinch of snuff, Morgenstern's poor old knee presents the spectacle of a body (or a part of it) seemingly oblivious to its owner's demise.

Poe's "Loss of Breath" is an equally fanciful tale of jovial grisliness. Based on a literalization of the metaphor of losing (and then catching) one's breath, the story is narrated by a figure whose "loss of breath" turns him into an anomaly who is "alive, with the qualifications of the dead; dead, with the propensities of the living." Inspite of being defunct, therefore, the narrator is able to recount the ensuing search for his breath, as well as the whole sequence of mutilations to which he is meanwhile subjected. And all this, of course, is in a tone of the utmost detachment. His skull is fractured, he reports, "in a manner at once interesting and extraordinary," and he finds the postmortem scientific tampering with his body especially fascinating:

> The apothecary had an idea that I was actually dead. This idea I endeavoured to confute, kicking and plunging with all my might, and making the most furious contortions – for the operations of the surgeon had, in a measure, restored me to the possession of my faculties. All, however, was attributed to the effects of a new galvanic battery, wherewith the apothecary, who is really a man of information, performed several curious experiments, in which, from my personal share in their fulfilment, I could not help feeling deeply interested.[36]

As in "The Predicament," a glaring contradiction is allowed to structure the narrative, a contradiction not only between tone and topic but between the seemingly disembodied narrator aloof from the troubles of his body and the narrator *as a* body: while the narrator constructs himself (of course) as an agent with intentions and a will ("I endeavoured..."), the galvanic battery retrospectively destroys any illusion of non-material volition and places him back inside the body that the act of narration appears to transcend. Even when, having been mistaken for a murderer, he is taken to the gallows, any awareness of suffering remains excluded from the narrative. The reader is confronted with the convulsions but without the pain, a caricature of any spectator's relationship to the observed death of *someone else* and a parodic armchair version of the voyeuristic cruelty involved in witnessing a public execution at first hand:

> I forbear to depict my sensations upon the gallows; although here, undoubtedly, I could speak to the point, and it is a topic upon which nothing has been well said. In fact, to write upon such a theme, it is necessary to have been hanged. ...
> For good reasons, however, I did my best to give the crowd the worth of their trouble. My convulsions were said to be extraordinary. My spasms it would have been difficult to beat. The populace encored. Several gentlemen swooned; and a multitude of ladies were carried home in hysterics.[37]

Morbid light-heartedness may also be channelled into wit, overcoming our preoccupations by being facetious, clever or waggish about them.[38] A witty disparagement of death – say, by bringing it into contact with the smelly and lowly realm of defecation and flatulence – (half-)triumphs over anxiety less by celebration than by denigration. Redfern cites the following piece of poetic flippancy:

If Death do come as soon as Breath departs,
Then he must often die, who often Farts;
And if to die be but to lose one's Breath,
Then Death's a Fart, and so a Fart for Death.[39]

The motif, again, is an old one. As Bakhtin reports, the interweaving of death throes with the act of defecation is an ancient form of degrading dying and death, going back at least to Seneca.[40] In Rabelais, the wind-consuming inhabitants of the Isle of Ruach (which – according to the *Briefve Déclaration* – is the Hebrew word for "wind" or "spirit") all pass away with a poop, a loud one for the men, a silent one for the women, their soul thus departing via the bum.[41] This century, Joyce's *Finnegans Wake* continues the tradition with the episode of a Russian general who was assassinated while doing his business.

A cavalier attitude towards one's own death in particular has a deflationary effect, taking the wind out of the pomposity and self-importance with which we may be prone to ponder our passing. The eponymous hero of Samuel Beckett's *Murphy*, who wishes to have his ashes flushed down a toilet, typifies such equanimity. As it happens, however, the dispersal of his remains is slightly less dignified even than this, for the bag containing them gets caught up in a pub brawl and goes under in a riot of sporting and festive carnage:

It bounced, burst, off the wall on to the floor, where at once it became the object of much dribbling, passing, trapping, shooting, punching, heading and even some recognition from the gentleman's code. By closing time the body, mind and soul of Murphy were freely distributed over the floor of the saloon.[42]

A precursor of Beckett in the Irish tradition of macabre humour is Jonathan Swift, whose *Verses on his Own Death* make light both of his approaching departure and the reaction of his friends and enemies to this occurrence ("H'as drop'd," they say, "and given the Crow a Pudding!"). A derisive awareness of the physical decay preceding death is articulated particularly graphically in *Gulliver's Travels*, where Swift paints a thoroughly unappetizing picture of the Struldbruggs, a race unfortunate enough to be condemned to immortality. In the light of the catalogue of their bodily malfunctions (loss of teeth, hair, taste etc.) and their general "ghastliness," death becomes a positive boon.[43]

It might seem, of course, that an openly disdainful or supercilious attitude to death is pure bluff, a show of bravura to mask our inevitable nervousness. The Jewish writer-performer Mel Brooks explains the need for comedy and humour as a way of shutting death out, keeping it at bay: "If you're alive, you've got to flap your arms and legs, you've got to jump around a lot, you've got to make a lot of noise, because life is the very opposite of death. ... My liveliness is based on an incredible fear of death. ... Most people are afraid of death, but I really *hate* it! My humour is a scream and a protest against goodbye."⁴⁴ The chirpiness of the comedian's wisecracks blocks out the deathly silence that is so hard to cope with, just as Falstaff resorts to jesting and roistering to forget or postpone death: "Peace, good Doll!" he says in a moment of tiredness, "do not speak like a death's head. Do not bid me remember mine end" (*2 Henry IV*, 2.4). The point, however, is that the comic bravura – bluff or not – would not even be necessary but for our underlying existential *concern* with the limits which de-fine us. Woody Allen, by contrast, refuses to bluff. His wit both exposes and makes fun of his (and our) fears. His response is thus that of the *eiron* rather than the *alazon*, the underdog rather than the boaster, and his admission of fear is a mode of overcoming it, expressed as it is with irony and ingenuity: "There is the fear that there is an after-life but no one will know where it is being held." Or "it's not that I'm afraid to die. I just don't want to be there when it happens." Asked whether his films are an attempt to achieve something lasting, he answers:"I don't want to achieve immortality through my work. I want to achieve it through not dying."⁴⁵

Alongside witty ditties, (feigned) indifference and (ironic) insight, the pun is one of the most controversial weapons in the fight against death, tending either to be dismissed for being mechanical (and therefore itself lifeless) or celebrated as a triumph of the creative, nonlinear spirit. Edgar Allan Poe says of the Englishman Thomas Hood – notorious for such lines as "The cannon-ball took off his legs / So he laid down his arms" – that his puns "leave upon us a painful impression; for too evidently they are the hypochondriac's struggles at mirth – the grinning of the death's head."⁴⁶ One of English literature's recurrent puns is that on "death" and the homophone or near-homophone "debt," which can be found, for example, in the two parts of *Henry IV* (Hal warning Falstaff: "thou owest God a death," *1 Henry IV*, 5.1, and Hotspur and Feeble producing similar wordplay, *1 Henry IV*, 1.3; *2 Henry IV*, 3.2). The motif is present in the medieval morality play *Everyman*, where the figure of Death warns Everyman that life is something which has been lent, not given, to him (ll. 161-64; cf. 437-40), while in Tobias Smollett's comic novel *Roderick Random* (1748) honest Jack Rattlin opines that death "was a debt which every man owed, and must pay now as well as another time," and the likeable Welshman Morgan muses, "we all owe heaven a Teath."⁴⁷ Although the death/debt pun is not available in the French language, the praise of debts (and profligacy) coming from the mouth of Rabelais's wise fool Panurge bids us exploit to the full the period of life we have borrowed from God. After all, he argues, "who knows whether the world will last another three years? And even if it were to survive longer, is there any man foolish enough to dare promise himself another three years of life?"⁴⁸ If we have debts, moreover, at least our creditors will care for our well-being. In the face of the uncertainty of death, debts represent the compensatory possibility of enjoying a Good Life. Again, death and debts are responsible for life's "precious texture."

Freud sees gallows humour as humour's ultimate accomplishment and humour itself as the ego's *tour de force*, the triumphant assertion of its invulnerability to the battering it may take at the hands of the outside world.[49] This is certainly part of the truth. To be able to bow out with a pun (as Shakespeare's Mercutio does) presupposes a degree of self-distance which is also a self-transcendence. Nowhere, however, does humour come closer to betraying a naked terror of nothingness, an existential nail-biting. It is well known how difficult it can be to keep a straight face at a funeral[50] (hardly a triumph of the ego's self-mastery), while psychologists have drawn attention to the laughter which may be provoked by the recital of a catalogue of human calamities.[51] More poignant is the war-report which portrayed Vietnamese women laughing vigorously on being shown photographs of the havoc and mutilation caused by bomb attacks in their home villages. Used to confirm propagandist stereotypes of Vietnamese callousness, the laughter was in fact a manifestation of acute distress and grief.[52] In the case of the sick humour – the jokes about disasters, pain, and physical and mental handicaps – which is so rife in twentieth-century Western culture, the fear and the attempt to come to terms with it seem to be allied with the self-assertion which comes from a breach of taboo or decorum, the desire to shock. All these examples exhibit an almost hysterical nervousness caused by liminal situations, by emotional extremities. Gallows humour, it seems likely, is both the outcome and the attempted overcoming of the same nervousness.

Lying and Standing

The instances of macabre comedy so far encountered have tended to denigrate or belittle death and to make fun of our attitudes or preoccupations. This is not the only manner of attempting to master our insecurity. The alternative is more celebratory, presenting death not as an end or limit but as something that is gone beyond, a part of a bigger process but not the final word. This applies most obviously to ritual resurrection and festive wakes, where death figures as but one stage in a cycle of creation and destruction, generation and degeneration, rising and falling. But the comic theatre too – though far removed from its highly contentious ritual roots – has an inherent reluctance to equate death with "curtains." The curtains in fact rarely fall until any death that does occur has been in some sense undone.

This results for a start from the theatrical or ludic nature of the proceedings. An acted death is necessarily followed by a "resurrection" of sorts: his role finished, the actor gets up, dusts himself off and returns to the business of life. In Gryphius's *Herr Peter Squenz* (1657), a baroque German adaptation of the Mechanicals' performance in *A Midsummer Night's Dream*, this consideration indeed leads the rather confused clown Pickelhäring to redefine the tragedy he is performing in as a comedy: "The play will end in merriment, for the dead will come back to life, sit down together, and drink a rouse full heartily: for this reason it is a comedy" (act 1). Stage performers have a knack of surviving the most gruesome theatrical carnage; nonetheless, in case we had forgotten this, Pickelhäring takes the precaution just before his suicide scene of reminding the spectators that it is only a play and they need not worry (they can even look the other way if they want), and the message is unwittingly underlined by his monumentally extravagant death throes, which entail him jogging round the entire stage. As with Shakespeare's Mechanicals, therefore, bad acting and bad theatre prove an especially good way of reminding us that the death is but a performance. Buckingham's burlesque *The Rehearsal* (1671) exploits a confusion very similar to Gryphius's. Having looked on as the hero Drawcansir slaughters everyone in sight, the spectator Smith asks the puffed up playwright Bayes how the corpses are to go off or be removed from the stage: "Go off!" exclaims Bayes, "why, as they came on; upon their legs: how should they go off? Why, do you think the people here don't know they are not dead? ... Come, Sir, I'll show you how they shall go off. Rise, rise, Sirs, and go about your business" (5.1). As if it weren't obvious. As with Gryphius, this "resurrection" is of course an aspect of the burlesque, mocking inferior tragic drama by blatantly and absurdly infringing the accepted dictates of illusionism. In "serious" drama the actors should at least be consistent in their pretence of death; comedy is not inhibited by such constraints.

The twin themes of death and acting feature centrally in Tom Stoppard's *Rosencrantz and Guildenstern are Dead*. While the Players – the troupe of actors who turn up to perform a mini-tragedy in *Hamlet* – are proud of their skill and know-how in the art of dying, Guildenstern objects that they do not and cannot *really* know death:

> Guil.: Actors! The mechanics of cheap melodrama! That isn't *death*! ... You scream and choke and sink to your knees, but it doesn't bring death home to anyone – it doesn't catch them unawares and start the whisper in their skulls that says – "One day you are going to die." ... You die so many times; how can you expect them to believe in your death?
>
> Player: On the contrary, it's the only kind they do believe. They're conditioned to it. I had an actor once who was condemned to hang for stealing a sheep – or a lamb, I forget which – so I got permission to have him hanged in the middle of a play – had to change the plot a bit but I thought it would be effective,

you know – and you wouldn't believe it, he just *wasn't*
convincing! It was impossible to suspend one's disbelief
– and what with the audience jeering and throwing peanuts,
the whole thing was a *disaster*!   (Act 2)

Guildenstern insists that death cannot be acted; in his view, it is not so much a spectacular departure to be accompanied by gore, gasps and rolling eyes as an absence, a failure to reappear. In his eagerness to prove his point, he snatches the Chief Player's dagger and stabs him with it, pushing the blade in up to the hilt: the Player "stands with huge, terrible eyes, clutches at the wound as the blade withdraws: he makes small weeping sounds and falls to his knees, and then right down. ... The tragedians watch the Player die: they watch with some interest. The Player finally lies still. A short moment of silence. Then the tragedians start to applaud with genuine admiration. The Player stands up, brushing himself down" (act 3). For all Guildenstern's disparagements, acting death is a way of keeping alive, keeping death at arm's length, in a sense even a route to immortality. Guildenstern's objection is that such histrionics are concerned only with the moment of death, the passage between being and non-being, ignoring the ungraspable and unperformable nothingness that comes afterwards. As such they are a form of self-deception, masking the real issue. Guildenstern has a point. But so has the Player: though the play itself represents the deaths of Rosencrantz and Guildenstern in the form of completely undramatic disappearances, even this is but a part –a trick – within a theatrical composition created by Tom Stoppard. And the two of them will be back again to perform on nights to come.

For Falstaff too, acting death is a means of preserving life, albeit in a more concrete sense, for "lying" here enables the life-loving rogue to avoid an untimely end on the battlefield. As with Stoppard's Player, his resurrection may startle both the theatrical audience and (some of) the fictive personages: dropping his "death-mask," Falstaff retrospectively reveals (to us, though not to Hal) that we have been taken for a ride. Cowardly though he is, however, Falstaff rarely provokes indignation. Nervous relief that the "trunk of humours" is back on his feet, admiration for his resourcefulness, or embarrassment at having been taken in are more likely responses, and Falstaff himself has little difficulty in justifying his course of action: "'Sblood, 'twas time to counterfeit.... Counterfeit? I lie, I am no counterfeit. To die is to be a counterfeit, for he is but the counterfeit of a man who hath not the life of a man; but to counterfeit dying, when a man thereby liveth, is to be no counterfeit, but the true and perfect image of life indeed" (*1 Henry IV*, 5.4). In the anonymous popular play *Locrine*, the clown Strumbo likewise plays possum to save his skin. In this instance Strumbo "lies" next to the fearless warrior Albanact, who has killed himself to avoid

the ignominy of capture, the clown's mock-death serving as an
irreverent burlesque of the real thing. It is also a pretext for Strumbo's
numbskull of a servant Trompart to launch into some hyperbolic
lamentation:

> Trompart: Look where my maister lies. Master, Master.
> Strumbo : Let me alone, I tell thee, for I am dead.
> Trompart: Yet one word, good master.
> Strumbo : I will not speake, for I am dead, I tell thee.
> Trompart: And is my master dead?
>   O sticks and stones, brickbats and bones,
>   and is my master dead?
>   O you cockatrices and you bablatrices,
>   that in the woods dwell:
>   You briers and brambles, you cookes shoppes
>   and shambles, come howle and yell. [53]

Yet up Strumbo gets ("Let me be rising") when Trompart alerts him to
the thieves who are on their way to purloin the dead man's purse.

Such incompetent acting is a notably effective way of reminding the
onlookers that the death they have before them is but the representation
of a death. This may come about through failure to maintain the illusion
in a play-within-a-play (as in *Peter Squenz* and *The Rehearsal*), an
inability to act the part consistently in a non-theatrical context (as with
Strumbo's "I am dead"), or simply through a farcical exaggeration of
the death-throes themselves (witness Pickelhäring's joggings or – in
Beaumont's *Knight of the Burning Pestle* – the fifty-line declamation
delivered by Rafe in spite of having a forked arrow impaling his head).
Analogous effects are achieved, however, not just at the level of drama-
within-drama, or fictive acting occurring *within* the frame-play, but also
when the illusionism of the frame-play itself is tampered with.
Aristophanes's *Frogs* is a case in point, breaching its own illusion by
having a corpse "come to life" on stage and conduct a perfectly
coherent conversation with Dionysus. Confounding our real-life
supposition that dead people do not talk, this short-lived mini-
resurrection both thwarts our expectations and, to the extent that it is
recognized as impossible or "not real," alerts us to the playfulness of the
play itself. As the "dead" corpse implicitly admits it is only someone
pretending to be dead, Aristophanes's comedy implicitly betrays its
own theatricality.

The comedy of shammed death may also be bound up with a
number of other comic moments, especially those resulting from the
spectator's ironic perspective. Seeing through the performance, the
onlooker can mock the gullibility or enjoy the duping of those who do
not. For a start, counterfeiting one's own demise is a near-infallible
method of unmasking the truth about other people's emotions. In

Molière's *Le Malade Imaginaire*, this device is used twice. Not only does Argan's younger daughter Louison, about to be given a birching for telling fibs, play possum in such a way as to bring out the "softy" in Argan, but the hypochondriac's own acted death prompts the scheming Béline to drop her mask of wheedling affection and expose both the disgust she really feels for him and her true mercenary motivations. The fool is saved from the rogue, and the comic death secures a happy ending. The "death" of Molière's charismatic rogue Scapin, by contrast, is a stratagem for gaining the forgiveness of the bad-tempered old *senex* he has run rings round during the entire course of *Les Fourberies de Scapin*. And although the old man initially only consents to forgive him *if* he dies, Scapin's "final" request to be placed at the head of the banquet table pending his actual passing suggests a coupling of "death" and festivity which will end up carrying the day. This same combination is also in Buckingham's *Rehearsal*, where Bayes's ludicrous play-within-the-play stages a "tear-jerking" funeral for the lovely Lardella. The sorrow is suddenly transformed into celebration with the entry of Pallas, who – just as the mourners are about to commit suicide for grief – reveals that it was all a set-up to test their ardour and inside the coffin is a banquet.

In many (though not all) of these instances much of the comic force derives from the fact that we, the audience, see through the imposture and are therefore in a position of *knowing better* than those who are taken in. This sense of superiority applies equally when the characters themselves believe that they are dead. Once again, this is a time-honoured motif, going back to Boccaccio's *Decameron*, whose Ferondo – guilty of the cardinal Boccaccian sin of failing to swive his gorgeous wife assiduously enough – is given some sleeping powder, laid to rest in a tomb, and on awakening made to believe he is in Purgatory (the Abbot meanwhile ministering to the wife's needs with unflagging energy and religious diligence). Interestingly, this story (3:8) also raises the ever-recurrent question of whether the dead eat or not. Bakhtin gives this account of a sixteenth-century farce called *The Living Corpses*, performed at the court of Charles IX of France:

> A lawyer loses his mind and imagines that he is dead. He gives up eating and drinking and lies motionless on his bed. In order to cure him, one of his relatives pretends that he too is dead and gives orders to be laid out on a table in the lawyer's room. All weep for the "dead" relative. Then he makes comic grimaces, and everybody laughs, including the supposedly dead man himself. The lawyer is surprised but is told that dead men laugh, so he forces himself to laugh; this is the first step in regaining his sanity. Then his relative begins to eat and drink. The lawyer is now persuaded that dead men also nourish themselves. He does so, too, and is completely cured. Thus, laughter, food and drink defeat death.[54]

In his history of madness/folly, Michel Foucault cites the case reported in the eighteenth century of a man who was cured of the same delusion in precisely the same manner,[55] and a strikingly similar anecdote even finds its way – in narrative form – into Ludvig Holberg's play *Jeppe From the Hill* (1722). Jeppe himself provides more of the same sort of comedy: having usurped and abused the position of the local Baron, Jeppe is condemned to "death" but given instead a dose of sleeping potion. The staged death is again part of something akin to a comedy-within-the-comedy, but this time everybody plays along *except* the deceased, who as a communal butt remains ignorant of the truth: as he sinks into oblivion, he makes a moving farewell speech to wife and family, horse, dog, cat, oxen, sheep and pigs. Waking up to find himself hanging (dead) from the gallows, Jeppe – suspended somewhere in a no-man's-land between life and death – is visited by his wife, discovers to his surprise that he can talk, and is almost beaten to a second death for asking her to fetch him a bottle of schnaps. Even when eventually condemned to life again by the Judge, Jeppe remains chronically uncertain whether he is alive or just a ghost (5.1/2).

As is suggested by Foucault's concern with people prey to the delusion of being dead, the themes of death and madness are closely interrelated. The simple fact that *we know better* reduces the sufferer to a sort of fool or gull, someone who lacks our knowledge of the "true" state of things. In a number of comedies, metaphorical "deaths" thus come to be symptomatic of a state of mental imbalance: having just discovered that he has been robbed, for example, Molière's miser Harpagon rants "I am dead" in a frenzy of paranoia and monomanic distraction, a symbol of the radical loss of self-possession that accompanies a loss of possessions for someone who *is* what he *has*. In Machiavelli's *Mandragola*, the thematization of death follows the various stages in Callimaco's attempt to conquer Lucrezia. His first "death" is a metaphor for his frustrated passion, the second a metaphor for his excitement at the prospect of the ruse's fruition, the third a threat should it all go wrong. In each case, his "dying" betokens a loss of self-control, the madness of someone who is "beside himself" for love (or lust, at least). It also anticipates the sexual "dying" to come.

Another side to this correlation of death and madness is the frequent association of chronic schizophrenia with playing possum as a final defence mechanism against an implacably hostile world. Plagued by a sense of inner nothingness, or of the chasm separating outer behaviour from "true" or "inner" selfhood, many schizophrenics strive to strip themselves of *all* behaviour and thus lapse into catatonic withdrawal. Literalizing a feeling of being nobody, they pretend not to be anybody: "to play possum, to feign death," writes R.D.Laing, "becomes a means of preserving one's aliveness."[56] The same words in a different context could have been written of Falstaff, himself an incurable actor, a Nobody who is locked in perpetual performance. Laing indeed sees in the "denial of being, as a means of preserving being" [57] one of the most basic defences for all forms of psychosis. One patient reports: "I tried to die by being catatonic ... I had to die to keep from dying." [58] Or, as Laing himself puts it, "being dead, one cannot die." [59]

Falling and Rising

If most of the examples so far have been situations in which the audience, enjoying an ironic perspective, is *aware* that the death is only a mock-death, an equally significant brand of deathly comedy contains a "resurrection" when the spectator least expects it. One remarkable instance of this is Corneille's seventeenth-century play *L'Illusion Comique*, where – having traced the sequence of adventures constituting Clindor's past life – the action comes to a violent close with his tragic death: that is, until the final act reveals itself to have been just a theatrical performance with Clindor, now a player, merely *acting* his death. Fooling the onlooker into believing that the events on stage are real, Corneille (the prankster!) deflates the tragic pomp and discharges the tragic tension with his final "comic" revelation of Clindor and his wife counting their receipts at the end of the production. In Beaumont's *Knight of the Burning Pestle*, death is a deceit used to ensure the happy ending of the two young lovers, as the roguish Jasper fakes it to regain the affections of his lady and then uses the coffin, from which he had surprised both her and us by popping up from the dead, as a vehicle for smuggling her out of her captivity.

The ruse plays an even more central role in Thomas Middleton's *A Chaste Maid in Cheapside* (1630), where the young couple Moll and Touchwood Junior – thwarted in their love by parental obstinacy – end up "dying" of sorrow. Middleton extravagantly piles on the pathos both of their deaths (Moll singing a final melancholy song as an expression of her grief, before mournfully expiring) and of the double funeral ("It makes a hundred weeping eyes," sobs Lady Kix), but this emotional climax serves only to make the comic relief and release all the more pronounced when they do indeed come back to life. Rising from the dead, Touchwood Junior and Moll are speedily united by an obliging parson, the funeral is reversed into a wedding celebration, and the tragedy converted into a comedy before scheming parents can get a word in edgeways. As those present enthuse, "Never was hour so filled with joy and wonder" (5.4). When completely unexpected, comic resurrections generate not the satisfying predictability of an ironic perspective, but awe and amazement, the *admiratio* seen by Renaissance theorists as crucial to the comic surprise. No wonder, then, that coming back to life is frequently associated with magic and sorcery, as is the case with Faustus, who revives after being beheaded by Benvolio and Frederick ("Give him his head, for God's sake," blubbers a panicky Frederick, but of course Faustus already has a spare one, [*Doctor Faustus*, 4.3]), or with the English Harlequin, whose magic bat "could reassemble the maimed and reanimate the dead when a patent steam carriage exploded, scattering its passengers." [60]

In a different tone is the wonder engendered by the resurrection in Shakespeare's *Winter's Tale*. Here Hermione – brutally accused of infidelity by her jealous husband Leontes – passes out and is universally thought to be dead; she recovers, however, and is hidden away unbeknown to the husband, returning to life only in the final scene many years later. Though the motif is not at all unusual in Shakespeare, this is in fact the one play in which he refuses to take the spectators into his confidence, withholding the sort of information which would have allowed them to appreciate the dramatic ironies resulting from the figures' lesser knowledge. Instead, the audience is put in the position of *sharing* the stupefaction felt by the fictive characters when what appears to be a statue of the deceased shows signs of being a real person. Objections to the episode's plausibility are forestalled by Paulina, who is in the know: "That she is living, / Were it but told you, should be hooted at / Like an old tale: but it appears she lives..." (5.3). As Paulina recognizes, the response provoked by such an unlikelihood hovers between silent awe ("Strike all that look upon with marvel," 5.3) and laughter (hooting). Were it simply narrated, such an absurdity would arouse mocking mistrust; in the flesh, it generates reverential astonishment; in the theatre, perhaps, the response is something inbetween, a frame of mind suspended between disbelief and a willing suspension of disbelief, credulity and incredulity.

Shakespeare's play is conspicuous for the seasonal symbolism which structures it: it is a tale not only *about* the metaphorical Winter created within and around himself by a suspicious husband, but also itself an *overcoming* of Winter. The season of darkness is vanquished both by the telling of the tale (story-telling or play-acting being a must for passing those long, cold Winter nights pending Spring's return) and by the occurrences within it, as the youth and warmth of the young lovers Florizel and Perdita in the second half of the play succeed in triumphing over the powers of gloom and destruction. These seasonal figures are reinforced by imagery of sickness and health, poison and cure, infection and purgation: accused of unfaithfulness, Hermione is treated "like one infectious" (3.2); Paulina regards herself as Leontes's "physician," seeking (but failing) to cure him of the destructive madness that wreaks such havoc, using her words as medicine "to purge him of that humour / That presses him from sleep" (2.3). As an overcoming of Winter, a victory over death, the comedy itself proves a purgation of the Winter in *us*, a laughing catharsis.

Such a play seems to offer concrete corroboration of those theories which would trace comedy back to its roots in a communal ritual representing the triumph of life over death, the festive religious sacrifice which preserved the community from the sterility of age in a celebration of youth and fertility. What starts out as the periodic slaying of an ageing king (god-man) or a dying tree-spirit is thus – it has been conjectured[61] – over the centuries modified by the substitution of a dramatic for an actual death. And indeed *The Winter's Tale* itself contains a "death" (the almost sacrificial killing of old Antigonus, bathetically and farcically narrated so as to distance its horror), which is pivotal to the symbolic transition from tragedy to comedy. In such a form, the overcoming of death appears intrinsically linked to the ritual overcoming or expulsion of the scapegoat, the sacrificial victim possibly functioning both as a symbolic representation of death or decrepitude and a *pharmakos* bearing the collective evils of the community. What many critics have celebrated as comedy's mythic vitalism does smack somewhat of involuntary euthanasia. Yet Frazer also connects the ritual "carrying out of Death" with the killing of Carnival, "Death" performing a role structurally analogous to the personification of festivity.[62]

It is clearly impossible to hope for anything more than a second-hand understanding of the "significance" of comedy's hypothetical ritual forefathers. Nonetheless, a whole semantic field of "negative" forces can be retrospectively arrayed as essentialized metaphysical undesirables to be overcome – death, age, evil, disorder. Each of these in some way symbolizes the Other, the Unknown. What is also clear is that these forces cannot *simply* and *unequivocally* be banished or annihilated: they remain essential to their opposites, if only for definitional purposes, just as a self cannot be defined without its other. The Carnival figure of festive disorder in particular betrays this ambiguity, and the "Death" who is vanquished in pre-comic ritual may accordingly be understood to embody a fundamental opposition as both a scapegoat (to be expelled) and a spirit of vegetation (to be renewed), a figure of festive abundance and of diseased sterility: "the pharmakos," writes Cornford, "is a representative both of the power of fertility and the opposite powers of famine, disease, impurity, death."[63] Such ambiguity helps explain the multiplicity of directions taken by the comic impulse, which may pursue its scapegoats with relentless malice or allow them to be literally or metaphorically resurrected.

Not all anthropologists or literary critics concur with the interpretation of the *pharmakos* in terms of seasonal change and the death and rebirth of nature. Girard, as has been seen, understands the scapegoat not as a symbol of death or infertility but as a victim of the violence we *all* have within ourselves, the "death" which lies hidden at the heart of the community. Again, however, the effect of sacrifice is cathartic, a purgation of the contagious, undifferentiated violence which

would otherwise consume the society, a re-establishment of the
communal well-being following the exorcism of the contamination
within us. As Girard argues, the kinship of scapegoating and catharsis is
underscored by the semantic contiguity of the Greek words *pharmakos*
and *katharma*, both of which denoted a human sacrificial victim. This
affinity is echoed in the medical terms *pharmakon* (poison/cure) and
katharsis (purgation). The related term *kathairo*, moreover, meant to
cleanse the world of its monsters, as well as to whip,[64] which recalls to
mind both the Athenian practice of flogging its scapegoats on the
genitals and the *comic* flagellation meted out by the corrective comedy,
say, of a Ben Jonson, whose Asper – speaking the Prologue to *Everyman
Out of His Humour* – claims to lash contemporary follies with "a whip
of steel" (line 19). Witnessing the verbal asperity of society's satirical
scourges or the thrashings and drubbings of farce (a Girardian model
might say), the community is protected from the contagion of death by
a communal laughing exorcism of all the brutality which might
otherwise prompt us to slaughter one another. In this case the comic
catharsis cleanses not so much our fear of death as our proclivity to
cause death.

Such a model is limited in its capacity to explain comedy on account
of its one-sided emphasis on violence at the expense of the other
metaphysical nasties a community may have reason to expel. It would
fail, for example, to do justice to the complexity of a character like
Falstaff, who in *The Merry Wives of Windsor* suffers the series of ritual
"deaths" which Northrop Frye equates with the ceremonial "carrying out
of Death." If Falstaff is a scapegoat and a devil on the one hand, he also
bears a resemblance to some sort of ageing fertility god (especially in his
fruitless efforts to tup the local ladies), suggesting that the themes of
violence and seasonal renewal cannot always be sundered as cleanly as
Girard would have it. Falstaff is both a devil and a "Death" who is
"carried out," and for all that one of the best loved of all festive fools.
The reduction of comic catharsis to the sphere of violence further fails
to account for the Oedipal tendency characteristic of the line of comedy
descending from Plautus. The fact that so much comedy represents
either (or both) the beating or the outwitting of a senescent father-figure,
coupled with the triumph of youth and a conjugal happy ending, implies
the predominance of a tendency to celebrate renewal, fertility and
procreation.

The revitalizing impulse has been perceived by theoreticians to be
fundamentally linked to a movement towards knowledge or self-
knowledge culminating in *anagnorisis*, or a recognition scene. Even if
only in parodic form, the recognition scene is as essential to the
traditional comic plot as Aristotle judged it to be to tragedy: lost
children, lost siblings and lost parents have a felicitous knack of turning
up (and being recognized) in the nick of time to procure the happy

ending, clearing up potentially destructive misunderstandings and guaranteeing future harmony. Shakespeare's *Comedy of Errors,* for example, conjoins a recognition scene with the final sweeping aside of the threat of death that has been hanging over the play from the outset, as a multiple *anagnorisis* involving two sets of siblings and a long-lost husband and wife is in effect what saves the life of the hero-victim Egeon. The comic epiphany permits the presage of sacrifice to be metamorphosed into a promise of rebirth, harmony and festivity: the overcoming of death is simultaneously an overcoming of (figurative) darkness and a progression towards enlightenment and a new order. The Cambridge anthropologist Gilbert Murray thus traces comedy's "somewhat tiresome foundling" back to archaic ritual origins in the discovery or recognition of the Year-Baby (i.e. the resurrection of the vegetation-god Dionysus);[65] Northrop Frye makes the sweeping assertion that "*anagnorisis,* or recognition of a newborn society rising in triumph around a still somewhat mysterious hero and his bride, is the archetypal theme of comedy."[66]

Rather conveniently,[67] the Bible is itself thus comedic in structure (and tragedy but an episode *within* the divine comedy). Or is it rather comedy – as some medieval poetic theorists thought – that is biblical in structure, imitating the Christian plot of history and the soul's progress towards God with its movement from adversity to prosperity? Whichever is the case, the medieval Corpus Christi dramatizations of the Christian story find room within their feast-day celebration of man's salvation both for the callous beating of the scapegoat/god-man *and* for the ensuing resurrection. Striking in this context is the parallel between Christ and Dionysus, the Greek god of fertility, vegetation and wine, in whose honour comedies and tragedies were performed at Athenian festival. Of all the Greek deities it is Dionysus who bears the greatest resemblance to Christ, and, like Christ, Dionysus is a god of resurrection: born of Zeus and Kore (as one version has it), the infant Dionysus was ripped to pieces and devoured by the Titans (on the instigation of the jealous Hera), but his heart was saved and he was born again. If Christianity had developed in a more celebratory and less nihilistic way, we would perhaps today be performing comedies for Christ, the scapegoat, wise fool and god of wine.

"Mythic" or "archetypal" interpretations of comedy tend to be distinctly conciliatory and optimistic, singing the praises of comedy's "natural vitalism" and its regulatory properties. But apart from ignoring the possibly oppressive and normalizing implications of such notions as "nature" and "vitality," this approach also fails to do justice to comedy's structural *ambivalence.* The overcoming of death – be it as the expulsion of the figure of "Death" or as a ritual resurrection of a hero-victim – need not simply be an unequivocal victory over or banishment of an unknown and unknowable enemy but also the *celebration* of something which cannot genuinely be separated from life. To acknowledge this is to acknowledge that life and death are mutually interdependent, two sides of the same mortal coil. The ambivalence felt towards death is embodied within the persona of the ageing fertility god, who stands both for ageing and fertility, death and life, or in the devil-cum-scapegoat, whose transgressions enact the disorder within us and who therefore stands both for disorder and for us.

It is perhaps the traditional Irish wake which most graphically expresses the festive attitude towards death. As Mercier describes in his account of the phenomenon, the wake combines merriment and mourning in the very presence of the corpse. The obscene horseplay, mimed fertility dramas, and bawdy games such as "laying the keel" and "erecting the mast" which originally brightened up the occasion all betray a ritual kinship with phallic ceremonial, and even though the playful licentiousness later came to be modified, the kissing games and mock marriages which persisted testify to a residual paganism. [68] Drawing a distinction between grotesque humour, which operates in the sphere of sex, and macabre humour, concerned with death, Mercier sees both types as an attempt to come to terms with death and belittle life. And both have their roots in fear: "Whereas macabre humour in the last analysis is inseparable from terror and serves as a defence mechanism against the fear of death, grotesque humour is equally inseparable from awe and serves as a defence mechanism against the holy dread with which we face the mysteries of reproduction." [69] If Mercier is slightly overstating the terror and awe, and understating the celebratory moment, this is perhaps because celebration itself is but a *response* to terror and awe. Whatever the case, the interdependence of fear and festivity, death and sex, proves crucial both to the spirit of the wake and to the tradition of macabre Irish humour which draws on it.

James Joyce's *Finnegans Wake* is very much in this tradition, pervaded as it is by a sense of the cyclicality or circularity of historical time (owing in part to the Italian philosopher Vico) which creates the novel's own "vicus of recirculation." The novel is all about falls (Adam's, Finnegan's, Humpty Dumpty's, Man's...). But it is equally about getting up (again), just like the New York Irish ballad "Finnegan's Wake," which recounts the story of one Tim Finnegan, a labourer who – somewhat the worse for wear – tumbles to his death from his ladder. Reminiscent of Beckett's *Murphy*, Tim's funeral develops into a drunken brawl:

Micky Maloney raised his head,
When a gallon of whiskey flew at him;
It missed, and falling on the bed
The liquor scattered over Tim.
"Och, he revives! See how he raises!"

And Timothy, jumping up from bed,
Sez, "Whirl your liquor around like blazes –
Souls to the devil! D'ye think I'm dead?" [70]

Unlike the ballad's title, the title of Joyce's novel does not have an apostrophe, allowing for the essential pun on "wake" (as verb and noun), a pun echoed in the name "Finnegan", which contains both "*fin*" and "again," both an ending and recommencement, death and resurrection. A sleep must be followed by a waking, a fall by a rise, razing by raising: "Phall if you but will, rise you must." In *Finnegans Wake*, Finnegan's funeral is thus a funferall:"... tap up his bier! E'erawhere in this whorl would ye hear sich a din again? With their deepbrow fundigs and the dusty fidelios. They laid him brawdawn alanglast bed. With a bockalips of finisky fore his feet. And a barrowload of guenesis hoer his head. Tee the tootal of the fluid hang the twoddle of the fuddled, O!" [71]

Not that the copulation of festivity and death is something exclusively Irish: it is central, for example, to Rabelais's comic vision, which has Gargantua's wife die in childbirth (not surprisingly, as Pantagruel's arrival is preceded by that of sixty-eight muleteers each with a mule heavily laden with salt, plus a whole cargo of other thirst-inducing wares). Gargantua himself is left not knowing whether to bewail the loss of his beloved or celebrate the gain of his jolly wee ballock of a son. [72] Later on, Pantagruel's own battle with the Andouilles, a grotesque cross-mixture of sausages, stoats, soldiers and huge animated penises, is both a fray and a feast, a great food-fight which comes to a close with everybody being showered with mustard. [73] Further afield, and from three millenia ago, one of the beautiful burial hymns of the ancient Hindu Rig Veda compilation (10.18) exhorts the mourners – once the body has been laid to rest – to a festive celebration of life:

These who are alive have now parted from those who are dead. Our invitation to the gods has become auspicious today. We have gone forward to dance and laugh, stretching farther our own lengthening span of life. [74]

The mood of the hymn is a far cry from Rabelaisian or Joycean anarchy, and the songs of the Rig Veda concerned with death are all in all permeated by a serene acceptance diametrically opposed both to brash bravura and to hysterical terror. Still, even here there are hints that the rituals themselves may have included a transgressive element, the dead man's wife lying down by her husband and possibly miming copulation. [75]

The most festive of deaths imaginable is the death itself *caused* by laughter: again, a topos with a history. An example is furnished by Arlecchino's "Despair Monologue" from the *commedia dell'arte*, transcribed in the seventeenth century. Having been spurned by Columbine, poor, poor Arlecchino, wallowing in self-pity, contemplates taking his own life. But entertainer that he is, he naturally wishes to go out in style. Hanging is too mundane, blocking up his nose and mouth too inefficient, so he turns to the audience for help:

> Gentlemen, if any of you would die to show me how it's supposed to be done, I'd be most grateful....Wait a minute, now I've got it! I've read that on occasion people have died laughing. If only I could die that way. That would be funny. And I'm terribly ticklish. If I was tickled for a long time, I'd die from laughing. I'm going to tickle myself to death! (*He tickles himself, laughs, and falls to the ground. Pasquariello enters and catches sight of him. He thinks he's drunk, calls his name, wakes him up, and comforts him. Then they both walk off together.*)[76]

Harlequin had presumably been reading up on his Rabelais, for nowhere is the celebratory association of laughter and death deeper-seated than in Rabelais's festive imagery. After listening to the latinistic gibberings of the sophist Master Janotus de Bragmardo, for example, Gargantua's companions Eudemon and Ponocrates all but give up the ghost for laughing,"like Philemon, who died of laughter when he saw an ass eating some figs which had been prepared for his own dinner."[77] Elsewhere Rabelais proudly displays his classical erudition with an enumeration of people reputed to have died for joy,[78] while in the *Quart Livre* he cites a whole catalogue of unusual and ridiculous deaths, again drawing on classical and contemporary anthologies of death. The list includes people choking on grape-pips, being hit on the head by a falling tortoise-shell, and holding in a fart for too long (for fear of kicking up a stink in the presence of the Roman Emperor Claudius). It also includes two cases of terminal laughter, both Philemon's killingly bad joke and the demise of the painter Zeuxis, alleged to have laughed himself to death at the sight of an ugly old hag he had painted.[79]

More recently, the topos has come back to life at the hands of such markedly Rabelaisian writers as Bonaventura (*15. Nachtwache*) and Jarry (*Ubu Roi*), while in Simpson's *One Way Pendulum* the morbid mass-murderer Kirby Groomkirby – single-mindedly providing himself with people to mourn – dispatches his victims by telling them a joke, waiting for them to laugh and then clubbing them on the head with an iron bar. Monty Python's "funniest joke in the world," devastating at up to fifty yards, was indeed an integral part of the British war effort. So lethal were its effects that experts working on a German translation in '43 were only allowed to come into contact with one word at a time, and when one translator was exposed to two he had to be hospitalized for a fortnight. In 1977, *The Goodies* on BBC television actually produced such a joke, in the form of the "Ecky Thump" episode. The sight of Bill Oddie, an adept of this Lancastrian black-pudding-based martial art, in conflict with an expert in the martial art of bagpipes caused one viewer to laugh so heartily throughout the entire programme that he died just before the closing titles. As revealed by the media reaction,[80] this festive death was widely felt to signal that – at a time of social gloom and great nuclear insecurity – one person at least had got his priorities right. To die laughing is to provide oneself with the most symbolic of happy endings.

The conjunction of festivity and a sense of impending doom is itself a traditional comic motif, laughter being associated here not with the death of the individual but with a more apocalyptic vision. The outlandish comic fancy of Friedrich Dürrenmatt is in this spirit: in his own words, "our world has led to the grotesque as much as to the atom bomb, just as the apocalyptic images of Hieronymus Bosch are also grotesque."[81] Though this may sound a rather sombre topic for comedy, there need be no contradiction: the humorous response is simply a manner of coping with the prospect of the definitive limit of (earthly) human experience. Mythology has even viewed the earthquake as the laughter of the earth;[82] and indeed human and seismic mirth share the same explosive, eruptive, ventilatory qualities. At its best, laughter itself can be a cataclysmic experience, a detonation and a deluge.

The theme of apocalyptic jolliness is present in the seventeenth-century comic pastoral *Le Berger Extravagant (The Extravagant Shepherd)* by the Frenchman Charles Sorel. This novel features one episode in which a small country village resorts to a huge festive orgy in the anticipation of the imminent fire and floods of The End Of The World. In the absence of detailed moral calculations with regard to an afterlife (and the need to settle one's account with the Almighty), the prospect of universal death in this context seems to function as a curious sort of unfettering, a release from the shackles of prudence, restraint and the long-term economics of social orderliness. And while for Nestroy's wise fool Knieriem – beset by a boozy double vision of social decline and cosmic doom – this sense of an end becomes a reason/excuse for systematic alcoholic excess (coupled with social criticism), Rabelais's more jovial Frère Jan sees the relentless approach of the Day of Judgement as a pretext for marriage (and sex) so as not to be caught with his ballocks full when the day of reckoning actually arrives. Rabelais himself provides catastrophic comedy of a light-heartedly gruesome nature, when the giant-hero Gargantua – antagonized by the gormless curiosity of the Parisians on his arrival in the capital – responds by undoing his magnificent codpiece, fetching out his john-thomas and pissing on them so fiercely that 260,418 of them (not counting women and children) drown in a sea of pee.[83] The fact that he does this "for a joke" (*par rys*) serves Rabelais for a show of mock-etymological wordplay that is more significant than the calamity itself, which remains just a joke.

Communal death forms the *framework* to Boccaccio's *Decameron*, which comprises ten days of jovial story-telling set against the horrific background of the Black Death. In the introduction to the stories of the first day, the narrator himself, alerting the reader to the interpenetration of grief and mirth ("just as the end of mirth is heaviness, so sorrows are dispersed by the advent of joy"[84]), gives a detailed account of the way the plague's baneful presence has led to a sportive indifference to death. Dignified mourning has come to be replaced by more frivolous customs

> for not only did people die without having many women about them, but a great number departed this life without anyone at all to witness their going. Few indeed were those to whom the lamentations and bitter tears of their relatives were accorded; on the contrary, more often than not bereavement was the signal for laughter and witticisms and general jollification – the art of which the women, having for the most part suppressed their feminine concern for the salvation of the souls of the dead, had learned to perfection.[85]

It is this confrontation with death to which the ten young Florentine ladies and men are responding in their narrative merry-making. Again, it is as though the spectre of the plague permits a loosening of certain bonds and restraints (though the conduct of the youths themselves – as far as we know – always maintains decorum and form): in the face of death a celebratory freedom of the imagination can flourish, allowing charming and sophisticated young ladies and men to tell racy tales of randy abbots, needy nuns and wives who get swived on the side. Silencing the official law, the plague creates a sort of Carnival context in which conventions can be breached and an alternative truth openly spoken.

Apocalyptic visions have also been associated with the festive/satirical motif of the topsy-turvy world, or the world upside-down, in which wife dominates husband, child beats parent, cart goes before horse, patient examines doctor, ox slaughters butcher, sheep shears shepherd, and a load of other impossibilities are actualized. Although such inversions – iconographically embodied, for example, in the European broadsheets and woodcuts of Reformation years – could be enjoyed as purely nonsensical flights of fancy, they were generally regarded as satirical or caricatural depictions of existent society in its perversion and corruption, and consequently interpreted as symptoms of social and moral degeneracy. As such they were felt to prefigure The End Of The World, when everything would be turned on its head. The image of the Day of Judgement and the Second Coming was likewise connected in the popular imagination with that of a great levelling, visualized in the *Apocalypse* of Dürer (1499) or Holbein's *Dance of Death* (1520s).[86]

The conception of levelling reinforces the implication that death need not have merely negative connotations. In the work of Lucian above all, death is celebrated for its egalitarianism, scything down as it does the high and the low, the great and the small, the powerful and the weak, with implacable indifference. As the Cynic Menippus cheerfully observes in *Menippus, or the Descent into Hades*, "it seemed to me that life is like a long pageant, and that all its trappings are supplied and distributed by Fortune, who arrays the participants in various costumes of many colours. Taking one person, it may be, she attires him royally, placing a tiara upon his head, giving him body-guards, and encircling his brow with the diadem, but upon another she puts the costume of a slave. ... For a brief space she lets them use their costumes, but when the time of the pageant is over, each gives back the props and lays off the costume along with his body, becoming what he was before his birth, no different from his neighbour."[87] Centuries later, Cervantes's wise fool Don Quixote makes precisely the same point (2:12). Death is the great leveller and the great unmasker, stripping us of all the accessories associated with rank, wealth and hierarchy in the comedy of life and reducing us to a lowest common denominator (nothing). As such it puts a welcome end to worldly injustice, tyranny and pomp.

Yet death creates not just *equality*: even better, the levelling impulse is inseparable from an inversive one. In Lucian's *Cataplus*, for example, the poor but honest cobbler Micyllus, who in life had been dying to die, makes the pleasant discovery that in Hades the cobblers actually fare better than the mighty despots. Not only, that is, is there an underlying fairness, but the element of laughter tips the balance in favour of the formerly disadvantaged: "All are at peace, and the tables are turned, for we paupers laugh while the rich are distressed and lament."[88] Whereas all other worldly trappings are prohibited in Hades, laughter is welcomed, allowing a power reversal benefitting in particular the Cynic (laughing) philosophers such as Diogenes, Menippus and Antisthenes, who had despised mundane fripperies – such as opulence and authority – from the outset. The cobbler Micyllus thus laughs both at the recently deceased tyrant now having such a miserable time in the underworld (bewailing the loss of his prosperity) and at himself for having previously been in awe of him. Menippus too is highly amused by the sight of the rich and powerful fairing so wretchedly, with "kings and satraps reduced to poverty there, and either selling salt fish on account of their neediness or teaching grammar, and getting abused and hit over the head like the meanest of slaves. In fact when I saw Philip of Macedonia, I could not control my laughter. He was pointed out to me in a corner, cobbling worn-out sandals for pay."[89] Laughter, both during and after life, is a signal of man's definitive triumph, and – again – the best means of procuring one's own happy ending. Those who take themselves and their life excessively seriously, by contrast, will be the long-term losers, exposed to the hearty derision of paupers and Cynics.

Rabelais too incorporates aspects of the Lucianic tradition, above all in the episode in *Pantagruel* where the hero's brave and beloved companion Epistémon has his "chop headed off" in battle (2:30) but is resurrected by the medical skill of Panurge in conjunction with the regenerative powers of Panurge's codpiece. Returning to the land of the living with a yawn, a sneeze and a fine fart kept in for a rainy day (indicating the return to form of his vital *spiritus*), Epistémon proceeds to give an account of his experiences in the other world. Once more, the underworld is envisioned as a world upside-down where philosophers such as the Stoic Epictetus and Diogenes the Cynic lord it, while former potentates are reduced to penury. Indeed, Rabelais treats us to one of his lists, cataloguing the fortunes of the notables of history, including Alexander the Great (now darning breeches for a pittance), Cleopatra (now an onion-hawker), Dido (now a mushroom-vendor), Pope Calixtus (now a fanny-shaver) and Pope Sixtus (now involved in the treatment of venereal diseases – always a ripe topic for medieval mirth). All in all, Epistémon has a rollicking good time down under. Hell is a place not just of Carnivalesque topsy-turvydom, but banquets, merriment, beatings and bodily humour; and even the devils are a laugh. It is perhaps this mood of convivial festivity that most clearly distinguishes Rabelais's from Lucian's underworld.

The egalitarianism promised by the afterlife also informs the medieval *danse macabre* or *Totentanz*, a motif dating from the fifteenth century and still evident in ecclesiastical frescoes and friezes (one particularly accessible example being the *Totentanz* in Berlin's *Marienkirche*, presumed to date from 1484). The church context of these dances implies that they on the one hand bear a more sombre message than anything purely comic, warning us of the vanity of worldly goods much as Dethe does in the morality play *Everyman* (lines 125-26): "I set not by golde, sylver, nor rychesse, / Ne by pope, emperour, kynge, duke, ne prynces." Within this frame of values, death is something best prepared for by a virtuous life. On the other hand, as Jane Taylor has pointed out, the *danse macabre* is also known to have been *performed* on at least three occasions in the fifteenth century (in Bruges, Besançon and Paris),[90] the celebratory circumstances in these cases possibly carrying the day over the moralistic impulse. Indeed, even in the wall-paintings, the Carnivalesque element is striking. While the quick stand rigid with fear, the skeletal dead caper and prance merrily around them, mocking them for the transience of their possessions and properties. On occasions they even don Carnival masks. Moreover, for all their didactic implications, the friezes remain remarkably free of any teleological dimension. The dead do not harangue or admonish the living, nor do they make promises of rewards or retribution, heaven or hell. What they do instead is simply point out the absurdities of temporal appearances, the impotence and hollowness of worldly riches, honours, learning and pleasure. The dead, in Taylor's words, "are retrospective, not prospective:

they invite their victims only to the immediacy of the Dance and not to any 'beyond.'"[91] It is once again impossible to tell to what extent the Dance is an expression of fear and to what extent an overcoming of it.

The pairing of death and festivity is also conducive to the sort of truth-speaking in evidence in the saucy story-telling of Boccaccio's *Decameron*. Or, as Gulliver has it (in Swift's own variation on the Lucianic theme), "lying [is] a Talent of no Use in the lower World."[92] As a universalized unmasking, death sees through verbal cloakings of the truth as easily as through the physical costumes worn in life's pageant. Yet the death-induced discarding of literal or metaphorical clothing may also be more goal-oriented.[93] This is the case in the light-hearted lunacy of Richard Brautigan's *The Hawkline Monster*. Set, tellingly enough, in the Dead Hills of Eastern Oregon, Brautigan's story relates the reign of puckish causal anarchy exercized by the eponymous monster, a "thing" of mutated light created during Professor Hawkline's experiments on "The Chemicals." A spirit of unmitigated madness comes to dominate the proceedings, seeing the professor transformed into an elephant foot umbrella stand, his two daughters inexplicably dispossessed of their clothes, and a range of other occurrences "too silly to recount."[94] In particular, the death of their beloved seven-foot-two butler provokes an immediate Carnivalesque response both in the two daughters (whose identities have by now become utterly interchangeable) and in the two professional killers come to get rid of the monster. Struck in unison by how nice it would be to "get fucked," this is precisely what they proceed to do (accompanied by an assortment of fearsome weapons), leaving the dear old butler lying dead on the floor.[95]

Going and Coming

The sparkling morbidity of *The Hawkline Monster* unearths a deep-seated (albeit taboo) relationship between dying and getting fucked, which – after the act – surprises even the sisters themselves. In Boccaccio's *Decameron* too, it is sexual rather than religious consolation that serves to overcome the grief of bereavement, St. Grow-in-hand coming to the rescue as the most comforting of God's ministers (2:7). The affinity of sex and death has long since been talked about by philosophers. Schopenhauer, Freud and Bataille all regard Eros and Thanatos, the sex-drive and the death-drive, as "essential correlates."[96] For Bataille especially, sex is a metaphorical enactment of death, in that both constitute an attempt to transgress or even dissolve the boundaries of the individual, to overcome the discontinuity that separates self from non-self: "We must never forget," he preaches in *L'Erotisme*, a philosophical amalgam of Schopenhauer and de Sade, "that the procreation of beings goes hand in hand with death. Those reproducing survive the birth of those they beget, but their survival is only a postponement."[97] Indeed, not everyone even survives. According to a Latin dictum alluded to by Rabelais's Frère Jan,[98] men who have sex with a nun die with a stiff john-thomas, while queen bees, black widows, bumblebee eelworms and female scorpions all dispatch their partner in the act. And of course – nudge nudge wink wink – what a way to go!

As a dissolution of boundaries, sex is thus inherently transgressive, and in this capacity correlative not only with death but with *moral* transgression (whence its persistent association with sinfulness and evil). This conjunction of sexuality and fearfully transgressive forces is embodied in the traditional Irish figure of Sheela-na-gig, whose grotesque, macabre form survives in a number of stone-carvings. Like the Greek goddess Baubo, Sheela-na-gig seems, in part at least, to personify male anxieties with regard to sex. A threatening man-eater, she was originally – as Mercier has speculated – a goddess of creation and destruction, perhaps even of war. Yet Sheela is virtually all vulva, coupled with a skull-like face and skeletal ribs, and not surprisingly, she does not become an unambivalently comic figure until herself portrayed with a smile. In this slightly more ludicrous guise she is not entirely dissimilar from medieval portrayals of the Devil himself, a kindred spirit in obscenity.[99]

Like death, moreover, coition can be understood as a form of madness, a "mild madness: for a man rushes out of a man," in the words of Democritus.[100] Bataille puts it less flatteringly. Not only do we become ecstatic (or beside ourselves) in the act, but sex requires the complete "death" of our personality: Bataille's lover is metamorphosed into a "rabid bitch,"[101] sex producing a "loss of self" in the sense of a loss of self-control, a loss of self-possession. If orgasm is a sort of mini-death, however, the repeatability of sex means that it simultaneously entails a mini-resurrection, a point recognized both by Donne ("Wee dye and rise the same," as he writes in "The Canonization")[102] and by Joyce ("Phall if you but will, rise you must"). The motif of sex as a "resurrection of the flesh" is at home in both the Boccaccian and the Rabelaisian systems of imagery, while a more macabre variant on the theme, the causal link alleged to exist between death (by hanging) and such penile resurrection, characterizes the thought of de Sade and Georges Bataille. Beckett's Estragon and Vladimir too, trying to kill time while waiting for Godot, contemplate stringing themselves up for a cheap thrill, but they don't manage it.

Seen as an act of love, however, sex may also transcend the boundaries of the self in a decidedly more utopian fashion. Shakespeare's poem "The Phoenix and Turtle" playfully focuses on the metaphor of two selves "made one" by love. Fudging notions of distinctive selfhood and separateness, this emerges as something deeply inimical to that sober mathematician, Reason:

So they lov'd, as love in twain
Had the essence but in one;
Two distincts, division none:
Number there in love was slain.

...

Property was thus appall'd,
That the self was not the same;
Single nature's double name
Neither two nor one was call'd.

Reason, in itself confounded,
Saw division grow together;
To themselves yet either neither,
Simple were so well compounded,

That it cried, how true a twain
Seemeth this concordant one! (lines 25-8; 37-46)

Blurring the distinction between thine and mine, thee and me, the act of love (on a good day) is an act of utopian folly (on a bad day, Bataille's foaming insanity).

As in the other areas broached in this essay, a deep-seated and multi-layered ambiguity comes to the fore in our attitudes to the margins which define our self. While the sexual act itself may seem to hover between blissful transcendence and threatening dementia, between a throwing off of limitations and a loss of control, the sexual *conquest* tends by contrast to function as a signal of mastery, self-assertion, a self-congratulatory token of the capacity to captivate the Other, to have or possess them, to make them "ours." These ambivalences are echoed in the range of laughing responses to sexuality and its power-play. As so much has already been written on the matter, however, the following account will be kept to a minimum. Indeed, the comic celebration of fertility and procreation is in a sense but the complement to the comic overcoming of death and age that has already been encountered.

If Cornford and others are to be believed, then comedy has its origins in dramatic rituals celebrating "the victory of the Spirit of life over the adverse influences of blight and death."[103] Aristotle suggested that comedy developed with the differentiation between a "leader" and the chorus in traditional phallic songs, the word itself being derived from *komos*, meaning a "revel" or the sort of drunken procession occurring at the festivals of Dionysus, while the treatise "De Fabula," attributed to the fourth-century grammarian Evanthius, claims that comedy, like tragedy, has its roots in rituals of prayer for a successful harvest. Ritual debauchery and playfulness seem to have been practised on the principle that periodic or delimited chaos is actually conducive to fertility and abundance, just as the obscene invective and magical abuse accompanying phallic processions was felt to exert a communally therapeutic effect, keeping evil spirits at bay and working as a fertility charm.[104]

Such buoyant phallic celebration is especially conspicuous in the Old Comedy of Aristophanes with its blatant bawdiness, its uninhibited verbal indecency, its sexual horseplay, and the gusto with which all this comes across. Yet the same impulse, albeit in sublimated form, also informs the New Comedy dating from Plautus, where the happy ending signals the triumph of youth over the obstacles presented by interfering old age. Schopenhauer sees the "success, victory and hope" typical of comedy's finales as an "incitement to continued affirmation of the Will-to-Life,"[105] an affirmation which manifests itself not simply in the form of self-preservation but as an urge to reproduce.[106] Illusory and transient the happy ending may be, but the sight of young couples pairing off and on the point of hopping into bed makes the spectator want to follow suit. The Oedipal pattern seen to be structuring the tradition of New Comedy means that the vexatious *senex* may not merely be a spoilsport but also a rival to the young lover, as is so often the case in the *commedia dell'arte*, where Pantalone embodies a comic contradiction of senility and lustfulness. But here comedy shows its normative teeth again, tending to be phallocentric, ageist and strictly heterosexual in its conventional leanings.

Another strand of comedy, however, has down the years compensated for comedy's habit of ending with marriage by being insistently anti-matrimonial in its orientation. The saucy stories of Boccaccio and Chaucer, as well as the Italian tradition of knavery and the cynical English comedy of manners, have all – implicitly or explicitly – been prone to cast doubt on the sexual satisfaction afforded by marriage and to champion either one-off or repeated scrogging outside the conjugal bed, celebrating the wit and wile with which this coup is brought off. A further aspect of comedy's disorderly anti-domestic impulse is its attitude to the offspring *resulting from* the procreation it so openly advocates. Nelson makes the point that "the comic attitude to children and childbirth has always been ambivalent. Comic celebration is directed towards irresponsible energy and fun rather than towards biological renewal. Babies in comedy are left on mountainsides, in baskets, on doorsteps, or even in the left-luggage compartments of railway stations; but the assumption, in all but the darkest works, is that they will turn up again when they are old enough to be interesting."[107] Comedy is in this case an enactment less of the triumph of immediate youthful procreation than of the (periodic) chaos required – in the long run – by any healthy society. Fun comes before the family.

The comic treatment of sexuality is by no means always so celebratory, however, nor so open. In a context of sexual inhibition and reticence, for example, a characteristic peeping Tom brand of comedy is able to exploit the involuntary half-exposure of tits and bums in the same startling way as funereal irreverence works in a society where death is a non-subject. Many of the *Carry On* sequence of films are thus dependent upon its public's hang-ups and furtiveness in the sphere of sex, while at the same time also permitting and encouraging laughter *about* those very hang-ups. As such the films are both voyeuristic and a parody of voyeurism, with the saucy puns and innuendoes strewn liberally throughout serving as a verbal re-enactment of this parodic interplay of exposure and concealment. By comparison with *Carry On's* Dick Turpin – "known as Big Dick because of the unusual size of his weapon" – who keeps his actual weapon tucked well and truly out of sight, Aristophanic comedy derived boundless comic pleasure from its farcical play with the long, floppy (but exceedingly versatile) artificial stage-dicks with which its (male) characters were endowed. But in both cases, of course, some degree of concealment is at play. An analogous principle of sexual coyness underlies the comedy of frustration, the anti-climactic comic chase where the half-promised baring of the vitals or the anticipated erotic encounter is deferred and deferred, and the plot simply refuses to come to the crutch.

Parody may attack not only prevalent social outlooks but also established theatrical conventions, caricaturing – for example – the optimism implicit in the happy ending or the dramatic sentimentalization of love. The King in Fielding's *Tom Thumb* provides a beautifully grotesque example, deflating the imagery of plenitude and sexual abundance customarily appropriate for a play's happy ending by contaminating it with a conceit evoking decay and decomposition:

> Long may ye live, and love, and propagate,
> 'Till the whole Land be peopled with Tom Thumbs.
> So when the Cheshire-Cheese a Maggot breeds,
> Another and another still succeeds;
> By thousands and ten thousands they encrease,
> Till one continu'd Maggot fills the rotten Cheese.
> (Act 2, scene 8)

Even less celebratory is the imagery pervading Samuel Beckett's comic vision, gloomy and blackly grotesque as this is. A sense of sexual and existential impotence limps through *Waiting for Godot*, while there could not be a much more extreme parodic counterpoint to conventional comic drama than *Endgame*, an apocalyptic piece in which the human race is on the point of (welcome) extinction. The nearest we have to a sexual encounter is the following exchange between the ageing couple Nell and Nagg, who seem condemned to live out their days in adjacent dustbins:

Nell:	What is it, my pet? (*Pause*) Time for love?
Nagg:	Were you asleep?
Nell:	Oh no!
Nagg:	Kiss me.
Nell:	We can't.
Nagg:	Try.
	Their heads strain towards each other, fail to meet,
	fall apart again.
Nell:	Why this farce, day after day?[108]

Hardly a celebration of fertility and abundance.

Schopenhauer perceived the *earnestness* lurking within the joking treatment of sexuality: "It would not be possible for the sexual relation to provide the easiest and most accessible material for jokes, available even for the weakest of quips, (as the abundance of dirty jokes proves it to do), were it not for the deep seriousness which lies at its very heart." [109] Nor is it merely as an existential boundary that it affects us: sex, together with all the fore- and afterplay that sandwiches it, is an essential cultural performance, an act, a grinding climax to the histrionic social comedy. While seeming to be a resistance to control, an escape from surveillance, a private mini-party where we can bare all and be ourselves, it is at the same time just another strand in society's infinite network of power relations, an intense game of domination and subordination, where the desire to captivate (to hold or possess the Other as a captive) and the desire to be captivated (to let oneself go or be possessed) can never be fully disentwined.

It is especially as a signal of power (and thus of weakness) that laughter thus steps in as an agent of normalization, mocking what is commonly seen to be deviant or aberrant. Comedy's generic hetero-sexuality is thus matched by a traditional joking disparagement of homosexuals, although the ambivalence even in this area is indicated by the celebratory transvestism colouring much popular festivity. Perhaps most important is the frequency with which humour – regardless of its derisive or celebratory bent – focuses on sexual topics otherwise treated as taboo or handled only with scientific/theoretical kid gloves, topics such as venereal disease (a sore point), oral sex (this too, a matter of taste) and bestiality (though nine out of ten cats said their owners preferred it).

Embarrassed laughter in particular indicates the way in which the laughing response may be used as a means of coping with a socially awkward or compromising situation. Boccaccio's ladies in the *Decameron* often respond to the racier of the stories they hear with blushes and giggles ("giggling" of course being a conventionally female activity, while the men boom and roar). Potential targets of personal and sexual anxiety especially suited for embarrassed amusement – or equally for displaying that you know it all and are therefore *not* embarrassed –

include virginity and sexual innocence, penis size ("mine's 12 inches long but I don't use it as a rule") and sexual ineptness. Martin Amis's account of condom incompetence in *The Rachel Papers* capitalizes on the theme:

> ... you seemed to need a minimum of three hands to get it on: two to hold it open and one to splint your rig. After thirty seconds my cock was a baby's pinkie and I was trying to put toothpaste back in the tube... Glancing downward, my rig, in its pink muff, looked unnatural, absurd, like an overdressed Scottie dog. [110]

And an old favourite in the sphere of mirthful embarrassment is male impotence. Amis's John Self crystallizes the problems associated with the resurrection of the flesh into a pun: "They're very difficult. They're not at all easy. *That's* why they're called *hard-ons*." [111] More on impotence is to follow in the coming chapter.

Chapter 6

Self as Body

In the "Croton" episode of Petronius's *Satyricon*, the impotence of the narrator Encolpius is exploited as a comic leitmotif dogging him throughout a series of sexual encounters. A deliberate parody of Homer's *Odyssey*, where Ulysses is pursued by the divine wrath of Neptune, Encolpius's quest is phallic in nature, as he strives far and wide to remedy the infirmity caused by the anger of the fertility god Priapus. Seeking support in his extremity, Encolpius subjects himself to the farcical hocus-pocus of a randy old witch, lavishly apostrophizes the irate phallic god, apologizes to him for past misdeeds, and even resorts to abusing and vilifying the flaccid bodily part that has left him so miserably in the lurch: "What have you got to say," he rants, "you insult to mankind, you blot on the face of heaven."[1] But his private part remains inscrutable:

> She held her eyes averted and down-cast,
> Nor altered aught her face at this address
> Than supple willow or drooping poppy-head.[2]

Not that Petronius was the only Latin author to use the motif. The group of classical Latin poems known as the *priapea*, which were either about Priapus, addressed to him, or uttered by him, contains one particularly salacious specimen, in which the poet, suffering from the same problem as Encolpius, inveighs firstly against Priapus for failing to patronize him and then against his own malfunctioning mentule: "Accursed cock! I'll make you pay for this..,"[3] he declaims, threatening to punish it with the cavernous and unsavoury genitalia of an old hag (another traditional – if somewhat heartless – comic motif, occurring three times even within the eighty poems of the *Carmina Priapea*).[4] And in seventeenth-century England, the Restoration rake Rochester has comparable problems with his pintle, problems that are divulged in his poem "On his Prick":

> Did she not take you in her ivory hand?
> Doubtless stroked thee, yet thou would not stand?
> Did she not raise thy drooping head on high
> As it lay nodding on her wanton thigh?
> Did she not clasp her legs about thy back,
> Her porthole open? Prick, what didst thou lack?   (lines 13-18)

Rochester angrily condemns the miscreant to shameful solitary confinement for this inexcusable display of sluggishness:

> Hide thy despised head and do not dare
> To peep, no not so much as take the air
> But through a buttonhole, but pine and die
> Confined within thy codpiece monastery.   (lines 3-6)

Such poetic self-abuse, like Encolpius's, produces a sort of comic self-duplication, personifying the plonker in question as an autonomous entity with a mind of its own.

Around two millenia after Petronius, and three centuries after Rochester, the writing of Martin Amis depicts the converse problem, an excessively hearty relationship with the god of the throbbing hard-on. Likewise personifying that impish little subself lurking restlessly down his Y-fronts, Amis's narrator in *The Rachel Papers* comically deflates another area of possible male anxiety in his description of their visit to the doctor:

> to give it its due, that organ had behaved immaculately the day before. As I stood beside Thorpe's white-sheeted chaise-longue, about as relaxed as a drainpipe, trousers frilling my shins, baggy but spotless Y-fronts midway down trembling thighs: as Thorpe cruised towards me, as he reached out his manicured hand, head down, saying "Well let's just take a look at the old codger then, shall we?" I was *convinced* he'd set off some awful glandular button, that my prick would spring to life joyfully in his fingers, that he would lift up his face to mine in eager recognition. But it couldn't have been better. I had wanted to buy it a bag of sweets or something afterwards.[5]

In Amis's later novel *London Fields*, the priapic comedy of an overjubilant penis is even more insistent. Guy's seditious willy – a dumb and hopeful bodybuilder, a "farcical animal," a "winking elf" – is permanently clamouring for attention, tipping up carefully balanced cups and saucers and blocking off virtually all access to the contents of trouser pockets.[6]

In such instances it is as if a separatist peninsular is splitting itself off from the mainland of the self, striving for independence and sticking up for its rights with a cocksure awareness of its sway and authority. The ancient idea that the phallus may possess a personality or identity of its own goes back as far as the ancient Hindu religion (which dates from the Neolithic age more than ten millenia ago),[7] and is perpetuated within modern Hinduism in the cult known as Sivaism, which acknowledges Siva in his capacity as *lingam* (or phallus) as an image of divinity. Siva says:

> I am not distinct from the phallos.
> The phallos is identical with me.
> It draws my faithful to me
> And therefore must be worshipped.
> Wherever there is an upright male organ,
> I, myself, am present, even if there is no other representation of me.[8]

Conveyed west by the Dravidian peoples of what is now India, this cult of the *lingam* and the *yoni* (the female genitalia) was to become the foundation for Greek Dionysianism,[9] the ecstatic worship of the resurrection-god in whose honour comedy and tragedy were performed at Athens. While the Dionysus of late antiquity came to surrender his bulging masculinity to the adolescent, exaggeratedly under-endowed ideal of late Hellenic and Roman aesthetics, however, it was left to Hermes and Priapus to keep the phallic flag flying. Like the mercurial Siva-figure, who was worshipped in the form of an upright stone or an ithyphallic image, the amoral rogue and trickster Hermes was frequently represented by the so-called herm, a plain wooden column comprising little more than a carved head on top and erect male genitals down below. There indeed appear to exist deep-seated affinities between the unruly wilfulness of the penis and the disorder associated with mythological trickster characters. The equally fluid and ambivalent Exù, the trickster in the Afro-Brazilian religions of Candomblé and Candomblé de caboclo, is likewise conventionally depicted as a huge, horned mud member,[10] while in ancient Egypt Babi (Baba), the god of the phallus in erection, was closely identified with Seth, trickster and anti-social god of confusion: according to one spell found in the Coffin Texts, a dead man can ensure sexual pleasure in the afterlife by associating himself with Seth and his phallus with Babi: "My phallus is Baba. I am Seth." [11]

Less hostile and more recent than the supernaturally aggressive Babi, the Winnebago Trickster of the North American Indians of central

Wisconsin and eastern Nebraska is also lumbered with an exceedingly large and an exceedingly lively limb, an overmuscular bed-partner with that unpleasant habit of snatching away all the sheets for itself:

> After a while he woke up and found himself lying on his back without a blanket. He looked up above him and saw to his astonishment something floating there. "Aha, aha! The chiefs have unfurled their banner! The people must be having a great feast for this is always the case when the chief's banner is unfurled." With this he sat up and then first realized that his blanket was gone. It was his blanket he saw floating above. His penis had become stiff and the blanket had been forced up. "That's always happening to me," he said. "My younger brother, you will lose the blanket, so bring it back." Thus he spoke to his penis.[12]

The Trickster and his penis are quick to make friends again after this minor contretemps. In a moment of magnanimity, the Trickster dispatches his plonker to go and have intercourse with the chief's daughter, sending him on his way with a friendly tip ("My younger brother, you are going after the chief's daughter. Pass her friends, but see that you lodge squarely in her, the chief's daughter"[13]).

As the example of the Winnebago Trickster makes clear, the comedy is compounded by distortion and exaggeration, the oversize organ belonging very much to the realm of bodily grotesquery. This brand of hilarity was particularly connected with the late classical figure of Priapus, son of Aphrodite, whose father was variously said to be Hermes, Dionysus, Pan and even Zeus. According to legend, Hera – either out of jealousy or fury at Aphrodite's promiscuity – caused him to be born with unrealistically copious wedding tackle, but in spite of his penis size Priapus is only ever a minor god, suspended somewhere between second-division divinity and garden gnomery. As a god of fertility, his image – in the form of herms or ithyphallic statues – was frequently set up in gardens and orchards, where his obtrusive weapon functioned as an apotropaic warder off of evil and a warning to thieves. Not surprisingly, however, the poems and stories about him became a pretext above all for comic obscenity, and the punishments he promises to mete out to thieves in the *Carmina Priapea* were jovial threats of *pedicatio* (sodomy) or *irrumatio* (oral sex) i.e. rape. While the Greek *priapea* did contain a number of relatively pious poems to Priapus the god of harbours and protector of mariners, the Latin songs were more than anything else facetious, parodic and crude. At least six of them, for example, derive amusement from the outlandish proportions of Priapus's penis.[14]

If antiquity presents Priapus as the god with the unfeasibly large tadger, an interesting "human" variant turns up in the modern-day comic *Viz*, where Buster Gonad's "unfeasibly large testicles" take on a life of their own, proving both useful and costly to their owner/companion. At the municipal tennis court, for example, Buster has to pay double ("These testicles constitute a person..."), while on other occasions they save the day, functioning as flexibly and as serviceably as the pendulous stage penis of ancient Greek Comedy. The topos of oversize orchids itself goes back to before Rabelais, who on two occasions refers to the horrifically big-ballocked people of Lorraine.[15]

Satirical caricature often resorts to the grotesque exaggeration of bodily cavities and promontories, mocking and uglifying its objects by amplifying noses, mouths and eyes until they reach absurd or fantastic proportions. But though directly derisive in the case of the huge beak-like noses with which celebrities and politicians are so often supplied, this is not the only effect. The nose especially is endowed with considerable *symbolic* potential. In a sixteenth-century treatise on popular medical superstitions, Rabelais's contemporary Laurent Joubert documents the commonly held conviction that the size of one's nose is an indication of the size and potency of one's genitals,[16] and the self-evident metaphorical bond between knobs and noses was reinforced by the unfortunate fact that the ulceration and eventual disintegration of the nose were well-known symptoms of tertiary syphilis. In the second half of the nineteenth century, indeed, the eccentric Berlin nose and throat surgeon Wilhelm Fliess (who also originated the theory of biorhythms) wrote a small treatise on the causal relations between the nose and the sexual organs.[17] Arguing for the existence of so-called "genital points" in the nose, Fliess claims that such sexual irregularities (!) as onanism and coitus interruptus have direct effects on these areas. In fact, the aetiological connection is a two-way affair, whence the success of nasal therapy (including an application of cocaine) for the treatment of genital complaints and dysmenorrhoea.

With the aid of such medical and metaphorical links, noses have thus traditionally been both a bawdy and a sensitive subject. The beloved Neapolitan Pulcinella of the *commedia dell'arte* is armed with a blatantly phallic nozzle, and in the medieval morality play *Mankind*, Nought makes fun of the goody-goody Mercy with a rather naughty anti-cleric quip:

Yt ys grawntyde of Pope Pokett
Yf ye wyll putt yowur nose in hys wyffis sokett
    ye xall haue forty days of pardon.   (lines 144-6)

Asked why he has such a fine conk, Rabelais's monk Frère Jan gives the obligatory bawdy response (his wetnurse's soft dugs allowed it to swell and prosper), before himself making the same thematic connection in irreverent monastic argot: Ad formam nasi cognoscitur ad te levavi,[18] or in other words the shape of the nose allows you to infer the dimensions of the bodily part lifted up in prayer towards God (nudge nudge).

In Rabelaisian vein is Laurence Sterne's *Tristram Shandy*, where the
whole saucy "nose" episode – the tale of Slawkenbergius – is preceded
by a series of completely unconvincing and counterproductive
asseverations that the episode is *not* bawdy and a nose is never anything
but a nose:

> I define a nose as follows – entreating only beforehand, and beseeching
> my readers, both male and female, of what age, complexion, and
> condition soever, for the love of God and their own souls, to guard
> against the temptations and suggestions of the devil, and suffer him by
> no art or wile to put any other ideas into their minds, than what I put into
> my definition. – For by the word *Nose*, throughout all this long chapter
> of noses, and in every other part of my work, where the word *Nose*
> occurs, – I declare, by that word I mean a Nose, and nothing more, or
> less. [19]

Like Sterne, Edgar Allan Poe was also to use the nose to signify (of
course) nothing other than a nose, as well as taking the opportunity to
parody academic pretension and empty erudition. In Poe's short story
"Lionizing," the otherwise insignificant Robert Jones and his unfeasibly
large proboscis are fortunate enough to live in the town of Fum-Fudge,
where social standing is a direct function of the magnitude of one's
conk. Himself an ardent nosologist, Jones and his nose become salon
favourites, but not without giving rise to patent sexual tensions:

> There was myself. I spoke of myself; – of myself, of myself, of myself;
> – of Nosology, of my pamphlet, and of myself. I turned up my nose, and
> spoke of myself.
> "Marvellous clever man!" said the Prince.
> "Superb!" said his guests; and next morning her Grace of Bless-my-
> Soul paid me a visit.
> "Will you go to Almack's, pretty creature?" she said, tapping me
> under the chin.
> "Upon honor," said I.
> "Nose and all?" she asked.
> "As I live," I replied.
> "Here then is a card, my life. Shall I say you *will* be there?"
> "Dear Duchess, with all my heart."
> "Pshaw, no! – but with all your nose?"
> "Every bit of it, my love," said I; so I gave it a twist or two, and found
> myself at Almack's.
> The rooms were crowded to suffocation.
> "He is coming!" said somebody on the staircase.
> "He is coming!" said somebody farther up.
> "He is coming!" said somebody farther still.
> "He is come!" exclaimed the Duchess. "He is come, the little love!" –
> and, seizing me firmly by both hands, she kissed me thrice upon the nose.
> A marked sensation immediately ensued. [20]

Though the narrator does not go as far as to put it in the Duchess's *sokett*, the phallic connotations of the nose are betrayed both in Poe's punning subtext and in the narrative rhythm itself (He is coming! He is coming!... He is come!). This too (minus the "arrival") is a typically Shandean trait.

Also influenced by Sterne was the Russian Nikolai Gogol, whose masterly comic tale "The Nose" was published in 1836 having been rejected by the *Moscow Observer* as "dirty and trivial." [21] Waking up one morning to find an absolutely flat surface where formerly his "fairly presentable and reasonably sized nose" had been, Major Kovalyov naturally enough goes in immediate search of the anatomical truant. When tracked down, however, this personified proboscis – now wearing a gold-braided uniform, sporting a sword at its side and masquerading as a state councillor – stubbornly refuses to acknowledge its previous possessor:

> "My dear sir," Kovalyov said, summoning up his courage, "my dear sir..."
> "What do you want?" replied the nose, turning round.
> "I don't know how best to put it, sir, but it strikes me as very peculiar ... Don't you know where you belong? And where do I find you? In church, of all places!"...
> The nose looked at the Major and frowned a little.
> "My dear fellow, you are mistaken. I am a person in my own right. Furthermore, I don't see that we can have anything in common. Judging from your uniform buttons, I should say you're from another government department." [22]

Snubbed by his own nose, the Major loses all social status and is condemned, even more frustratingly, to the humiliation of sexual failure ("he remembered that instead of a nose he had nothing, and tears streamed from his eyes" [23]). No nose, no sex.

Gogol's narrative grotesquery hovers tantalizingly between dream and reality, madness and sanity: like the barber who finds the spare nose in his breakfast roll one morning, the Major wonders whether he is drunk or sleeping, and the tale ends with the nose returning to the Major's face as inexplicably as it had departed, like a dream snapped out of. The same causal aberrancy occurs in Philip Roth's *The Breast* (1972), where the bemused narrator is metamorphosed into a six-foot mammary gland, the sort of mammary gland that could only appear in "a dream or a Dali painting." [24] Here too, the borderline between madness and sanity is ultimately impossible to ascertain. Preferring to be a madman than a mammary gland, the narrator ends up *wanting* to believe he is insane and actually deludes himself that he is deluded. Or perhaps he really is...

These comic personifications or quasi-personifications of the

sticking-out bits of the body are all grotesque transformations of a
marginal or liminal *part* of our self into an autonomous *whole*, a fraction
of our body into an independent unit. Yet this rather disconcerting play
with the boundaries of the body and the not unproblematic relationship
between body and self need not result in a duplication of selves (primary
self versus wayward cock or conk). Indeed, it may seem to hint at a
dissociation of self and body altogether, exemplified in particular by the
way the resilient comic hero can in many cases survive dismemberment
and mutilation and still come bouncing back into the fray. Baudelaire
relates the deep impression made on him by the English comic thug
Pierrot, who remains completely unperturbed by his own decapitation
and is such an unrepentant kleptomaniac that – even after being
guillotined – he surreptitiously pockets his gorily severed head.[25] Poe's
tale "A Predicament" is equally remarkable for the cool indifference
with which the air-headed narrator recounts the severance of her head
from her body. Of course such occurrences are plainly "absurd," far-
fetched enough to be recognized and enjoyed as flights of comic fancy.
But precisely through its capacity to show the absurdities which occur
when thought and volition are divorced from brain or head, such
comedy both embodies and implicitly parodies the counter-intuitive
dualism which clumsily sunders mind and body.

   Grotesque fantasy may take on a more unsettling aspect when
combined – as in the case of science fiction or the fashionable subgenre
cyberpunk – with a greater measure of plausibility, or a lesser one of
implausibility. In "The Man that was Used Up," Poe's comic vision
conjoins satiric near-plausibility with a characteristic sense of the
bizarre, making fun of military hero-worship by merely amplifying
absurdities already felt to be in existence. In this short story the dashing
appearance of the truly splendid fellow Brevet Brigadier-General John
A. B. C. Smith initially has Poe's narrator in raptures: the gloss of his
hair and whiskers, the brilliance of his teeth, the clarity and
melodiousness of his voice are all quite unrivalled; the deep hazel lustre
of his eyes renders "either one of such a pair ... worth a couple of the
ordinary ocular organs."[26] Calling by to interview The Man Himself,
however, the narrator is confronted with "a large and exceedingly odd-
looking bundle of something" lying at his feet,[27] a bundle which – when
unceremoniously kicked out of the way – voices its disapproval with the
puniest of squeaks. This pile of odds and sods in fact turns out to be the
disassembled General himself, a mere heap of prosthetic devices, false
organs and limbs, a wig, a glass eye and a set of false teeth, who is
reassembled before the narrator's very eyes by the General's valet. The
comic disparity between appearance and reality hits the reader (like the
narrator) as a retrospective revelation that what had seemed to be a
bundle of junk is in truth a man, and what had seemed to be a man is in
truth a bundle of junk. The *grotesque* occurs at the point of transition

between the two states, where the boundary between man and machine becomes blurred, where it cannot definitively be said whether the machine has started being a man or the man stopped being a machine. The military satire is compounded moreover by a more general satirical thrust: the comic repetition in the conversational responses prompted by the hero and in the tales told about him – the vacuously reiterated "Bless my soul!" or "prodigies of valor!" – implies that not only is he a sort of automaton, but his past history itself is but an automatically regurgitated party piece and we too (who respond so vacuously) are but machines and puppets. Our machine-like nature may be less obvious than the General's (for he is shown in his constituent parts), but it is betrayed in our predictably stereotypical reactions and the dog-eared clichés we churn out.

Far from being a quirk of Poe's eccentric imagination, however, the motif of prosthetic/cosmetic grotesquery has been of satiric relevance in both the preceding and succeeding centuries. Derisive criticism of a society where the artificial is allowed to be mistaken for the natural, where beauty is only skin-deep and appearances mask a much less attractive reality, can be found in Lesage's *Le Diable boiteux* (1707), in which what don Cléofas has imagined to be a ravishing young belle turns out to be a superannuated coquette armed with artificial hips, waist and breasts, and said to have accidentally parted company with her buttocks on a recent visit to church. In Martin Amis's *Money*, Lorne Guyland embodies the wonders of twentieth-century technological advance and bodily homogenization:

> the old prong was in good nick, you had to admit, with that tan-and-silver sheen of the all-American robot-kings. Yeah, that was it: this isn't a man, I kept thinking, it's a mad old robot, all zinc and chrome and circuitry coolant. He's like my car, he's like the fucking Fiasco – way past his best, giving everyone grief, and burning up money and rubber and oil.[28]

The comedy of a prosthetic or mechanical self (which again recalls to mind Bergson's theory that laughter is provoked when a human being behaves like an automaton) is a consequence of the ambivalent status of the self as something simultaneously free and causally determined, creative and reiterative, spontaneous and pre-programmed. Erasing or expunging the one half of this equation, it takes the other half – the mechanized half – to the point of absurdity. Equally, it arises from the impossibility of anatomically *localizing* the self, which therefore always runs the risk of becoming detached as a separate entity (a "soul") or of disappearing altogether, leaving a mechanical body either severed from its owner or even ownerless. To the extent that the soul is understood to be divorced from its body, indeed, the *whole* of the human body is potentially comic: any part of it can be seen as a mere appendage contingently attached to something "deeper" or more essential.

In practice, of course, it is the margins and extremities that are especially prone to cause mirth. Insofar as we normally identify ourselves with our body in its entirety, it is the points of interchange between organism and environment that thus acquire heightened ritual and comic significance. The bulges, swellings and orifices of the body clearly come into this category, and our hair, fingernails and toenails, which seem to be both a part of the body and independent of it (for they continue to grow after death), have commonly enjoyed magical status. Unlike a static, hermetically sealed off system, moreover, the human organism is in permanent dynamic interaction with its surroundings, and the whole gamut of goos and sludges, draughts and breezes issuing from it tend to provoke a potent but equivocal mixture of disgust, anxiety and amusement. This applies to faeces, urine, semen, (menstrual) blood, as well as to vomit, saliva, cerumen, sweat and the sometimes rather unsavoury winds emitted as belches and farts. Nor should the degree of this exchange be underestimated. As a rule we fart between three hundred and two thousand millilitres of gas a day, attaining a daily average of 13.4 actual pumps. Composed as they usually are of such odourless gases as nitrogen, oxygen, hydrogen, methane and carbon dioxide, it is only a mindless minority of poops that earn the whole strain its notoriety. In the words of Dr. John Collee, "as with fine wines, it is mere traces of other chemicals which conspire to give the fart its original aroma." [29] Hydrogen sulphide, volatile fatty acids and the so-called "mercaptans" are the culprits here.

Bakhtin's account of what he terms the "grotesque body" successfully captures the phenomenon in question. According to the Russian literary theorist:

> the grotesque body is not separated from the rest of the world. It is not a closed, completed unit; it is unfinished, outgrows itself, transgresses its own limits. The stress is laid on those parts of the body that are open to the outside world, that is, the parts through which the world enters the body or emerges from it, or through which the body itself goes out to meet the world.[30]

Spanning the borderline between self and other, life and death, creation and destruction, such topics as copulation, death, eating, drinking and defecation are viewed with a deep-seated ambivalence, an ambivalence which is generally hidden behind the mask of silence created by taboo. The association of the bodily functions with *filth* is thus counterbalanced by their equally compelling association with *fun*. Defecation, to take one graphic example, can be an act both of defilement and of deliverance, rejection and relief. As with other forms of cathartic release, it may be both a poison and a cure. Sited somewhere between celebration and denigration, the laughing response to the extravagantly churning and chundering human organism with its emissions and exudations is simultaneously the expression and the overcoming of anxiety.

Whereas the bodily comedy encountered so far has mainly consisted of surreal soarings of the imagination, the very mention of taboo substances or activities – in the right context – also has the power to shock, surprise or even repel a reader or listener into laughter. Given a context in which taboo hushes up all open reference to bodily wastage and masks the way human beings actually interact with the world, the gesture of unmasking is a moment of comic *truth*. Take the crusty, down-to-earth understatement characteristic of Beckett's *Watt*: "Finding himself now alone, with nothing in particular to do, Watt put his forefinger in his nose, first in one nostril, and then in the other. But there were no crusts in Watt's nose, tonight." [31] A far cry from the hyperbolic excesses of penile or personified noses, Beckett's prose focuses quietly but unmistakeably on the snot which even Sterne, Poe and Gogol leave out of their accounts, creating a style which is comic for its uncompromising honesty. Of course, the element of taboo-rupture is not excluded from the more absurd or bizarre examples of bodily humour, which combine naughtiness with the sort of conceptual grotesquery that teases and toys with the very notion of identity. But Beckett's grotesquery, by contrast, is earthy and minimalistic.

As with Beckett, it is as an irreverent speaker of home truths that Lenny Bruce derived so much comedy from talking about snot, at one and the same time exposing the yuck that is concealed by society's cosmetic sheen and making fun of the fascination and repulsion exerted by this yuck. All he needed to do was say the "s-word," blow his nose, steal a furtive glance at his used handkerchief or demonstratively *not* steal a glance at it; the effect would be to nauseate his snot-hating audience into laughter.[32] But Bruce was himself aware of the fine line he was (perceived to be) treading between loathing and laughter: "he's not funny," he would say, imitating past and anticipating future audiences, "he's just disgusting." [33]

The same ambivalence characterizes faecal humour, leaving us caught between two stools in our response to the phenomenon. On the one hand, excrement is a traditional means of denigration and debasement, and its effect is indeed so contaminative that for many people it seems to befoul any literature or drama which makes reference to it. For the eldest comedy involving a mishap with a chamber pot we have to go back to Homer's lost burlesque *Margites* ("Madman"), and the same motif occurs in satyric dramas by both Aeschylus and Sophocles, this tradition of bedpan humour continuing to run (albeit intermittently) through Boccaccio, Smollett and via Jarry into the twentieth century. Panurge's malicious pranks are regularly scatological in nature, and over a quarter of a million Parisians meet their Waterloo in the torrent of urine nonchalantly passed by Gargantua without so much as a by-your-leave. Following in Rabelais's giant footsteps, Swift too capitalizes on the comic grotesqueness which ensues when bodily functions are magnified to such an extent that those unfortunately placed are threatened with at best a drenching and at worst a drowning. Even relatively harmless flatulence – a symptom both of windy pretension and of undignified terror – is traditionally diabolical in association.

On the other hand, farting may equally betoken a natural candour or the sort of festive bodily honesty which could not give a hoot for the rigid social niceties which are often allowed to fetter us. One French commentator highlights this more celebratory aspect by designating the fart "anus-laughter" (and laughter, conversely, is a "mouth-fart"!?),[34] while Walter Redfern alerts us to the scatological impulse underlying so much wordplay by pointing out the affinity between punning and the number two.[35] A shaft of wit is but a spoonerism removed from the flagrantly lavatorial, and one of the technical terms for a double entendre, "cacemphaton," speaks for itself in this context. The ritual and carnivalesque significance of excrement comes to light especially concretely in the coprophagy practised by certain of the ceremonial clowns of Africa and North America. Unlike the relatively restrained participants of the traditional European Feast of Fools, the "funny men" of the Zuni tribe of Pueblo Indians in North Mexico do not merely go through the motions in this licensed flouting of taboo.[36]

Faeces and farts are thus also felt to possess generative or beneficial qualities. Bakhtin writes: "such debasing gestures and expressions are ambivalent, since the lower stratum is not only a bodily grave but also the area of the genital organs, the fertilizing and generating stratum. Therefore, in the images of urine and excrement is preserved the essential link with birth, fertility, renewal, welfare." [37] The multi-functionality of the reproductive organs brings together the sexual and the urinary in a pun-like copulation, but this coupling is itself equivocal: is it a celebration of the excremental, or a downgrading of the procreative? In all probability, it is both. Joyce's *Finnegans Wake* illustrates the punning affiliation of the two bodily functions in its own inimitable way, micturition and masturbation becoming as good as indistinguishable in the all-encompassing narrative flow. In Rabelais (where else?), Pantagruel's farts are prolific in their reproductive capacity. Trying to emulate one of Panurge's pumps, Pantagruel's response has far-reaching meteorological and demographic repercussions:

> one fart he blew made the earth tremble for nine leagues around, and the
> foetid air from it engendered more than fifty-three thousand little men,
> dwarfish and misshapen. And with another poop he engendered just as

many stumpy little women ...

"What!" exclaimed Panurge. "Are your farts so fruitful? By God, here are fine ballocky men and fine stinking doxies. Let them get married together, and they'll breed horse-flies." [38]

The hyperbolic comedy which exaggerates bodily breezes to hurricane force also assails the unfortunate Winnebago Trickster, who has wind problems of a gargantuan order after eating a laxative bulb. Even once the rumpus has started, Trickster is unwise enough to doubt the bulb's potency:

> Once more he broke wind. This time it was very loud and his rectum began to smart. ... Then he broke wind again, this time with so much force that he was propelled forward. ... The next time he broke wind, the hind part of his body was raised up by the force of the explosion and he landed on his knees and hands. ... Then, again, he broke wind. This time the force of the expulsion sent him far up in the air and he landed on the ground, on his stomach. The next time he broke wind, he had to hang on to a log, so high was he thrown. However, he raised himself up and, after a while, landed on the ground, the log on top of him. He was almost killed by the fall. [39]

And this is just a foretaste of the mess to come. In a different context, Martin Amis's lavatorial overstatement works in a similar way: "I was pure turbo power," reports John Self, the narrator in *Money*, "a human hovercraft over the bowl. Oh, I had lift off..." [40]

In the context of medieval conviviality, moreover, diabolical flatulence is but a parodic complement to the divine afflatus, bodily winds but a comic counterpart to the breath or *spiritus* animating the creative mind. Repetitions may imply both airy windiness and festive fulness, stagnation and fecundity alike. Banqueting itself provides an age-old framework for comic business. In Rabelais, as in the Corpus Christi plays of Towneley and Chester, gargantuan feasts are related by means of gargantuan enumerations listing all the foodstuffs to be consumed, a graphic enactment of the abundance which makes revelry possible. Curtius claims that "kitchen humour" is in fact the most popular source of pleasantry in late antiquity, taking the form of farcical disputes and wrangles between cooks or slaves, as well as the perennial comedy of greed. [41] The goliards of the twelfth century, wandering (ex-) scholars who left their mark by composing bawdy and satirical Latin verse, were living manifestations of this trait, renowned for the riotous gluttony which on the one hand signalled excess and intemperance but on the other revelry and carousal. Falstaff is just one in a long line of sinfully and festively foolish gluttons, a lineage of folly perpetuated by Jarry's Père Ubu and by Monty Python's fattest man in the world, who eventually explodes after having one mouthful too much. Like excrement, though much less openly nauseous, food and drink can themselves therefore have a distinctly grotesque set of connotations. After all (as Feuerbach quipped in German), we are what we eat.

Just as stomach-churning and just as cathartic as other such issues is the comedy connected with spots, boils and zits. The matter rears its (black)head in Martin Amis's *The Rachel Papers*, for example, where one of Charles's pustules – like a wilful willy or a personified proboscis – seems to assume an almost autonomous identity:

> My chin seemed curiously mis-shapen, or off-centre. Suddenly my hand flew to my face. A Big Boy...
>
> The day was going well, particularly in view of the fact that Rachel's first words were:
>
> "Hi. You've got an enormous spot on your chin."
>
> I laughed with her, in a way relieved that we weren't going to spend every second of the afternoon not mentioning it.
>
> "I know all about it, thank you," I said. And I did, too. That morning, man and spot had become one, indivisible. Now, it felt like a surgically implanted walnut. But Rachel didn't seem to mind, or was good at seeming not to. I would have minded.[42]

The word "comedo" (the technical name for a blackhead) itself stems from the Latin *comedere*, meaning "to eat (with)," and implies the presence of an unwanted party-guest. The German word *Mitesser* has the same effect, evoking the ancient comedic figures both of the parasite and the glutton. The boil in Bruce Robinson's *How to Get Ahead in Advertising* is very much in this spirit.

Chapter 7

Self as Rational Unity

Divisions and Doubles

In *How to Get Ahead in Advertising,* what starts out as a small macula develops into a monstrous alter ego which eventually takes over its owner. The carbuncle's cathartic nature is in evidence from its first appearance, when the highly successful advertising agent Bagley – who spends his life racking his brains for catchy jingles about acne, boils and skin complaints – has a breakdown-cum-transformation that leads to his utter rejection of the exploitative commercialism structuring his life so far. The imagery is of contamination and the curative expulsion of a malignancy: "I'm going to cleanse my life," he tells his boss, "I'm going to rid my mind and body of poisons." [1] Whence the boil. Yet things prove not to be as straightforward as Bagley has envisioned, as the spot grows from a pea to a "fucking tomato," [2] before assuming an autonomous personality of its own, a bullying, manipulative, tyrannical personality, the sort "that sells toothpaste and soup." [3]

Dissociating himself from his poisonous sales-jargon, Bagley becomes a speaker of Truth (however much he may give the appearance of being a nutter talking to his neck), but the ruthless liar who has previously been internalized *within* him concurrently wins his independence as a separate being, and there ensues the comic spectacle of a manichean duel between the two faces of a radically split self. Bagley's wife and associates remain notably unaware of the furuncle's vitality, even as it grows a moustache and starts to look more and more like Bagley. For the world it is Bagley, not the Boil, who is mad:

Bagley:	Do you think I'm going mad, Julia?
Julia:	Goodness gracious, no. Doctor Gatty says you're simply paying the price for your creativity. You have such an active imagination it's taking advantage of you.
Bagley:	What did he say about the Boil?
Julia:	He said it's perfectly normal.

She consoles him with a tiny smile. Takes the lid off the casserole.

Boil:	Mmmm – smells good – smells thumb-suckin' good.
Julia:	Thank you, darling.
Bagley:	I didn't say anything.

Another sweet smile from Julia as she attempts to go along with him.[4]

A trip to the psychiatrist Mendlebaum presents the self-division in even more graphic form:

Mendlebaum:	Has the Boil spoken this morning?
Bagley:	Yes, I had a row with it. And it got very heated when I refused to shave.
Mendlebaum:	Tell me about your parents?
Bagley:	Not part of the plot. As far as I know they were completely normal. I come from a completely normal family.
Boil:	Tell him about your grandfather.
Bagley:	That was the Boil! Ignore it!
Mendlebaum:	I don't think we should do that. It's the first time it's spoken in front of me, and it might be important.
Bagley:	It has nothing important to say. It is destructive, self-satisfied, and abusive.
Boil:	You cunt.
Bagley:	You see. Don't listen to it.
Boil:	Come on, fair's fair. You've had your say, now I'll have mine.
Bagley:	Don't listen to it. Don't listen to it.
Mendlebaum:	Why don't you tell me about your grandfather? If you tell me, the Boil may be quiet.[5]

In the end the battle between the Social Conscience and the Amoral Entrepreneur is won by the latter. The Boil takes over as an identical full-sized replica of Bagley's head, and when the time comes for medical treatment it is the wrong head that is lanced: the newly revitalized Bagley is a sex-mad Machiavellian, and now it is the Boil who is the idealistic environmentalist. This role-reversal – with the resultant inversion of values – is a vivid demonstration of the moral equivocacy of the bodily and spiritual "poisons" at our margins.

People caught talking to themselves or to any personified part of themselves are commonly perceived to be at best eccentric, at worst mad. Such behaviour is in blatant contradiction with the image which we – as human beings – like to cultivate of ourselves, the image of a single, rationally sovereign agent in complete control of all our actions and thoughts. Our laughter at the folly of self-division comes from the security of what we believe to be our own unitary self-consistency: *our* boils are not allowed to get as big as Bagley's. But this is not the whole truth. The case of Bagley is all the funnier because it echoes the conflict within ourselves, the ongoing running battle between the lecherous egoist and the caring altruist. To this extent, our laughter may be something akin to a cathartic admission and surfacing of the utterly unpleasant homunculus squatting behind the philanthropic self-projection we put on public display. Not unlike Bagley's boil, it is a physical expulsion of our unwanted psychic "poisons", and it may be every bit as two-faced.

Personified furuncles are a literary rarity. Not so with penises. We have already encountered the "penisolate war"[6] waged between man and a wilful wanger bent on having its way. Even the great Greek rationalist Plato was aware of the problem, writing in *Timaeus*: "in men the nature of the genital organs is disobedient and self-willed, like a creature that is deaf to reason, and it attempts to dominate all because of its frenzied lusts."[7] Nor is it only on the human rung of the evolutionary ladder that such bodily autonomy comes to light: witness, for example, the ability of the male praying mantis to continue copulating even while being steadily gobbled up (headfirst) by the female.[8] In the case described by Plato, what the penis wants tends to coincide neither with what is willed by our socially or morally responsible self nor with the rational or prudential option. The interests of our phallic subself, that is, stand in defiant opposition to those of the narrating self (or subself), and the result is a comic conflict, as in Amis and Petronius. On occasions, indeed, the comedy arises when the damage has already been done. In the following medieval Welsh poem, the fourteenth-century bard Dafydd ap Gwilym bids his unruly rod quieten down and behave itself in order to avoid any further troubles:

> I consider you the vilest of rolling-pins,
> horn of the scrotum, do not rise up or wave about;
> gift of the noble ladies of Christendom,
> nut-pole of the lap's cavity,
> snare shape, gander
> sleeping in its yearling plumage,
> neck with a wet head and milk-giving shaft,
> tip of a growing shoot, stop your awkward jerking;
> crooked blunt one, accursed pole,
> the centre pillar of the two halves of a girl,
> head of a stiff conger with a hole in it,
> blunt barrier like a fresh hazel-pole.[9]   (lines 9-20)

The poet chides his vile rolling-pin for its indiscriminate excesses ("There is an eye in your pate / which sees every woman as fair," [10]) and for the hassle and inconvenience caused by these excesses ("Consider that there is a writ and an indictment, / lower your head, stick for planting children"[11]), but as the translator Dafydd Johnston points out, the complaint serves also as an ironic means of blowing his own trumpet ("You are a trouserful of wantonness" [12]). A less hyperbolic variant on the theme of the mischief-making member is the popular limerick:

> There was a young man from Stamboul,
> Who soliloquized thus to his tool:
> "You took all my wealth
> And you ruined my health,
> And now you won't *pee*, you old fool." [13]

The penis is indeed a particularly anthropomorphic appendage. Dafydd ap Gwilym refers to its "snout," its "neck" and "head," the "eye in its pate," and calls it "leather-headed one." [14] In more modern times, the affinities with polo-necked skinheads or pink-helmeted UN troops have not gone unnoticed. Yet it is not the exclusive right of the phallus to take on a comic life of its own. Among the implausible tales of Bürger's *Münchhausen*, there is one episode in which it is the entire hind part of the Baron's trusty steed which enjoys a period of autonomy (the beast having been sliced in two during battle), first of all wreaking havoc among the enemy and then proceeding to have the time of its life among a harem of local mares. The Winnebago Trickster of North American Indian mythology personalizes not only his penis but also his anus, whom he sets the task of keeping watch over some roasting ducks while he snatches forty winks. When the anus fails in its task, the Trickster's furious reaction (he applies a piece of burning wood to it) testifies once more to his inability to differentiate self and other, the folly of an as yet lawless or undiscriminating consciousness.

While the male genitalia are by nature not only headstrong and refractory but extraverted and outgoing, the more inwardly-oriented female genitals (traditionally at least) lend themselves less obtrusively to personification. When the medieval Welsh poet Gwerful Mechain writes a eulogy to the quim in response to the courtly decorum of male poets who ignore the most vital part of the female anatomy, the metaphorical richness of the lyrics focuses much more on its natural and sensual qualities than on any capacity to "come to life":

> the sour grove, it is full of love,
> very proud forest, faultless gift,
> tender frieze, fur of a fine pair of testicles,
> a girl's thick grove, circle of precious greeting,
> lovely bush, God save it. [15]   (lines 46-50)

Even so, owing to its oscular nature (as a "lower" mouth), the vagina may come to incarnate a capacity for gossiping and giving secrets away. This is the case in the comic novel *Les Bijoux Indiscrets*, written by the great French philosopher and encyclopaedist Denis Diderot, where the eponymous *bijoux* or "jewels" are a transparent euphemism for the female genitals. Here the reproductive organs serve above all – like Bagley's boil in its later days – as organs of truth, as embodiments of a subversive nature which insistently undermines the hypocrisy and sexual duplicity on which "cultivated" society is founded. It is the power of a magic ring which brings the women at whom it is directed to talk from "the frankest part of the body,"[16] and of course the truths that are unearthed are of a different order from those normally admitted by the dictates of social propriety. As one lady puts it, "a jewel speaks without passion and adds nothing to the truth," while another one's *bijou* – preferring the lackey to the master – claims: "Everyone has their philosophy, and ours consists above all in distinguishing the merit of a person, the true merit, from that which is only imaginary."[17] Nor are the comic effects of the situation restricted to satirical sauciness, as the female jewels betray a whole range of previously hushed over desires, peccadilloes and escapades: the comedy of self-division itself is grotesquely enacted when one lady, Ismene, is brought by a skilful manipulation of the magic ring to indulge in a revealing dialogue with her own vagina. Initially confident of her insusceptibility to the prattle of artful slanderers, Ismene's confidence proves premature, as a little "perhaps" pipes up from beneath the table:

> "What do you mean, 'perhaps'?" Ismene replied, piqued by this insulting doubt. "What might I have to fear from them?" – "Everything, if they knew what I know." – "And what do you know?" – "Lots of things, I can tell you."[18]

And out comes the truth. Another purple passage depicts a sequence of European conquests which are fruity enough for Diderot's bashful narrator (like the *bijou* itself) to feel obliged to recount them in the languages of the countries in question (English, Latin [!], Italian, Spanish). But the eroticism is mixed with a measure of philosophical raillery, as Diderot makes fun in particular of Cartesian ideas on the location of the soul. Aware of the relative autonomy of the female *bijou*, the cynical Sultan remarks:

> The jewel makes a woman do a hundred things without noticing it; and I have observed on more than one occasion how a woman who believed she was following her head was obeying her jewel. A great philosopher placed the soul (ours of course) in the pineal gland. If I were to grant one to women, I know where I would place it.[19]

The sultan's favourite by contrast espouses the view that the soul – starting at the feet – migrates through the human body until it finds a more permanent residence according to the dominant trait of the person in question: while the virtuous woman's soul divides its time between head and heart, therefore, the tenderhearted woman's is split between heart and *bijou*, and that of the voluptuous woman is permanently ensconced in her vagina.

By personifying the body's margins and extremities (where self coincides with non-self) and attributing a will to this personalized extremity, a situation is produced in which self is in conflict with self. Of course – as with Bagley's boil – the conflict may appear to be between a true self and a false or marginal self, but the question – as with Bagley's boil – can always be asked *which* is the true self? In the case of Diderot's voluble vulvas, it is the physically marginal part which proves to be the mouthpiece of genuine feelings and sexual truth. Yet although carnal openness may be felt to be a revelation of our "true" selves, the act of copulation, like the state of infatuation, can just as easily be experienced as a "loss" of self-control and self-possession, a mini-madness during which we go out of our minds while our genitals jump at the opportunity to fill the breach. The literary conceit whereby two people "become one" through the reason-defying act of love is a time-worn one, and love itself, concentrating the mind to the point of obsession, has made of the stock lover a stock fool, an unsuspecting ninny as blind to the world of wile and intrigue as he is to everything else. Love and Reason are thus at traditional loggerheads, in comic as in non-comic drama and literature. In the words of Follywit, the lovable rake from Middleton's *A Mad World, My Masters*: "Man's never at high height of madness full / Until he love and prove a woman's gull" (4.5). One of the most memorable expressions of the damage inflicted upon reason by amorous rapture is the parodic one in Henry Fielding's *Tom Thumb*. When heroic Tom enthuses "I know not where, not how, nor what I am, / I'm so transported, I have lost my self," Huncamunca chooses to take his figure literally: "Forbid it, all the Stars; for you're so small, / That were you lost, you'd find your self no more" (2.8). Even worse is the madness of unrequited love experienced by Orlando in *Orlando Furioso*. This reaches an unparallelled height of hyperbolic extravagance when the hero – able to recognize neither himself nor others – takes his fury out on anything that comes within his range, uprooting trees, massacring the locals, kicking one donkey so hard that it lands on a nearby hill,and decimating a third of the population of Malaga. The narrator, not without private problems of his own, muses:

> love, in the universal opinion of wise men, is nothing but madness.
> Though not everyone goes raving mad like Orlando, Love's folly shows
> itself in other ways; what clearer sign of lunacy than to lose your own

self through pining for another? The effects vary, but the madness which promotes them is always the same.[20]

Ecstatic lovers appear foolish to sober spectators, and in this respect the laughter provoked by the absent-minded incompetence of an emotional transportee once again bears witness to the self-assurance of a rationally sovereign ego in full control of mind and body. Or so it might seem. But the very fact that love is a madness with which we are likely to sympathize or in some sense identify betrays a simultaneous admission of the potential for lunacy within ourselves. In other more graphic or racier instances, where the self-division involves vivified vaginas or animated anuses, our laughter testifies even more explicitly to our dual nature, tending to be earthier or dirtier or more rip-roaring, tearing upwards from our own innards, rocking our foundations and shaking us to the roots. For all our pretensions to unity and consistency, such side-splitting ecstacies of hilarity hardly betoken a sovereign *cogito* distancing itself from whatever deviates from the rational ideal. As ever, things are more equivocal than that.

The precise nature of the split is of course contentious. It may be understood (for example) in terms of a metaphysical or theological conflict between good and evil, soul and body, or reason and the senses; a psychological rift between conscious thoughts and unconscious bodily drives, between an ego concerned with the future and an id intent on short-term pleasures, or between contradictory impulses both to emulate and supplant the father or figure of authority; a physiological division between various functional subsystems of the brain or an anatomical one between the left and right cerebral hemispheres; or it may simply be understood as a succession of roles, personae or moods picked up in the course of our development within a complex network of social relations. Clearly, however, the potential for comic business will depend upon how the divided self is conceived. If overladen with heavyweight moral and theological implications, our dual nature is likely to be a source of *angst* and possibly revulsion, the "lower" half of the equation (the one connected to the genitalia) being felt to be something that must be negated or subdued. When Mankind, in the morality play of the same name, introduces himself as someone in crass contradiction with himself, he is not playing for laughs:

My name ys Mankynde. I have my composycyon
Of a body and of a soull, of condycyon contrarye.
Be-twyx them tweyn ys a grett dyvisyon.   (lines 194-6)

Calling his flesh "that stynkyng dunge-hyll" (line 204), he metonymically associates his body with the most peripheral and transient part of it, and one half of his dual self is thus automatically debased as something to be overcome and its influence expelled, rather like Bagley's boil but with an afterlife hingeing on the success of the enterprise. In a sense, it is this division that gives rise to the very possibility of comic conflict in the play, as the split self is torn between the bore Mercy and the boors Nought, New-gyse and Now-a-days, who entertainingly despise and deride one another. Indeed, it is the fact that neither we nor Mankind are uniformly rational, wise or good – for we are necessarily trapped in our bodily imperfection – that permits us to enjoy comedy at all, both as laughers and as objects of laughter. These divisions and ambivalences are reflected in the contradictory combination of play (the non-serious) and theology (officially, the very serious). Yet overtly at least, the play advocates an overcoming of phallic, festive, secular fun, and the "happy ending" – which is also by allegorical implication "our" happy ending – depends on the triumph of the soul over the body (a triumph, moreover, of infinitely long-term interests over short-term distractions, of prudence over improvidence). The split can and must be vanquished, and the danger of Mankind's failure always coincides with a veering towards seriousness.

By the time of Shakespeare, the internalized conflict between Vice and Virtue has taken a turn for the parodic, as the medieval dualism comes to be ridiculous for its rigidity. In *The Merchant of Venice,* the Clown Launcelot Gobbo, trying to make up his mind whether or not to leave Shylock's service, indulges in an imaginary dialogue between his conscience and the Devil, a send-up of the personified virtues and vices of the moralities:

> The fiend is at mine elbow, and tempts me, saying to me, "Gobbo, Launcelot, Gobbo, good Launcelot," or "good Gobbo," or "good Launcelot Gobbo, use your legs, take the start, run away." My conscience says, "No; take heed, honest Launcelot, take heed, honest Gobbo," or, as aforesaid, "honest Launcelot Gobbo; do not run, scorn running with thy heels." Well, the most courageous fiend bids me pack, "Fia!" says the fiend, "away!" says the fiend.... well, my conscience says "Launcelot, budge not!" "Budge!" says the fiend. "Budge not!" says my conscience. "Conscience," say I, "you counsel well; fiend," say I, "you counsel well."
> (Act 2, scene 2)

The issue is complicated because Gobbo regards Shylock himself as "the very devil incarnation [!]," and, as the fiend is obviously equally infernal, either option appears to entail some kind of compromise with the devil. Given that the entire episode is a comic turn performed by a clown/entertainer (whose vocation is in turn diabolical in origin), this is perhaps not inappropriate. The comedy arises above all from the sight of Gobbo as the servant of two internalized masters, a puppet played by two puppeteers. Tugged to and fro between autonomous and contradictory subselves, he ends up going for the soft option: "the fiend gives the more friendly counsel: I will run, fiend; my heels are at your commandment; I will run"(2.2).

Where the phallic, or vulval, or hedonistic/disorderly subsystems within ourselves are interpreted in terms of sin or evil, we are more prone to land on the non-comic side of the borderline between the funny and the frightening. Evil is at best something – like the Devil – to be laughed *at*. Officially at least. Where these associations are absent, by contrast, laughter can be acknowledged as relief as well as rejection, a release for the unconscious drives normally suppressed and regulated by social structures. The "split self" of this chapter is to this extent but an internalization of the conflicts between (social) order and (anti-social) disorder encountered in earlier chapters. The claim that the person laughing and the person being laughed at are one and the same [21] allows for this subtle interplay of cathartic self-recognition and self-rejection, identification and distance. Laughing at the antics of the fool (whether roguish, gullible or festive), we are laughing at and with the fool within ourselves.

Yet other constraints exist which may put a brake on our laughing reaction to inner disunity. In particular, some degree of emotional dissociation or detachment from the "victim" is a prerequisite for the humorous response, and – as with "madness" in general – the absence of this stops laughter in its tracks. Susan Purdie notes the definitional proximity of "mad" behaviour and "funny" behaviour, for both signal a failure to make sense of and control oneself or the world: "Not only is comic behaviour quite often produced in plots through some temporary mental aberration – such as drunkenness or 'a blow on the head' – but all broad comic behaviour would read as madness if it were read with serious implication." Conversely, "what texts present as disturbing madness will inevitably be funny if it is not accepted implicatingly." [22] Whenever disunity is felt to be traumatic for the victim, or wherever it is presented as a bewildering neurological disorder rather than just weakness of character, then the onlooker's empathetic association with the suffering or the confusion tends to preclude the possibility of mirth. [23] Context and cause are here paramount, as brought to light by the example of medical disorders connected with loss of proprioception. The word "proprioception" refers to the self-regulating, unconscious feedback system which, as a continuous sensory flow, monitors and adjusts the movement and position of the movable parts of the human body. As something which in the normal run of events is taken for granted as a harmonious relationship between mind and body, it is like a sixth sense, an automatic familiarity with the posture and alignment of our muscles and limbs. In "The Man Who Fell out of Bed," however, Oliver Sacks recounts the effects of a malfunction in this normally unnoted bodily mechanism. Waking up to find what seems to him to be a severed human leg in his bed, the patient in question initially assumes that it has been put there as a rather tasteless and disgusting practical joke. When he tries to throw it out of bed, however, he is outraged and bewildered to find that it is in fact attached to his own body and that he has thrown himself out of bed:

> "Look at it!" he cried, with revulsion on his face. "Have you ever seen such a creepy, horrible thing? I thought a cadaver was just dead. But this is uncanny! And somehow – it's ghastly – it seems stuck to me!" He seized it with both hands, with extraordinary violence, and tried to tear it off his body and, failing, punched it in an access of rage.[24]

If this tale of disharmony between mind and body tends to provoke feelings of empathetic perplexity as much as anything, this can be attributed to its clinical context and to the traumatic quality it has for the patient concerned. Had Sacks's mini-narrative found its way into a story by Poe or Gogol, by contrast, our heartstrings would presumably have been at least partially anaesthetized.

Reflections

Hegel writes that the truly comic hero knows himself to be above his inner self-difference. The comic vision comprises, that is, an "infinite light-heartedness and confidence felt by someone raised altogether above his own inner contradiction and not bitter or miserable in it at all."[25] Ultimately indifferent to and cheerful in spite of the necessary dissolution of his foolish or "subjective" activities, the comic fool – as opposed to the butt of satire – achieves in Hegel's eyes a higher level of consciousness. In these terms, comic self-difference implies a triangular configuration, one of the axes denoting vertical rather than merely horizontal self-distance, i.e. the intellectual detachment which liberates us from emotional implication and worries about consequences. "Humour" in particular suggests a capacity to stand not just outside oneself and one's immediate situation but *above* it, smirking down on life's vicissitudes from a position of emotional if not physical invulnerability. Baudelaire, himself keenly aware of our duality and the comedy this duality can occasion, expressly admires the ability of the "philosopher" to laugh at himself, the capacity for rapid self-duplication that allows him to "look on as an impartial spectator at the phenomena experienced by his self."[26] Such assured and specifically human self-detachment implies control, intellect and dispassionate rationality. Yet the element of rationality should not be over-estimated, for this faculty has a happily megalomanic knack of overvaluing its own importance and claiming integrative centrality in a way that fails to do justice to the mind's many other cognitive subsystems. Indeed, *excessive* self-reflection – a tendency to look at or think about oneself too much – can end up taking us in the direction of insanity rather than insight.

A number of Martin Amis's comic figures illustrate this tendency. In the case of the sophisticated and brilliant Charles Highway, the perpetual self-reflection results in a critically heightened awareness of his own role-playing, a constant directing and organizing of the personae he plays in his social dealings. Unable to stop being a spectator at his own emotional performances, to stop reading himself as a character in a book, Charles reaches the paradoxical state where spontaneity is something that can only ever be feigned (and he cannot help but see through the pretensions to spontaneity and naturalness with which others deceive themselves). Even the emotional crisis sparked off by Rachel's departure betrays the intricacies of Charles's self-duplication: not only does the first-person narrative formally entail that the same person is both narrator and narratee, but this is a doubling encouraged by the narrator himself. He muses:

> Who can say how I got through the weekend? My heart really goes out to me there.
> Charles listened to the car drive away and walked up the stairs like a senile heavyweight. "Seven o'clock," his watch told him. In the master bedroom he rifled through drawers, examining bottles of pills. Back in the sitting room, he washed down a fistful of hypnotics with a quarter of lukewarm vodka. He complained to the mirror that this only made him feel worse.[27]

As if to underline the doubling that allows his heart to go out to himself, self-pitying Charles obtrusively switches from the normal first-person perspective to the third person, as he splits himself into a "narrator" watching himself – as someone else – ham out the clichés of forlorn love. The "mirror" image itself reflects this extravagant mental doubling, as Charles turns into a self-conscious parody who histrionically fails to wash, sleep or clean his teeth and wallows in a carefully cultivated morass of smelly self-neglect.[28]

Yet it is not just at times of ruminative self-awareness that Charles's self-observations expose and deflate the theatricality of his existence. Even when seducing Rachel (when his "phallic" subself might have been expected to be in total control), he remains a highly amusing combination of the automatic and the reflective. Charles's body seems to have a mind of its own as it works towards its "conquest" of Rachel's:

> Meanwhile the hand is creeping on all fours. At the edge of her panties it has a rest, thinks about it, then takes the low road. The whole of me is along with those fingers, spread wide to salute each pore and to absorb the full sweep of her stomach. Mouth toils away absently, on automatic.

> I nudge her with my right knee and give a startled wheeze as she parts
> her legs wide. Still, the hand moves down, a hair's breadth, a hair's
> breadth.
>   On arrival, it paused to make an interim policy decision. Was now
> the time for the menace? Had the time come to orchestrate the
> Lawrentiana? [29]

In such circumstances the comedy of a divided self is clearly much less
the disparagement of bodily autonomy than the acknowledgement of
narratorial insight, as the readers are put in a position to recognize both
their own fleshly subselves and their directorial attempts to control
and integrate them. But this need not coincide with maximal rationality
any more than does "yielding" to the whims and urges of a particular
subsystem. As Charles puts it, "Me, I'm devious, calculating, self-
obsessed – very nearly mad, in fact." [30] And he on one occasion comes
even closer to madness when he gets tangled up in the vicious circularity
of unchecked introspection:

> I experienced thrilling self-pity. "What will that mind of yours get up to
> next?" I said, recognizing the self-congratulation behind this thought
> and the self-congratulation behind that recognition and the self-
> congratulation behind recognizing that recognition.
>   Steady on. What's so great about going mad?
>   But even that was pretty arresting. Even that, come on now, was a
> pretty arresting thing for a nineteen-year-old boy to have thought. [31]

The problem here is that Charles's reflections do not grant him access to
any "true" or "inner" self but just to yet another in the sequence of
performances that constitute his life, in this case the performance of
introspective reflection. Once they have reached this state, Charles's
cerebral reflections resemble the mirror reflections of two looking-
glasses placed opposite one another with nothing in either of them
except images of each other in infinite regression. And even the madness
that this entails can only ever be a self-aware performance.

In *Money*, John Self has even more pressing and disconcerting
problems with selfhood and loss of identity, which become a key and
often non-comic thematic issue. Prey to an unsettling awareness of his
own fictional nature and a not entirely unwarranted feeling that he is
being controlled or manipulated by someone else, Self even resorts to
adopting the identity of his author, "Martin Amis," [32] as if a sense of not
being a Self were triggering off an unarticulated yearning to assume
authorship of and authority over his own life. Yet his self-disunity and
inner disharmony prove simply too deep-seated. This disharmony is on
one level a bodily malaise. At times desiring a wholesale "body
transplant," he on other occasions feels as though he must have already
had one but it went wrong. [33] Even toothache – a symptom of a

prematurely wrecked body – is something from which Self can comically dissociate himself: "Around five in the morning I reached a point where I felt an outsider's sadness for that poor tooth of mine, which after all was suffering its own death agonies, dying young and violently and by its own hand, long before its time."[34] But Self's inner disharmony goes deeper even than this, coming dangerously close to madness:

> I disclaim responsibility for many of my thoughts. They don't come from me. They come from these squatters and hoboes who hang out in my head, these guys who stroll past me like naturalized, emancipated rodents (passport and papers all in order), like gentrified rats, flapping a paw and saying "Hi, pal," and I have to wait and not mind while they make coffee or hog the can – there's nothing I can do about them. The place I have to shuffle around is a two-room flat with no hall or passage, a student gaff full of books I can't read. The people in here, with me among them, no better and no worse and with complete equality of powerlessness, are like sick bats or threadbare monkeys wearing hippie loons and jaded T-shirts with three buttons up the throat. There's nothing I can do about them, these unknown Earthlings.[35]

With his wayward thoughts personified in the same way one might personify an over-animated willy or a twittering twat, Self's self proves to be just one among a whole hippy community of crashers and dossers ("with their milk cartons on the windowsill"[36]). Not even landlord in his own home, his "I" thus finds himself forced to relinquish any rights to control or domination and must muck in on a basis of equal impotence. Once more, however, Self is not merely held up to ridicule: the relative powerlessness of his responsible, rational, narrative subself is something with which the reader is encouraged to empathize, and possibilities for self-recognition coincide with the poetic skill of the narrative extravagance.

A further dimension of self-difference may be opened up by the factor of time, but this too tends to be a (comic) problem only on reflection, or in Alice's reflectively inverted worlds through the looking-glass or in Wonderland. In Simpson's *One Way Pendulum*, the Prosecuting Counsel's allegation that the Groomkirby of a few months ago has gradually been replaced by a different person is founded on a line of argument which flies in the face of "common-sense" assumptions of personal continuity over time, belying what we take for granted in all notions of social or ethical responsibility. Its comedy lies in its very absurdity (coupled with that perverse truthfulness which may emerge on reflection). It is our continuity within the flux of permanent self-modification, the specificity underlying our plasticity,[37] moreover, that provides for the possibility of memory and explains the essential role played by memory in the constitution of our identity. Accordingly, though a memory may fail to correspond to a past reality (and here external evidence and other people's memories will be required for corroboration or refutation), the question whether this particular memory is *mine* or not is simply daft. My memories do not consist in a contingent relationship between a present "me" and a past "me" who was perhaps really somebody different; they are a present product of my unremitting self-creation, and in a sense I *am* my memories (in the same way that I *am* my hopes, desires and fears). Distortive and self-deluding they may be, but they are always mine. Memory – and its loss – plays a crucial role in the reflective/philosophical madness of Wonderland.

Alice's self-divisions are in fact as varied and as complex as John Self's, and even when not in Wonderland she has a habit of conducting dialogues with herself, internalizations of a duality composed of an authoritarian or parental voice and its mischievously childish counterpart:

> She generally gave herself very good advice (though she very seldom followed it), and sometimes she scolded herself so severely as to bring tears into her eyes; and once she remembered trying to box her own ears for having cheated herself in a game of croquet she was playing against herself, for this curious child was very fond of pretending to be two people.[38]

In the early stages of her adventures in Wonderland, the telescopic distortions undergone by her body provoke misgivings lest she should lose contact with her feet altogether, and she contemplates bribery as a way of keeping a modicum of volitional control over them: "I must be kind to them," she ponders, "or perhaps they wo'n't walk the way I want to go."[39] But as disconcerting as anything are the identity crises resulting from Alice's doubts about her memory and her continuity. Alone in the hall early on, her reflective introspections succeed in reducing her to tears:

> I wonder if I've been changed in the night? Let me think: *was* I the same when I got up this morning? I almost think I can remember feeling a little different. But if I'm not the same, the next question is "Who in the world am I?" Ah, *that's* the great puzzle![40]

Wondering whether she has perhaps turned into one of her less knowledgeable friends Mabel (which her own loss of memory seems to support), Alice acknowledges: "*she's* she, and *I'm* I."[41] Yet this still doesn't help, and she decides to ask someone else who she is. The conversation with the hookah-smoking Caterpillar deepens Alice's identity problems:

> "Who are *you*?" said the Caterpillar.
> This was not an encouraging opening for a conversation. Alice

replied, rather shyly, "I – I hardly know, Sir, just at present – at least I know who I *was* when I got up this morning, but I think I must have been changed several times since then."

"What do you mean by that?" said the Caterpillar, sternly. "Explain yourself!"

"I ca'n't explain *myself,* I'm afraid, Sir," said Alice, "because I'm not myself, you see."

"I don't see," said the Caterpillar.[42]

As with Simpson, the comedy lies in the absurdity (for a sober reader *not* in Wonderland), in conjunction with the cognitive puzzles unearthed by excessive reflection or introspection. From the "common-sense" point of view, Alice's position is clearly contradictory. If she (now) can remember who she was (this morning), then her memories form the necessary guarantee of continuity however much she may have "changed" in the meantime, and – from the "common-sense" point of view – she *is* who she was this morning. The Caterpillar appears to share this realization that memory is the key to knowing who we are, and he bids Alice recite a poem. But he does not help matters with his contention that her recitation is wrong "from beginning to end," [43] and the questions remain unresolved.

The split entailed by the metaphor of self-reflection – the split into an observer and a mirror image – can further lead to problems of misrecognition. If the over-zealous reflections of solitary, self-obsessed, introspective characters may on occasion produce a situation where nothing is seen except the act of reflection (the "mirror"), under-efficient reflections can prove equally misleading and equally comic. Failures of self-recognition have been graphically enacted in the tradition of comic play with mirrors: mirrors create a similar "splitting" of self, and my mirror image is in a sense both me and not me. This split lends itself to exploitation for laughs. Tony Staveacre provides a brief history of this much-loved and time-honoured slapstick gag:

> The premise is simple: servant has broken master's mirror and, to prevent him finding out, impersonates his reflection in the frame. A bit of detective work, and we find an account of the same piece being performed by Charles Manetti and Rhum, in the Cirque Olympique, 1848. The Hanlon-Lees (six tumbling Irish brothers) did it at Niblo's Gardens, New York, in 1860. They also claimed to have invented it. According to Lupino Lane, it was his grandfather, George Lupino, who had originated it for a Harlequinade at Drury Lane. The routine recurs in films: Max Linder's *Seven Years' Bad Luck,* the Marx Brothers' *Duck Soup,* Abbott and Costello's *The Naughty Nineties,* Woody Allen's *Sleeper.* And who really started it? The smart money's on the anonymous author of a seventeenth-century Spanish play, *The Rogueries of Pabillos.*[44]

In the scenario depicted by Staveacre the comedy derives from a failure to recognize that the image is in fact *not* the self, nor even a reflection of it. The laughter is thus the sort that is directed at a gull taken in by a piece of trickery, coupled perhaps with admiration for the mimetic virtuosity of the fake "image." The superiority of the audience is presupposed: we must know better than the deluded fool.

This superiority is also assumed in the case of the *Viz* character Biffa Bacon, who falls foul of an even more ludicrous type of self-misrecognition. A caricature of the British tendency to beat one another senseless, Biffa is a model of mindlessly aggressive irrationality, the arch-bonehead interested in nothing except whether you spilt his pint or called him a puff. Lacking anyone else to lay into, Biffa is on one occasion inspired to beat himself up in the local chippy. On another, his "Fatha" provocatively informs him "my pint called you a puff," inciting Biffa to nut the said pint ("naebody calls me a puff") and thus lay himself open for the anticipated return trashing. With the predictability of a haywire puppet, one holiday issue of *Viz* even sees Biffa headbutting his own mirror reflection ("Who the *fuck* are you looking at?"). Smashing mirror and face alike, the misrecognition in this typically bloody mini-episode drastically enacts Biffa's refusal to reflect and his utter incapacity for self-knowledge. But this is not something I would tell him to his face.

Irrationality

With Biffa, part of the comedy is the comedy of irrationality, as we are presented with the spectacle of someone behaving in blatant contradiction with his own interests. Yet Biffa is not unique in this respect. We have already come across the self-damage inflicted by our genitally-oriented subselves, where it is above all our longer-term interests that go for a burton. But states of ecstasy, possession, frenzy and rapture may produce more immediately self-damaging behaviour, be it the folly of religious rapture, the ecstatic self-abandonment of love and sex, the transports of drink- or drug-induced intoxication (being "out of one's head" or "out of one's skin"), or the theatrical self-abdications of clinical "madness." Clearly, not all such states of self-loss are equally prone to induce laughter, and once more the context is crucial. Nonetheless, love's lunacy is a well-worn comic commonplace;[45] drunkenness has proved timeless fodder for badly-acted imitations in the search for easy laughs; madness and mental illness in the past frequently served as a source of voyeuristic amusement; and even the ecstatic religious folly of the early Christians aroused mirth in non-believers. There appears to be something deeply comic in the sight of people failing to act in what we see to be their own interests.

Irrational self-damage or self-conflict à la Biffa is most graphically represented in the comic image of physical antagonism between two parts of the human body. As with the various forms of "possession," of course, a clinical or non-play context may show such self-difference in a decidedly more disconcerting light: the occurrences of physical division following commissurotomy, for example, which is in one instance reported to have led to the situation where a patient's right arm embraced his wife while his left arm pushed her away,[46] show how comedy stops where "affective implication" starts. Even so, the motif has cropped up in the most varied of circumstances. The immature and chaotic folly of the Winnebago Trickster is signalled by precisely such a dispute, as Trickster's left arm looks to get in on the booty after his right arm has captured a buffalo:

> In the midst of these operations suddenly his left arm grabbed the buffalo. "Give that back to me, it is mine! Stop that or I will use my knife on you!" So spoke the right arm. "I will cut you to pieces, that is what I will do to you," continued the right arm. Thereupon the left arm released its hold. But, shortly after, the left arm again grabbed hold of the right arm. This time it grabbed hold of his wrist just at the moment that the right arm had commenced to skin the buffalo. Again and again this was repeated. In this manner did Trickster make both his arms quarrel. That quarrel soon turned into a vicious fight and the left arm was badly cut up.[47]

In Molière's *L'Avare*, where Harpagon's farcical loss of self-control after the theft of his money-box expresses the folly of his monomanic avarice, the mad old miser likewise catches hold of his own arm in his frenzy to find the felon: "Give me back my money, you rascal," he jabbers, "Oh! it's me. My spirits are troubled – I no longer know where I am, who I am, and what I am doing" (4.7). Nowhere does Molière paint a more vivid picture of mental imbalance, an imbalance shared almost verbatim by Harpagon's precursor Euclio in Plautus's *Pot of Gold*. The Inferno in Dante's *Divine Comedy* contains one of literature's most grotesque images of identity-loss, as the sinful folly of the thieves – those who in their lifetime refused to acknowledge the distinction between "mine" and "thine" – is punished by their transformation into hideous formlessness. Dante looks on as one of them is "swallowed" by a shapeless reptile, an amorphous and unstructured being in a state of permanent dissolution. He watches in awe as their two heads become one, their faces fuse, as their legs and arms, belly and breast merge into a horrific non-shape that is both and neither of the former forms.[48]

As these examples suggest, there is a recurrent thematic association between self-conflict and theft, and unity is often linked with metaphors of ownership. Euclio, Harpagon and Dante's thieves (as well as Trickster's left arm) all infringe accepted norms in their relationship to property and possessions and are rewarded by a loss of *self*-possession. Ancient mythology underscores the bond in the shape(s) of the trickster-god Hermes, who was not only a god of fertility represented by one of man's most insistent subselves but the most mercurial of all gods and – among other things – a god of thieves. Yet it is perhaps the anarchic English clown-thief Pierrot who takes the biscuit and steals the show, when he furtively pockets his own disembodied head after being guillotined. Even that unglamorous subself the furuncle is not just a gluttonous parasite but, etymologically speaking, a petty thief. Musing on the romantic urges felt by dissonant selves to fly or flee or steal away from the shackles binding their other halves, Karl Miller indulges in revealing flights of word-play:

> Romance is stealth, and theft, and it is flight. If time flies, so does the thief, and in the Latin tongue the matter is given the appearance of a tautology: *fur fugit*. In English, "steal" and "fly" reveal an approximation in meaning to which the ambiguous relationship between "fly" and "flee" has contributed. The Latin verb *fugio*, I flee, stands close to *fur*, a thief, and can be translated into English verse by the figurative "steal." In French, the same word, *voler*, signifies both stealing and soaring. The Latin verb *volo* means both soaring and wishing.[49]

To the extent that we are never quite in full possession of ourselves, therefore, we are our own thieves: perpetually trying to steal away from or catch up with ourselves, we are – as Sartre and Ryle recognized – in constant flight.[50] As with Bagley's boil, the boundary between human being and furuncle is rather hard to tell.

While comic forms associate irrationality and loss of self-possession with the whole gamut of festive, sinful and existential modes of folly, racist jokes most commonly work by attributing irrational action to a marginal ethnic minority. Here the sense of "irrationality" extends to incorporate more general concepts of functionally inefficient behaviour (or stupidity). The original "light bulb" joke illustrates the point: "How many Irishmen does it take to change a light bulb? Three – one to hold the bulb and two to turn the table."[51] In communist Eastern Europe, by contrast, jokes about irrationality were in general directed at those in power – those at the centre rather than at the margins of the social order – and the political system itself was lampooned for its self-defeating irrationality. In this spirit are the two following Polish jokes: Why do the Poles build their meat shops two miles apart? So that the queues won't get mixed up. What do the Polish and American economies have in common? In neither can you buy anything with zloties.[52] As Christie Davies has argued, these jokes highlighted the irrationality *within* the excessive "rationality" of the political systems themselves: "the irrational aspects of East European societies can be seen to be the inherent result of attempts to extend ostensibly rational forms of bureaucratic planning and control beyond what is possible and beyond what is rational to attempt." [53] Yet this does not only apply to the former communist bloc. Any obsessive slavery to a purely "rational" world dominated by the work ethic and inflexibly dogmatic order sets itself up for humorous deflation, producing jokes – as Davies writes –

> about work-addicted Americans, jokes about rigid, pedantic, over-obedient Germans and jokes about stingy, over-rational, humourless Scotsmen. In each case the joke-tellers mock the members of another ethnic group for their excessive subordination to the world of work, money and duty. ... Their very rationality is irrational, for their methodical manipulation of means towards ends robs their lives of the possibility of human joy and freedom. [54]

In all these instances, the joke-tellers and their listeners use the jokes to reinforce and confirm their own rationality by contrast with the ineptness and incompetence of "Them" or to justify a "corrected" rationality as opposed to more rigidly self-defeating variants. These self-defeating versions of rationality in fact add a new dimension to the question of irrationality, for as acts of individual or collective self-deception, they unearth the potential for discrepancies between *having* reasons and *giving* reasons. The irrational is here passed off as rational and reasonable: behaviour that has its roots in bodily drives, cognitive habits, or short-term egoism is thus rationalized away by our self-important rational subself and only becomes questionable or comic to the observant outsider. It may, of course, be to our long-term advantage to be irrational now and again. In A.O. Rorty's words, "a creature whose only beliefs and motives are derived from the principles of critical rationality would be a very boring and short-lived creature." [55] But this is not the point here. As regards comedy, the point is rather the disparity between what we say about ourselves and what someone else (the spectator) can recognize to be true, between the wishful thinking or unconscious desires motivating some piece of conduct and the apparently objective reasons given to justify it. The very term self-deception implies an internal *splitting* into deceiver and deceived, knave and dupe. While an understanding of the self in terms of a relatively loose conjunction of largely independent subsystems allows for a functional separation of rogue and fool and thus for our capacity to hold contradictory beliefs or adopt conflicting policies, however, it is less the rebellious subself that is the deceiver than the rational "I" with its claims to integrative centrality. Self-deception is concerned primarily with perpetuating and preserving some appropriate *self-image* and in particular with the maintenance of our self-image as a rational, coherent and responsible agent. The comedy of self-deception is thus concurrently the comedy of self-ignorance and again assumes the onlooker's superiority.

Such self-deception emerges in the stock figures of the traditional comic stage, whose own justifications for the vice or "humour" structuring their behaviour can be taken to diverge from *our* interpretation of their motivation. The monomanic avarice of the Miser, rationalized as prudence and foresight, is seen as rooted in desire or sheer inflexibility. The hoarded learning of the Scholar or Pedant, rationalized as a love of knowledge or truth, is exposed as grounded in an urge for control and mastery. The pious devotion of the Spoilsport or Hypocrite is deflated for the self-importance underlying it. Part of the comic effect of these obsessively one-tracked figures, moreover, is the repeatability and predictability of their behaviour as they slip into pre-set or purely habitual modes of action and pre-scripted attitudes towards themselves and others. Self-deception in this sense comes to coincide with a lack of awareness of one's own *role-playing*, a failure of critical reflection to notice as the individual becomes engulfed within the inflexible mechanisms of a particular subself, a refusal to admit any other aspect of oneself except what one assumes to be central to one's identity and how others perceive it. Reduced to a single performative routine, the Miser, the Pedant and the Killjoy become mechanical self-parodies, just as the classical self-deceiver Don Quixote "loses himself" in his performance as a chivalrous knight and Gogol's "madman" gets absorbed in his role as the King of Spain.[56]

Immersed in their role-playing, actors are people who are "not themselves" and to this extent acting itself constitutes a loss of selfhood. Or, more accurately, it involves a splitting of self, for actors – partitioned into a mask and a face, a true and a false persona – both are and are not themselves. Comedy in particular tends to exploit this histrionic self-difference: while more naturalistic forms seek to swallow us up in their illusion and hide the theatre's dual nature, comedy by contrast constantly reminds us of the contradictions, betraying that the fictive figures are really just actors acting, the props are but props and what may seem to be real is in fact just performance. A distance or gap is thus opened up in the relationship both of the comic actor to himself and the spectator to the comic actor.[57] It is this very self-division and self-duplication, however, that has made of the actor, and especially the comic actor, a figure traditionally suspicious to authority. In Plato's *Republic*, Socrates's principles that "a man can only do one thing well" and "no man is to be two or more persons or a jack of all trades"[58] prescribe not just a socio-economic division of labour but a more deep-seated unity of identity which is manifestly infringed by the mutability of the mimic (who should therefore be politely kicked out of the ideal city-state). Such mimesis moreover – like Plato's ungovernable genitalia – is a threat to reason and may prove dangerously infectious with its raucous ribaldries.[59] The antitheatrical polemic of English Puritans in the late sixteenth and seventeenth centuries likewise took issue with the radically subversive potential of the actor – as a convincing impostor or dissembler – to undermine authority and flout conventional discriminations of rank, status and gender.[60]

Yet acting is nothing if not ambivalent. What on the one hand is associated with treachery, deceit and devilry can on the other be embodied in charismatic comic rogues and wits who elicit admiration for their benevolent flexibility. Plautus's Pseudolus, the *commedia's* Brighella or Molière's Scapin are all highly skilled actors and plot-weavers who share their ironic distance and reflective superiority with an audience that, unlike the gulls, can recognize and enjoy the discrepancy between mask and face. While Pseudolus and Scapin are shown to have a benign and warm-hearted core beneath their many faces, however, other comic heroes prove even more fundamentally protean: Falstaff, Panurge, Harlequin and Brighella are characterized as much as anything by their mercuriality. They are permanent performers and oxymoronically embody the ambivalence implied by amiable devilry. Though often diabolical, their self-difference – being successive rather than simultaneous – lacks the horrific grotesqueness, say, of Dante's thieves and seems to signal self-creation instead of self-destruction. Like the Hegelian comic hero, they "stand above" their own contradictions and savour their natural theatricality. Indeed, to the extent that we all (as Morton Prince puts it) "have as many selves as we have moods, or contrasting traits, or sides to our personalities,"[61] these protean heroes offer a vicarious victory for our own protean nature; to the extent that we are all performers, they unearth and celebrate the potential for self-creation within every one of us. Their mercuriality, like their amorality, is a release for those parts of the human psyche mythologically symbolized by Hermes or Siva, parts normally hushed up and hidden away by the dictates of propriety and the regulative principles of continuity, stability and self-possession.

Yet the fluidity of the protean fool may have its negative side too. What in comedy is a pretext for entertainment and fun and an opportunity for resilient self-invention may in real life be experienced (as in the case of the schizophrenic) as a traumatic lack of any genuine or "serious" self, a gaping absence beneath a fragile surface. Being everybody or anybody can thus flip over into a feeling of being nobody. A multiple self may be felt to be *not* a self. More than anyone else it is Beckett's non-character by the telling name of Mr. Knott who exemplifies the negativity of a protean nobody. Knott is described from the outset almost exclusively either in negative terms (what he was not) or in vacuously tautological terms (sometimes he was or did this, sometimes that, sometimes the other, and so on and so on...). One passage gives a more than usually succinct idea of his fluid identity:

The figure of which Watt sometimes caught a glimpse, in the vestibule, in the garden, was seldom the same figure, from one glance to the next, but so various, as far as Watt could make out, in its corpulence, complexion, height and even hair, and of course in its way of moving and of not moving, that Watt would never have supposed it was the same, if he had not known that it was Mr. Knott. [62]

Later on, however, we are treated to more exhaustive and exhausting accounts of Mr. Knott's non-appearance:

With regard to the so important matter of Mr. Knott's physical appearance, Watt had unfortunately little or nothing to say. For one day Mr. Knott would be tall, fat, pale and dark, and the next thin, small, flushed and fair, and the next sturdy, middle-sized, yellow and ginger, and the next small, fat, pale and fair, and the next middle-sized, flushed, thin and ginger, and the next tall, yellow, dark and sturdy, and the next fat, middle-sized, ginger and pale ... [63]

And so it continues for a very long time. Knott's identity is so mercurial that it is unknowable, for recognition depends upon fixity of identificatory criteria (and although Watt somehow can recognize him, he cannot describe him). To this extent Beckett's tautological litanies, saying nothing, say as much as can be said.

Chapter 8

Self as Persona

Acting and role-playing may represent either a release or a loss, self-creation or self-destruction. Once more the context is centrally important. When limited to a periodic play-frame, self-duplication glosses over the threatening or traumatic potential of what may otherwise be experienced as existential destabilization. Carnivalistic festivity allows just such periodically defined play with identities in the form of its disguises and masquerades, while theatre – modern theatre at least – places even stricter formal and artistic restrictions on its role-playing, as the subversive possibilities of improvisations are "contained" by the identity-defining authority of an author. Even in this displaced and often rather sanitized context, the actor symbolizes the capacity for creative self-difference, but it is the comic actor – the one who, like a fool, draws attention to his fictive or theatrical status – who takes the further step towards a *reflective awareness* of inner contradiction. Baudelaire writes admiringly of the men "who have made a profession of developing within themselves a sense of the comic and drawing it out of themselves for the diversion of their fellow-men, a phenomenon which comes into the class of all those artistic phenomena denoting the presence in human existence of a permanent duality – the ability to be simultaneously oneself and another."[1] Comedy accordingly has a marked tendency to thematize acting, whether by focusing on strategic pretence and role-playing within its plot, by self-consciously incorporating a theatrical performance into the action or by explicitly breaking with the established conventions of theatrical illusionism.[2]

In such instances, of course, the spectator is usually in the privileged position of "seeing through" the comic disguise. Although the role-swapping may involve the exchange of obtrusive identificatory criteria (such as dress or mannerisms), this exchange is as a rule imperfect, and the spectator, enjoying access to certain key "giveaways" (such as the accent that cannot be camouflaged, the tell-tale signals of gender or social standing, or simply a knowledge of what is or is not feasible), is reassuringly allowed to maintain an overview of who is who. The comedies of Plautus are especially explicit in this respect. When Philocrates and Tyndarus, master and slave, swap identities in *The Prisoners*, the Prologue hammers home the exchange that has taken place with a heavy-handedness that casts doubt on the audience's powers of discrimination.[3] Philocrates and Tyndarus themselves reinforce the point: "Now, you are pretending to be my master, and I am pretending to be your slave"; "for the present I am you and you are me."[4] The formulation which replaces the relationship of pretence (I am pretending to be you) with that of identity (I am you) adds a dimension of folly by infringing the rational presupposition that I am myself and you are you; and in *Pseudolus* the virtuoso rogue Simia is so skilled in his powers of imitation that he can induce such madness in the person he is impersonating: "I'll make a better Harpax than he is, you see if I don't. ... I'll have some tricky patter ready for this foreign soldier man, that'll scare the life out of him and make him admit that he's not himself but I am!"[5] In *The Swaggering Soldier* a conspiratorial refusal to recognize the dim-witted Sceledrus likewise brings the poor man to doubt whether he is himself or somebody else's self instead.[6]

The rational superiority of the onlooker – whose identity remains unquestioned – is often underscored by a flattering interplay of light and darkness. While deceptions and trickery on stage may thus be favoured by an obscurity which thwarts processes of identification *within* the play, this presumably does not interfere with the spectator's view from "outside" the play, and narrative confusions are even more frequently set against a context of metaphorical and literal unenlightenment. In tales by both Boccaccio (9:6) and Chaucer (*The Reeve's Tale*), night-time rumpy-pumpy flourishes in small dark rooms packed with beds which get swapped like musical chairs, while – in contrast to the fumblings and gropings of the figures – the readers enjoy the enlightenment of narrative omniscience, like torch-bearing voyeurs permanently conversant with who's shagging whom. Bodily identifiability proves to be dependent on light, as well as on sound (the swonking is done in silence), and in the absence of these, sexual partners are exchanged in cheerful oblivion: the tactile, olfactory and gustatory functions which might in non-comic circumstances permit a wife to know roughly what her husband feels, smells and tastes like are left out of account either for narrative convenience or through fictive self-deception (or both). The element of fictive self-deception is particularly patent in Cervantes's *Don Quixote*, where the deluded Don, mistaking inn for castle and the innkeeper's daughter for a beautiful damozel, seems able to block off or misread his entire range of sensory organs:

> he felt her shift and, although it was of sackcloth, it seemed to him of the finest, most delicate satin. The glass beads that she wore on her wrist had for him the sheen of rare orient pearls. Her hair, which was coarse as a horse's mane, seemed to him strands of the most glistening gold of Arabia, whose splendour eclipsed the very sun. And her mouth, which, no doubt, reeked of the stale salad of the night before, seemed to him to breathe out a sweet and aromatic odour. ... And so blind was the poor knight that neither her touch nor her breath nor anything else about the good maiden revealed his mistake to him, though she would have turned the stomach of anyone but a carrier.[7]

The fact that she is herself expecting not Don Quixote but her own lover (who overhears what happens) in the starlit barn and that she flees to the nearby bed of Sancho Panza (who in his confusion lashes out at random) leads predictably enough to a mass-brawl of quite stunning ferocity. More recently, Tobias Smollett's *Adventures of Roderick Random* (1748) describe a similarly Boccaccian scenario, with similar confusions arising for similar reasons, but – like *Don Quixote* – without the multiple sexual consummation, which is replaced by a more excremental element. In Smollett's novel, the narrator's friend Strap the barber unwittingly errs not only into the room where Captain Weazel, his wife and Miss Jenny are quartered for the night, but into the very bed temporarily vacated by the Captain, who has gone in search of a chamber pot. Strap of course is completely ignorant of his crime when the freshly produced contents of said chamber pot are flushed unceremoniously over his head.[8]

The ultra-ascetic, manichean association of darkness with sexual transgression, evil and sin is, particularly in Chaucer and Boccaccio, positivized into an association with fornicatory fun, but what the two understandings of darkness have in common is the waylaying of differentiation and a loss – in this sense – of personhood. Indeed, the rather random rogering that goes on, much savoured though it is, does testify to the "blindness" of bodily urges oblivious to vows of wedlock or chastity. In its turn, however, manichean dualism, like any compartmentalization of the world into black and white, is itself blind to nuance and subtlety and fails to account for the ambivalence either of darkness or of the deception and confusion to which it can give rise. As Hegel puts it, "in absolute clarity one can see as much and as little as in absolute darkness. ... Pure light and pure darkness are two emptinesses which are both the same."[9] Differentiation depends upon determinate light, which is also determinate darkness. Like acting itself, darkness and light are essentially equivocal. While diabolical impostors and evil rogues may be understood as agents of confusion and gloom, it is the benign tricksters – whose wile relies upon the unenlightenment of their fools and gulls – who are traditionally responsible for impelling the plot towards its happy ending. Admittedly, the happy ending is in turn traditionally conceived as a moment of *cognitio*, of enlightenment and recognition, as the entanglements of swapped identity are unknotted, disguises laid aside, long-lost relatives identified, and order re-established. And it is the guarantee of a *cognitio* to come which counteracts the more unnerving aspects of short-term misunderstandings and identity-loss: even when we don't know who is who, the likelihood of a happy ending is also the likelihood that we (and they) will at some stage find out. Nonetheless, although the recognition scene signals an overcoming of conflict, pretence and misidentification, it also signals the end of the play and a return – for the audience at least – to workaday reality.

Within the fictive context as much as outside it, darkness and the confusion of identities may be experienced as a boon or a bane. The darkness that in Chaucer and Boccaccio is equated with sexual abundance and satisfaction has a more disconcerting effect in Tom Stoppard's *Rosencrantz and Guildenstern are Dead*, where it further unsettles identities already in crisis:

Rosencrantz:	... I can't see a thing.
Guildenstern:	You can still *think*, can't you?
Rosencrantz:	I think so.
Guildenstern:	You can still *talk*.
Rosencrantz:	What should I say?
Guildenstern:	Don't bother. You can *feel*, can't you?
Rosencrantz:	Ah! There's life in me yet!
Guildenstern:	What are you feeling?
Rosencrantz:	A leg. Yes, it feels like my leg.
Guildenstern:	How does it feel?
Rosencrantz:	Dead.
Guildenstern:	Dead?
Rosencrantz:	(*panic*) I can't feel a thing!
Guildenstern:	Give it a pinch! (*Immediately he yelps.*)
Rosencrantz:	Sorry.
Guildenstern:	Well, that's cleared that up. (Act 3)

Caught up in the sub-plot of a play they are not really too enthusiastic about being part of (*Hamlet*), Rosencrantz and Guildenstern suffer continually from a painful sense of emptiness and lack of orientation. Symptomatic of their identity-loss is not only the "proprioceptive" muddle regarding leg-ownership, but also the widespread confusion as to who is Rosencrantz and who Guildenstern, an infectious uncertainty regarding name-ownership which gives rise to some very funny problems of identification:

> Claudius: Welcome, dear Rosencrantz ... (*he raises a hand at Guildenstern while Rosencrantz bows – Guildenstern bows late and hurriedly*) ... and Guildenstern. (*He raises a hand at Rosencrantz while Guildenstern bows to him – Rosencrantz is still straightening up from his previous bow and half way up he bows down again. With his head down, he twists to look at Guildenstern, who is on the way up*).
>
> . . . .
>
> Claudius: Thanks, Rosencrantz (*turning to Rosencrantz who is caught unprepared, while Guildenstern bows*) and gentle Guildenstern (*turning to Guildenstern who is bent double*).
>
> Gertrude: (*correcting*) Thanks, Guildenstern (*turning to Rosencrantz, who bows as Guildenstern checks upward movement to bow too – both bent double, squinting at each other*) and gentle Rosencrantz (*Turning to Guildenstern, both straightening up – Guildenstern checks again and bows again*). (Act 1)

Rosencrantz and Guildenstern are equally unsure in the matter and wistfully recall the days when they could both remember which name was whose. Guildenstern at least looks on the bright side: "we are comparatively fortunate; we might have been left to sift the whole field of human nomenclature, like two blind men looting a bazaar for their own portraits" (act 1). They make their plight worse, however, with the word-games and mini-plays with which they pass their (and our) time. One of these mini-plays-within-the-play is supposed to see Guildenstern playing the part of Hamlet and Rosencrantz interrogating him in order to "glean what afflicts him." But the confusion proves simply too contagious:

> Rosencrantz: Are you afflicted?
> Guildenstern: That's the idea. Are you ready?
> Rosencrantz: Let's go back a bit.
> Guildenstern: I'm afflicted.
> Rosencrantz: I see.
> Guildenstern: Glean what afflicts me.
> Rosencrantz: Right.
> Guildenstern: Question and answer.
> Rosencrantz: How should I begin?
> Guildenstern: Address me.
> Rosencrantz: My dear Guildenstern!
> Guildenstern: (*quietly*) You've forgotten – haven't you?
> Rosencrantz: My dear Rosencrantz!
> Guildenstern: (*great control*) I don't think you quite understand.
> (Act 1)

While an excess of performance can be felt to undermine one's sense of having a stable identity, however, on other occasions the opportunity to swap one's persona can serve as a cathartic release from the restrictions imposed by our social role-playing. The criteria of gender and social status lend themselves especially to such exchange. Of course, the comedy inherent in watching a woman play a man, or a man play a woman, or in the sight of master and servant switching roles, is traditionally grounded in the *imperfection* of the adopted identity: the underlying assumption is that man and woman, servant and master, have an essential character which can only be provisionally pasted over. Even so, this is just half the story, for it ignores the extent to which our sexual and social identity are themselves roles or performances, cultural constructs mastered by imitation during our integration into social relationships, and in so doing it masks the protean potential of the human being for self-creation. On the one hand comedy may thus portray its female men as failing in their roles (say, by fainting at the sight of blood as Rosalind does in *As You Like It*[10]), and there is always the possibility that bodily appendages of one sort or another may betray biological gender (as with Mnesilochus's whopping stage penis in Aristophanes's *Thesmophoriasuzae*). Breasts and beards can be equally treacherous. Likewise, comic servants raised above their station may prove unable to hide their rough edges, and down-at-heel masters simply too refined for their own good. On the other hand, however, the swapping of roles may open new perspectives, bringing to light the interdependence of master and slave, allowing both parties to see life through the eyes of the other and betraying the arbitrariness of the conventional hierarchy. And male-female transvestism too may not only expose the superficiality of sexual prejudice and custom but also give vent to "a deep yearning among men and women type-cast by themselves or their fellows to break free of the costume that symbolizes that constraint."[11]

Above all, cross-dressing signifies a liberation, and the comic pleasures of transvestism are evidenced by popular festivities, fancy-dress parties and the celebrated Dame of Drury Lane pantomime (immortalized by Dan Leno). Yet there are certain asymmetries in the comedy of the phenomenon. Festive gender-swapping has tended to be a male prerogative, and the comedy generated by men-disguised-as-women veers towards a much crasser grotesquery than that of women-as-men, which has as a rule been both more literary and more reliant on irony. Whereas men usually turn themselves into ugly old hags, therefore, women have a habit of becoming men with fine features and a gentle, youthful complexion, and for some reason the sight of a brawny, bearded, big-booted Dame seems much more likely to raise a laugh than that of a clean-shaven and delicate man (where the sexual imposture may be scarcely noticeable). This whole idea of ugliness and aesthetic norm-infringement cannot be divorced from the context of a phallocentric society which has customarily excluded women from the domains of joke-making and potentially subversive public performance.

Perhaps the point therefore is not so much that women-as-men make a less incongruous sight than men-as-women as that – in the past at least – it has been considered "unseemly" for women to create humour, to play for laughs, to tamper with identities, to make themselves grotesque, in short to do anything except be beautiful, attractive and in full conformity with male sexual desires. So when women do make so bold as to disguise themselves, decorum should remain intact.

Shakespeare's treatment of the several young women who at some stage resort to a male disguise in his plays is accordingly subtle and ironic rather than broad and farcical, and even in the merry madness of *Twelfth Night*, where the folly of role-playing and mistaken identity is played off against the folly of love, drunken revelry, court clownery, Puritan vanity and natural idiocy, the theme of identity is handled in paradoxical and whimsical but not grotesque fashion. It is for the gently comic undertones of its dramatic irony that Viola's disguise as the page Cesario is above all exploited, as the Duke – commenting on "Cesario's" youthful appearance – comes closer to the truth than he realizes:

> ... they shall yet belie thy happy years,
> That say thou art a man; Diana's lip
> Is not more smooth and rubious: thy small pipe
> Is as the maiden's organ, shrill and sound,
> And all is semblative a woman's part. (Act 1, scene 4)

And later on, when the Countess Olivia has fallen in love with Cesario/Viola, who in turn has fallen for the Duke, it is the seeming absurdities of self-difference and self-ignorance that are dwelt upon:

> Olivia: Stay:
>   I prithee tell me what thou think'st of me.
> Viola: That you do think you are not what you are.
> Olivia: If I think so, I think the same of you.
> Viola: Then think you right; I am not what I am.
> Olivia: I would you were as I would have you be. (Act 3, scene 1)

With its pervasive folly, Illyria is from the outset a realm where the law of identity is given short shrift, where people are not themselves and things not what they are. The wise fool Clown, himself acting the part of a learned curate, parodies the pedant's law of identity by clothing it in the gobbledygook of mock authority:

> As the old hermit of Prague, that never saw pen and ink, very wittily said to a niece of King Gorboduc, "That that is, is": so I, being Master Parson, am Master Parson; for what is "that" but "that"? and "is" but "is"?
>
> (Act 4, scene 2)

But of course Clown is not *really* Master Parson, so the law proves flawed. When Viola's long-lost twin brother Sebastian enters the scene and is mistaken by Clown for Cesario (to the bewilderment of both of them), Clown comes closer to Illyrian truth with his "nor this is not my nose neither. Nothing that is so, is so"(4.1). It is left to the enlightenment of the *cognitio* to provide coherence, re-establish order and – with the mutual recognition of each other by the twins – to explain away the confusions caused by their near-indiscernibility as persons. Once again, the language is primarily paradoxical: "One face, one voice, one habit, and two persons!" exclaims the Duke, "A natural perspective, that is, and is not!"(5.1).

Viola and Sebastian seem to violate a philosophical law which has since been termed "the identity of indiscernibles," the principle that if a group of things share all their properties in common (one face, one voice, one habit and so on), then they are really only one thing: they are numerically identical (here: one person, not two). Of course, in *Twelfth Night* the violation is only seeming: the conclusion, by bringing the twins together, establishes that they do not really share all their properties, for at a given time they occupy perceptibly different positions in space (and the question of what they have lurking down their hose could at a pinch serve as a further criterion of identifiability[12]). Nonetheless, the philosophical problem – whether there is a difference between numerical identity and exact similarity, between some person being me and his being merely absolutely like me in every physical and psychological respect – remains both unanswered and unanswerable, and has led to the most bizarre flights of speculative fancy. Imagine a scenario, for example, in which the information contained within my brain could in some way be "read" onto a computer and then reproduced in two further brains. Imagine, moreover, that these brains are then transplanted into the bodies of my two identical twins and that my original brain and body both die. Each of the resulting people would not only look exactly like me, but also have my character, memories and intentions and indeed believe that he is me.[13] But which of them would be right? Parfit argues that the concept of identity is inapplicable in such an instance. It is an empty question whether "I" am now one, or the other, or both, or neither, of these resulting people: it is "not what matters."[14] The alternatives are simply different ways of describing the same outcome, namely that "there will be two future people, each of whom will have the body of one of my brothers, and will be fully psychologically continuous with me."[15] In practice, problems will remain. Even though the twins will presumably start to "grow apart" psychologically from the moment of transplantation on, it can be assumed that there will ensue both disconcerting and comic conflicts and confusions about such matters as my name and possessions (some of the *external* criteria by which I was formerly identified), as well as the responsibility for my past misdemeanours and rewards for my past achievements. Moreover, if the two brothers do both insist on keeping my name and manner of appearance, situations may arise in which one of them is held accountable for misdeeds committed by the other: the archetypal comic case of mistaken identity. Nor is such confusion necessarily to our disadvantage: if nobody can tell the two new me's apart, our identities gain a fluidity which undermines all legal control: a whodunnit simply cannot be solved if no one even knows who are the who's who might have dunnit.

It is perhaps owing to this subversive potential that twins have traditionally elicited such strong but ambivalent ritual responses. Signalling a dissolution of difference, they embody the lack of differentiation which may be felt both to undermine social order and to be necessary for its periodic renewal. In the words of Réne Girard, "in numerous primitive societies twins inspire extraordinary fear. It comes to pass that one of them is put to death or, even more often, both of them are done away with. ... In societies where twins are not killed, they often enjoy privileged status."[16] And twins may indeed give rise to comedy of a distinctly grotesque order, not so far removed from the spooky doppelgänger figures of nineteenth-century literature. In Gogol's *The Government Inspector*, the indistinguishability of the twins Peter Ivanovitch Dobchinsky and Peter Ivanovitch Bobchinsky is underscored both by their virtually indistinguishable names (they both refer to one another as Peter Ivanovitch) and the mechanical predictability with which they repeat and interrupt one another in word and deed. Seeming to share not only their external characteristics but also their personality, they lack the vitality and autonomy necessary to distinguish either of them from a mere echo of the other. Ultimately they are but puppets or machines, and their duplication is thus also a dehumanization. Yet this effect is not always so noticeably present. Twins are a timeless pretext for knockabout farce, flourishing from Plautus's *Menaechmi* or *The Brothers Menaechmus* onwards, proliferating manically in the early scenarios of the *commedia dell'arte* (where twin Pantalones, twin captains, twin masters and twin servants and on one occasion even sextuplets are to be found), and translating effortlessly into the cinematic mode in Laurel and Hardy's masterly *Our Relations* (1936). More often than not the comedy derives from the sheer chaos, the riot of misidentifications which result when twins (unbeknown to one another) are on the loose. For the duration of the comic confusion at least, being one of a pair is a decidedly unenviable fate, entailing responsibility for the misdeeds of the other, yet without knowing why.

This is classically the case in Shakespeare's *Comedy of Errors*. By contrast with comedies where intentional disguise and trickery are involved, twins are more conducive to situations where the characters are *unintentionally* invested with identities other than their own. And although the audience may remain to some extent more knowledgeable than the bewildered fictive figures, the absence of a sovereign plot-weaver tends to mean that we are never granted quite the same reassuring overview allowed by other more controlled and less chaotic comic modes. *The Comedy of Errors* is thus marked by what for Shakespeare is an unusually high level of farcical aggression, as twin servants and twin masters baffle and beat one another in an atmosphere of befuddled frustration. As in *Twelfth Night*, the misrecognitions are thematically linked to the issue of madness (as people come to doubt their sense and their selves), and this recognitive loss of selfhood is tied up with a loss of selfhood caused by love. Antipholus of Syracuse is indeed beset from the beginning with an identity crisis, for the life-long search for mother and brother that has brought him to Ephesus has also, he feels, deprived him of a sense of self:

> I to the world am like a drop of water
> That in the ocean seeks another drop,
> Who, falling there to find his fellow forth,
> (Unseen, inquisitive) confounds himself.
> So I, to find a mother and a brother,
> In quest of them, unhappy, lose myself.   (Act 1, scene 2)

In Ephesus, however, Antipholus finds himself assailed with an alien identity, as the wife of his long-lost twin brother (who lives there) stubbornly misrecognizes him as her husband. Herself confounded by his unresponsiveness, she possessively "claims" him as hers (and as a part of herself):

> How comes it now, my husband, O, how comes it,
> That thou art then estranged from thyself? –
> Thyself I call it, being strange to me,
> That undividable, incorporate,
> Am better than thy dear self's better part.
> Ah, do not tear away thyself from me;
> For know, my love, as easy mayst thou fall
> A drop of water in the breaking gulf,
> And take unmingled thence that drop again
> Without addition or diminishing,
> As take from me thyself, and not me too.   (Act 2 , scene 2)

Yet while "losing" his identity to an overpossessive and jealous wife, Antipholus surrenders it more willingly in falling in love with the wife's sister, herself confounded by his overresponsiveness:

> Luciana: Why call you me love? Call my sister so.
> Antipholus: Thy sister's sister.
> Luciana :   That's my sister.
> Antipholus: No,

> It is thyself, mine own self's better part,
> Mine eye's clear eye, my dear heart's dearer heart,
> My food, my fortune, and my sweet hope's aim,
> My sole earth's heaven, and my heaven's claim.

Luciana: All this my sister is, or else should be.
Antipholus: Call thyself sister, sweet, for I am thee. (Act 3, scene 2)

The theme of identity-loss is comically echoed in the fortunes of the servants, who share one another's perplexity as – unbeknown to one another – they are each beaten by their masters for botching orders given to the other one. Like his master, moreover, Dromio of Syracuse falls victim to the loss of selfhood produced by possessive love, but here Nell forms a grotesque counterpoint to his master's new "wife":

Antipholus: Why, how now Dromio, where run'st thou so fast?
Dromio: Do you know me sir? Am I Dromio? Am I your man?
Am I myself?
Antipholus: Thou art Dromio, thou art my man, thou art thyself.
Dromio: I am an ass, I am a woman's man, and besides myself.
Antipholus: What woman's man? and how besides thyself?
Dromio: Marry, sir, besides myself, I am due to a woman, one that
claims me, one that haunts me, one that will have me.
(Act 3, scene 2)

Without ever being in total control, the spectator does remain "above" the self-doubts of the Dromios and Antipholuses, suspecting that their transformations are but the product of a lack of distance or knowledge. And the final enlightenment of the *cognitio*, tidying up identificatory loose ends even more exhaustively than could have been hoped, retrospectively underlines that they never "really" stopped being themselves. Yet as ever, ambivalences persist: not only has our overview as spectators been at best provisional and partial, but even the happy ending with its almost parodically excessive coincidences is ultimately too good to be true. Perhaps self-ignorance and self-difference is the norm after all, and recognition and self-harmony but festive dreams. What Terence Cave has written of recognition scenes in general is applicable here in particular:

> [They] are by their nature "problem" moments rather than moments of satisfaction and completion. Anagnorisis seems at first sight to be the paradigm of narrative satisfaction: it answers questions, restores identity and symmetry, and makes a whole hidden structure of relations intelligible. Yet the satisfaction is also somehow excessive, the reassurance too easy; the structure is visibly prone to collapse. ... Recognition may easily turn out to be an impostor, claiming to resolve, conjoin and make whole while it busily brings to the surface all the possibilities that threaten wholeness.[17]

Plautus's *Amphitruo* and many centuries later the *Amphitryon* plays
by Molière and Kleist are all built on the comedy of gemination, though
here the "twins" are not earthly siblings but divine impostors, as Jupiter
turns himself into the spitting image of Amphitryon in order to enjoy
the latter's wife while Mercury adopts the identity of Amphitryon's
servant Sosia. Being divine, this dual imposture naturally lacks the
imperfections of most human disguises, and in Plautus the divine
Amphitryon and Sosia are even provided with small signs – plumes or
tassels – to help the spectator tell them apart from the real ones. Minor
shifts of emphasis apart, the plays indeed have so much in common that
they are themselves near-identical triplets, and in all three cases it is the
Mercury/Sosia configuration that gives rise to the comic business. In all
three, Mercury's usurpation of Sosia's identity leads to puzzlement and
self-doubt in the servant, who allows himself to be persuaded – first by
force and then by argument – that he is not himself but somebody else
is instead. In all three, the playwrights revel not only in the confusions
and misunderstandings but also the paradoxes and logical contradictions
of the situation, as a bewildered Sosia tells a bewildered Amphitryon
that "he," Sosia, is both here talking to his master and at the same time
elsewhere (back at home), and the master assumes the servant is either
mad, dreaming, drunk or joking. In all three, we have Sosia's comic
description of how "he" beat "himself" up. And in all three, this
recurrent play with split selves and double selves is supported by the
(mis-)use of the word "I" in a way which obscures rather than reveals
identity. In Plautus this is restricted to a small exchange between
Amphitryon and Mercury-as-Sosia, in which the latter – barring the
former's entrance to his own house – pretends not to recognize his
voice:

Mercury:	Who's there?		
Amphitryon:		I am.	
Mercury:			I am who?	(line 1020)

Molière and Kleist repeat not only this episode[18] but other cases where
it is Sosie whose identity is deliberately not recognized. The differences
between the French and the German version are small but telling. While
Molière's exchange is a relatively straightforward:

Mercure:	Qui va là?		
Sosie:		Moi.	
Mercure:		Qui, moi?	
Sosie:			Moi.	(Act 1, scene 2)

Kleist's substantivization of the "I" perhaps hints at a more heavyweight
philosophical subtext underneath the farcical surface:

Merkur:	Halt dort! Wer geht dort?
Sosias:	Ich.
Merkur:	Was für ein Ich?
Sosias:	Meins mit Verlaub.

(Act 1, scene 2)

The phrasing of both the question ("What sort of an I?") and the answer ("Mine, by your leave") implies possibilities of self-difference (there could be an I which is not mine) which are not present in the French exchange and which more explicitly anticipate the duplications to come.

The deictic nature of the word "I" is a positive invitation to comic misunderstanding, for its reference depends on the context in which it is being used and, more specifically, on who is using it. This is an essential difference between it and other personal pronouns. In the words of Gilbert Ryle:

> "I," in my use of it, always indicates me and only indicates me. "You," "she," and "they" indicate different people at different times. "I" is like my own shadow; I can never get away from it, as I can get away from your shadow.[19]

If anything, it is in fact yet more persistent than my shadow, which can after all get shaken off in the dark, whereas "I" am "here" even in pitch blackness. Nonetheless, the "shadow" metaphor is significant, for it turns the word into another sort of doppelgänger or twin, a verbal double which pursues us, or which we pursue, on our journey through life. But it is not (normally) a shadow that lends itself to misidentification. Though we may well make mistakes in our first-person statements, we cannot make the mistake of misidentifying the person whom we are referring to (it can only be me).

As a deictic, however, it *is* open to the possibility of misuse by those who refuse to acknowledge the context. As with "now" and "here," successful communication relies upon the conventional recognition of when and where it is being employed. If I write, for example, "it is now ten past five on Tuesday 22 June 1993," then the argumentative, literally-minded or playful reader may be sorely tempted to ignore the contextual disparity opened up by the relationship of writer to reader and to appropriate "now" for the time of reading, turning a truth into a falsehood and creating a confusion. The same indexical ambiguity promotes the sort of conflict that could be caused by the word "my" in the following enquiry: "I did not have sex with my wife till after we were married. What about you?" And lost on one occasion in a maze, half-witted Laurel and Hardy – out of sight but within earshot of one another – get into a dispute which runs along the lines: "Where are you?" "Here!" "No, you're not. I am!"[20] For the enlightened onlooker there is of course no contradiction in them both being where they are.

The information given by the statement "I am here" is in fact about neither me nor the place where I am, for "I" am always "here" regardless of where it is that I am: the sentence is instead a purely demonstrative gesture *drawing attention* to my presence or location. In order to make the statement I need to be acquainted neither with my whereabouts (for I could be in utter darkness) nor even with my "self" (for I could be suffering from total amnesia). I need know, in short, neither who nor where I am. Nor is it a statement that allows of contradiction, for again "here" is where "I" always am. Except, that is, in the disconcertingly mad world of comedy, where discursive conventions are flouted in the general lawlessness, and the self-difference and self-doubt we normally suppress are playfully allowed out on parole. The exchanges between Rosencrantz and Guildenstern undermine the conversational habits that are generally taken for granted and at the same time throw the courtiers' (and our) selfhood into question:

Guildenstern:	Are you there?
Rosencrantz:	Where?
Guildenstern:	(*bitterly*) A flying start....
	(*Pause*)
Rosencrantz:	Is that you?
Guildenstern:	Yes.
Rosencrantz:	How do you know? (Act 3)

Rosencrantz, it seems, is so confused as to his identity that he *does* need to know where he is in order to say "I am here." The act of querying whether "I am here" is a signal of deep-seated doubt regarding one's unity or personhood. Plautus's Sosia, who has been convinced that he is not himself by his other self Mercury, explains the situation to his master in terms that defy all deictic self-evidence: "I am here and I am there, I positively am. ... So help me heaven, I didn't believe my own self, Sosia, at first, not till that other Sosia, myself, made me believe him" (lines 594-8).

In spite of the contradiction it holds, the claim that "I am not (only) here, but there" is not one that comedy merely derides as a logic-defying aberration, the delusion of a wayward or naive mind. Not only is such self-distance essential to all performative self-projections, to the play context, to the theatrical, joke-telling or festive framework in which laughter itself is born, but – whether consciously or not – it also hints at a truth about the human condition that a tyrannical rationality would prefer to keep tucked away out of sight.

Conclusion

Changing the Subject

Comedy is concerned with the ways in which we fail to coincide with ourselves. It gives voice to our disobedient, disorderly subselves, to the mercurial impostor and to the transvestite in us; it betrays how much "I" depend on "you" for identification and personhood, on earthy gunge for my bodily survival, on death for a sense of being alive, on letting myself go for the possibility of ever finding myself. Such self-difference, captured in Sosia's "I am not (only) here, but there," is an existential condition. Unless mastered and subordinated within an integrative unity, however, it is not a state compatible with the claims of rational (self-) control. The infectiousness of the disunity enacted and encouraged in *play* situations was recognized nearly twenty-four centuries ago by Plato, who saw in actors a potential disruption of civic order. And traditionally, changeability is associated with folly, madness or even sin. Impermanence and inconsistency, fickleness and inconstancy are negative attributes betokening the absence of a true self; an inability to take a stance or adopt a position in matters of opinion or value is seen as ethically dubious; self-contradiction is irrational.

But who says so? If self-difference really is an existential condition, who is it that determines *when* it is to be called mad or irrational? On being consigned to Bethlehem Hospital, the seventeenth-century playwright Nathaniel Lee protested: "They called me mad, and I called them mad, and damn them, they outvoted me." [1] Yet if madness and sanity are but a matter of consensus, then what about the acts of collective self-delusion that structure social co-existence? Marx's central idea that ideology subjects people to systematic illusions and distortive falsifications of reality in the interests of certain social groups, like Freud's unmasking of the delusions upon which social order is founded, universalizes self-deception just as medieval and Renaissance thought universalized folly. But to universalize such a concept is also to relativize it, depriving what is negatively evaluated of an "uncontaminated" positive yardstick against which measurement and appraisal can take place. In the matter of "irrationality," this applies both to the having and the giving of reasons. Even allowing a provisional definition of rational behaviour as behaviour that is "in one's own interests" (and waiving the question why it is rational to behave in one's own interests as opposed, for example, to the common good), there remain insuperable uncertainties as to what our interests consist in (pleasure? happiness? self-fulfilment? knowledge? survival?) and what to do when different interests are in contradiction, as well as – in the case of complex bundles of semi-autonomous subselves such as human beings – which of our subselves should have priority if conflicts do arise. Fortunately for us, we are not always even aware of what is in our "best interests." An infallible and inflexible rationality would deprive us of some of the benefits of limited self-deception, obsession, cognitive selectivity, automatism and intuition.[2] It is not rational always to be rational. It is not in our own interests.

Problems also arise with the *giving* of reasons. Any attempt to provide a rational justification for deductive reasoning, for example, itself presupposes the validity of deduction and so proves circular or infinitely regressive in its reliance upon the principles of inference that are at stake. If logical reasoning is founded upon the application of rules of logic, it may be asked, then how do we know how to apply these rules of logic. Presumably there must be rules telling us how to apply the rules. But how do we know how to apply these meta-rules?[3] No step of argumentation, it would seem, can be performed without the help of some higher-level rule to justify the step in question; but the higher-level rule is itself a step of reasoning and in turn presumably requires justification, which presumably itself requires justification... The result is an infinite regress which in theory appears to paralyze any rule-application, but in practice clearly does not. The same applies with attempts to justify induction (i.e. to prove that empirical generalizations derived from past experience will also hold in the future), which themselves appeal to some such empirical principle as the uniformity of nature or the success of induction in the past, and so rely upon the very sort of inductive moves whose validity they set out to establish. As Nozick argues, believing something in spite of coercive arguments to the contrary can be penalized by charges that it is irrational to do so, but so what!: again, the question *why* one shouldn't be irrational can only be answered in circular fashion, i.e. by giving reasons. It is senseless to seek to "justify" reasoning (whether inductive or deductive), for the idea of justification itself presupposes what it aspires to validate. Nor can the law of identity (I=I) ultimately be justified or explained. If the explanatory preconditions for the possibility of the law do not obey the law, then they contain a contradiction, and the law will not have been explained. If they do, then they themselves presuppose the law and so fail to explain it.[4]

This is to deny neither the possibility nor the desirability of rationality, for the act of writing about it in itself presupposes a commitment to *some* notion of rationality.[5] There is a sense, indeed, in which practical rationality comes not from "above" (from a justificatory meta-argument) but from "below": cognition, or life itself, *is* a form of inductive self-maintenance, operating predictively and repeating only what is successful or works in the cognitive system's interests, and the human ability to engage in reasoned arguments is but a result of the astonishing complexity of our cognitive structures and powers of verbalization. The human mind, as Locke recognized, "can reason without being instructed in methods of syllogizing; the understanding is not taught to reason by these rules; it has a native faculty to perceive the coherence or incoherence of its ideas."[6] And in practice, our reasoning remains relatively unconcerned with reason's incapacity to defend itself except in circular fashion. What can be asserted, however, is that our own incarceration within the limitations of our bodily perspective and a culturally determined system of beliefs – with all the attendant delusions and blind spots – does deprive us of the enlightenment of a rationally "pure" meta-perspective from which to judge either ourselves or others. This applies both to apparent aberrations within our own social system, where the "madness" of the madman is often not only definitionally dependent upon the "sanity" of the system but also causally determined by it, and to the seeming irrationalities within the belief-systems of other cultures. Entrenched as we are within our own cultural structures and their inadequacies, there is simply no non-circular way of appraising either our system or any other; there is no meta-reason which can justify us more than anyone else.

In the medieval topos of universal folly, one way of achieving limited wisdom was acknowledged to reside in a recognition of one's own folly. This was the Socratic response to human ignorance, but it is also the comic response. It involves, especially in the case of Socrates, a dual impulse: firstly, an awkward and untimely questioning of established values, a critical awareness of our capacity for self-deception and the seductive falsifications of dogma, but, coupled with this, a refusal to place oneself *above* this quagmire of ignorance (except, perhaps, through this knowledge of our lack of knowledge). Of course, the capacity to question or negate has been understood to lie at the heart of *all* human consciousness. As a facility to respond to the belief-systems constitutive of our self-understanding in a relationship of circular interdependence, it coincides with the very possibility of change, taking place ceaselessly as the dynamic bodily subject modifies the seemingly static structures of language and thought. Negation is indeed inseparable from all cognition, as even the capacity to recognize, define or determine an entity goes hand in hand with an ability to distinguish it from what it is *not*. The specifically human faculty of negativity, however, consists not simply in the verbalization of the distinctions we make, but in the reflexive activity of querying these distinctions and of *re*defining what is and what is not. The Socratic or comic "fool" – in the idealized sense I am using here – radicalizes this human potential for questioning and negating, by denying what (officially at least) cannot be denied, by calling into question The Truth, by contradicting the law of identity.

The Devil is here the archetypal fool and denier, and the comic fool is to this extent diabolical. Without necessarily even reaching a level of reflective self-awareness in the figure himself, the activity of the playful fool is the negation of a negation, an undermining of the binary oppositions (such as good/bad, foolish/wise, normal/abnormal, positive /negative) by which social values can be controlled and institutionally confirmed. And above all, it is an undermining of the binary schematization at the heart of all the others, the distinction between self and other which permits us to suppress or contain the otherness within ourselves (for a good, wise and orderly person knows exactly who and what he or she is and is not). Figures of disorder and folly, amoral and mercurial tricksters and rogues, cast a parodic shadow over these comfortable oppositions, showing how standards of good and bad, folly and wisdom, may fail to do justice to the infinite subtleties of experience. Comedy "positivizes" what is otherwise negative,[7] over the centuries transforming its comic devils from objects of derision into lovable Harlequins, Panurges and Falstaffs. And even where comedy lacks the central charismatic fool, a more general universalization of folly within the fiction, as in Shakespeare's *Twelfth Night*, exposes and celebrates the lunacy that is normally marginalized in "serious" day-to-day dealings, playing off against one another a whole multitude of different manners of madness.

It may be countered, of course, that comedy itself constitutes a sort of containment and delimitation of the disorderly negative. Not only is comedy's folly, like the transgressions of Carnival, restricted to a periodic play-context, but in its more normative and less festive variations it is concentrated within a single figure who stands out like a sore thumb against the consensual normality and more often than not receives an unpleasant comeuppance at the end. As the butt of the joke, the comic fool is here the victim of a consensus which, if not in existence beforehand, is specially created for the purposes of collusive and exclusive derision. Indeed, much comedy and joke-making does serve the interests of those keen to uphold complacent distinctions between "ourselves" and other, lesser people who should be either encouraged to become like us or, if not, expelled from our company or society. Yet play-situations in themselves have a habit of undermining pretensions and suspending otherwise straightforward distinctions, and few are the fools who are not ambiguous in their folly and in the responses they provoke. This point is what sets comic transgression apart from unsanctioned transgression, which – as an infringement of that most fundamental of social directives "Don't do that!" – is likewise the negation of a negation. Insofar as unreflective transgression constitutes a *stepping beyond* the limits of what is deemed reasonable or permissible, it leaves unquestioned the boundary itself and tends accordingly to be viewed as threatening, bad or mad. Festive transgression, by contrast, has already displaced the element of fear and threat, and to the extent that theatrical performance adds to this play-context the distance created by the separation of audience and actor, it becomes possible to view the mimed madness with an ambivalent alloy of critical distance and sympathetic identification which may throw the boundary itself into question.[8]

The unfunny discursive transgressions of poetry or fantasy can be distinguished from joke-telling or comic flights of fancy in analogous terms. Joking especially involves what Susan Purdie refers to as a "marked" transgression of discursive law, one which constitutes the tellers as "masters" of discourse, "able to break and to keep the basic rule of language, and consequently in controlling possession of full human subjectivity." It is the reinstatement of the law when its transgressions are marked as such that "crucially defines the extent to which an utterance feels 'funny' as opposed to utterances whose unmarked transgressions are enjoyed in a predominantly poetic or phantasising mood."[9] Yet in drawing attention to or acknowledging the boundaries of the permissible, joking need not necessarily leave these boundaries unaltered. Within everyday work situations for example, humour is seen to function as a method of "testing the atmosphere" or negotiating potentially sensitive themes in unfamiliar situations. In the words of Steve Linstead:

> Humour allows the exploration of new ideas in situations of uncertainty or unfamiliarity. Similarly allowed are the negotiation of taboo topics, sensitive issues, and marginal serious content. The possibility of the retrospective definition of actions as either "serious" or "non-serious," "real" or "joking" imparts an ambiguity and risk to such negotiations which can be exploited.[10]

And although the interaction in theatrical comedy is unilateral rather than bilateral, this element of re-definition may be equally present. Laughter is in either case a means of coming to terms with a potential for change, a potential which may of course be either realized or rejected. Just as festive transgressions may thus serve either as the ventilatory releases of a harmoniously self-regulating system (and therefore as a hindrance to actual radical change) or as infectiously subversive play which may at any stage flip over into genuine riot and disorder, so comedy may represent its negativity and disorder as an aberration to be overcome and contained, a cathartic but uncritical/ unreflective discharge (pure fun), or an ultimately rational critique of a situation which needs changing.

The self-aware or playful folly of Socrates and the comic fool returns us to a series of paradoxes which nestle at the heart of play, comedy and laughter. The unspoken assertion "I am a fool" is paradoxical in that it can be understood to contain an implicit *negative* meta-statement ("I am a fool, so it is not worth attaching value to any statements I may make, including this one") which invalidates the content of the statement itself. If I am a fool, that is, you may as well write off anything I say, including this. Aware of the impossibility of a "meta-level" from which to evaluate folly and wisdom, the declaration of self-conscious folly in effect replaces it with an implied negative meta-level which turns the declaration into a paradox. The paradoxicality is echoed in the oxymoronic notion of a wise fool, the fool who knows nothing except that he knows nothing. This paradox is closely parallelled in the paradox of the liar ("this statement is a lie"), where an implicit negative meta-statement again undermines the statement itself, and in the related paradox of play ("this is play" i.e. not to be taken seriously),[11] both of which characterize the propensity of comic drama to focus on its own theatricality or fictionality. Whereas realistic and tragic drama as a rule seek to "swallow" the spectator into the illusion, the comic mode tends to hover in an in-between zone which questions and confuses the distinction between performance and reality and to promote a (reflective) distance in stark contrast with the identification encouraged by naturalism. These paradoxes are parallelled yet again in the paradox of surprise, which can be formulated in its most simple form as "Now I am going to surprise you,"[12] and where the enunciation of the statement once more interferes with the meaning of it. Comedy itself – with its promise of abnormality, eccentricity and the outlandish – embodies this paradox, but it is the punch-line in a joke which epitomizes it. Failing even to provide the punch-line, the shaggy-dog story goes one step further, surprising us by not surprising us (but often becoming pretty predictable in the process).

Akin to all these paradoxes is the rather tricky near-paradox "I am not the producer of this sentence." In this proposition as in the others, the act of enunciation conflicts with the content of the enunciation; in this proposition as in the others, we are faced with a negative meta-statement ("this statement is not made by me") which nullifies the statement itself, here by breaching the convention that a first-person proposition can be attributed to the person assumed to have produced the self-reflexive token "I." Seen pragmatically, the proposition "it is not me saying this" – like the proposition "I am now hereby lying" – is a way of disowning what one is saying (the proposition itself) in a manner that infringes the conventional assumption that a speaker takes responsibility for the truthfulness of what is spoken.[13] And this sentence is central to the comic moment. "I am not the producer of this sentence" is the language characteristic of a realm where – both for the comic fool and laughing spectator – it is my body, not my rational "I" that holds forth, where some mad and normally overlooked homunculus within me gets its hands on my vocal chords, and my genitals do the gabbing. It is a realm where performance and misrecognition carry the day and faces are covered by masks which speak in our stead. It is a realm where doppelgängers, twins and alter egos finally get the chance to have their say.

Rather like the Gödelian sentence, which displays the incompleteness of any formal axiomatic system once it has the power to reflect on itself, all these paradoxes seem to signal the inevitable limitations to human and non-human rationality and self-knowledge. Just as human beings are never able to view their own faces except via the mediation of (for example) mirror images, so our self-understanding is necessarily trapped within the limits of its own perspective.[14] We are limited both as bodies and as systems of beliefs, both as havers and as givers of reasons. Yet this does not mean that we do not *strive* to overcome these limitations. The philosopher Thomas Nagel speaks of incompleteness in terms of "work to be done" and the possibility of potentially interminable advances on a path towards objectivity and self-knowledge. But this path is not one that will ever be completed, for every new attempt at objectivity will bring with it its own new blind spot: "each step to a new objective vantage point, while it brings more of the self under observation, also adds to the dimensions of the observer something further which is not itself immediately observed. And this becomes possible material for observation and assessment from a still later objective standpoint. The mind's work is never done."[15]

It is precisely the awareness of our conceptual limitations that provokes the desire to question and transcend them, just as it is the fool's understanding of the inadequacies of binary schematizations that prompts his search for those blind spots where self and other, good and bad, coincide as well as clash. The metaphors of negativity, quest and pursuit again prove pertinent. As we have seen, negativity – in its "concrete" sense as the negation of a negation[16] – has been judged to be crucial to all impetus, life and change. Contrasted with the lifelessness of pure, static self-identity, contradiction is "the root of all movement and vitality: only to the extent that a thing has a contradiction within itself does it move or have a driving force and activity." [17] It need not, therefore, be the pathological abnormality for which it is usually held, but is the very principle of self-movement and the foundation of freedom.[18] Without self-conflict, there is no change. It is the comic fool who is able to enjoy this self-conflict, the Socratic fool who is able to exploit this negativity.

Notes

These endnotes contain all secondary and theoretical sources, together with all primary ones except some references to drama and poetry. In the case of drama and poetry, I have wherever possible given act and scene numbers or line numbers within the text itself. Translations are mine, except where I have cited an English translation.

Introduction

1. Stephen Priest, *Theories of the Mind*, (Harmondsworth: Penguin, 1991), 221.

2. Robert Nozick, *Philosophical Explanations*, (Oxford: Clarendon Press, 1981), 79. For Nozick, an act of reflexive self-reference is the intentional production of the token "I" in the knowledge "that its sense is such that in any possible world, any producer X of it refers to X in virtue of a property [being the producer] bestowed upon him in the producing of the token 'I'."

3. Priest, 221.

4. Immanuel Kant, *Kritik der reinen Vernunft*, (Hamburg: Felix Meiner, 1956), 274.

5. See Stuart Hampshire, *Thought and Action*, (London: Chatto and Windus, 1959), 47-8, 51.

6. Johann Gottlieb Fichte, *Über den Begriff der Wissenschaftslehre*, in vol. 2 of *Gesamtausgabe*, ed. R. Lauth and H. Jacob, (Stuttgart: Friedrich Frommann, 1965), 121.

7. John Locke, *An Essay Concerning Human Understanding*, ed. P. H. Nidditch, (Oxford: Clarendon Press, 1975), 595.

8. Charles Baudelaire, "De l'essence du rire," in *Oeuvres complètes*, 11 vols., ed. J. Crépet, (Paris: Conard, 1923), 1.377.

9. Thomas Hobbes, *Leviathan*, ed. C. B. Macpherson, (Harmondsworth: Penguin, 1968), 125.

10. See Renate Jurzik, "Die zweideutige Lust am Lachen. Eine Symptom-analyse," in *Lachen, Gelächter, Lächeln*, ed. D. Kamper and Chr. Wulf, (Frankfurt-am-Main: Syndikat, 1986), 42.

11. See T. G. A. Nelson, *Comedy: The Theory of Comedy in Literature, Drama and Cinema*, (Oxford: Oxford University Press, 1990), 8.

12. See the introduction to my *Madness, Masks, and Laughter: An Essay on Comedy*, (London: Associated University Presses, 1995).

13. Johann Gottlieb Fichte, *Grundlage der gesamten Wissenschaftslehre* (1794), (Hamburg: Felix Meiner, 1988), 31.

14. Ibid., 132. It is a question, of course, of a *conceptual* as much as a *physical* boundary.

15. Georg Wilhelm Friedrich Hegel, *Wissenschaft der Logik*, in *Werke*, 20 vols., ed. E. Moldenhauer and K. M. Michel, (Frankfurt-am-Main: Suhrkamp, 1986), 5.136-37.

16. Elizabeth Wright, *Psychoanalytic Criticism: Theory in Practice*, (London: Methuen, 1984), 179.

PART ONE: THE HUMAN SUBJECT

Chapter 1: Defining the Subject

1. Charles Taylor, *Sources of the Self: The Making of the Modern Identity*, (Cambridge: Cambridge University Press, 1989), 27.

2. Ibid., 28.

3. Ibid., 29, 31.

4. Ibid., 27.

5. Jonathan Culler, *Structuralist Poetics*, (London: Routledge and Kegan Paul, 1975), 28.

6. Julia Kristeva, "The System and the Speaking Subject," in *The Kristeva Reader*, ed. Toril Moi, (Oxford: Basil Blackwell, 1986), 33.

7. Ibid., 30.

8. George H. Mead, *Mind, Self, and Society*, ed. Charles W. Morris, (Chicago: University of Chicago Press, 1962), 199-200.

9. Ibid., 214.

10. Taylor, 36.

11. See Maurice Merleau-Ponty, *Phénoménologie de la perception*, (Paris: Gallimard, 1945), 467.

12. Thomas Nagel, *The View from Nowhere*, (Oxford: Oxford University Press, 1986), 40.

13. J. Z. Young, *Philosophy and the Brain*, (Oxford: Oxford University Press, 1987), 90.

14. John R. Searle, "Minds, Brains, and Programs," in *The Mind's I: Fantasies and Reflections on Self and Soul*, ed. Douglas R. Hofstadter and Daniel C. Dennett, (Harmondsworth: Penguin, 1982), 363.

15. Ibid., 371.

16. Ibid., 372.

17. See Steven Rose, *The Making of Memory*, (London: Bantam, 1992), 313. A purely formalistic approach plays down the whole array of biochemical processes that give rise to the structural modifications of the brain's neurons and their synaptic connections. As Rose describes, the changes undergone by the cells of the central nervous system during and after learning can indeed be measured not only physiologically (in terms of changed electrical properties) and morphologically (in terms of persistent structural alterations), but also dynamically (in terms of localized and transient changes in cerebral blood flow and energy use) and biochemically (in terms of protein and glycoprotein synthesis). The claim that such molecular processes pertain to the "hardware" of mind or memory but not what it is "about" seems to miss the point, for the information-processing metaphor is equally unable to describe what mind feels like "from the inside." They are all objective attempts to approach what can only be "grasped" subjectively. As such they are equally viable and equally limited.

18. Roger Penrose, *The Emperor's New Mind*, (London: Vintage, 1990), 566-8, 141-6, 529-34. It is such insight from outside the system, Penrose argues, that allows us to *see* the validity of the famous Gödel proposition – by reflecting on the meaning of the axiomatic system and rules of procedure – even though it cannot be derived from the axioms or produced by any sequence of the system's algorithmic operations.

19. P. F. Strawson, *Individuals*, (London: Methuen, 1959), 97.

20. Taylor, *Sources of the Self*, 525.

21. Colin McGinn, *The Character of Mind*, (Oxford: Oxford University Press, 1982), 108.

22. Martin Heidegger, *Sein und Zeit*, (Tübingen: Niemeyer, 1986), 260, 266.

23. Ilya Prigogine and Isabelle Stengers, *Order out of Chaos*, (London: Flamingo, 1985), 127. For an exceptionally clear account see also Peter Coveney and Roger Highfield, *The Arrow of Time*, (London: Flamingo, 1991).

24. E. Schrödinger, *What is Life?*, (Cambridge: Cambridge University Press, 1946), 77.

25. Hegel, *Wissenschaft der Logik*, in *Werke*, 6.78.

26. Ibid., 6.76.

27. Prigogine and Stengers, 14.

28. Young, *Philosophy and the Brain*, 7-8, 47, 178.

29. Humberto R. Maturana and Francisco J. Varela, *Autopoiesis and Cognition: The Realization of the Living*, (Dordrecht: Reidel, 1980), 87.

30. Ibid., 48, 9-10.

31. Ibid., 27.

32. Richard L. Gregory, *Mind in Science*, (Harmondsworth: Penguin, 1984), 166.

33. Maturana and Varela, 13.
34. Ibid.
35. Locke, *An Essay Concerning Human Understanding*, 341.
36. Nozick, *Philosophical Explanations*, 108-9.
37. Derek Parfit, *Reasons and Persons*, (Oxford: Oxford University Press, 1986), 7-8.
38. David Pears, "The Goals and Strategies of Self-deception," in *The Multiple Self*, ed. Jon Elster, (Cambridge: Cambridge University Press, 1986), 59-60.
39. See Parfit, 201.
40. See Amélie Oksenberg Rorty, "Self-deception, *akrasia* and irrationality," in *The Multiple Self*, ed. Elster, 131.
41. David Hume, *A Treatise of Human Nature*, in *The Philosophical Works*, 4 vols., ed. T. H. Green and T. H. Grose, (1886; reprint, Darmstadt: Scientia Verlag Aalen, 1964), 1.541.
42. Of course, the possibility of this sort of self-ascription of thoughts does suggest a facility of linguistic formulation which, while applying to human experience, need not apply to all modes or levels of cognition.
43. Locke, *An Essay Concerning Human Understanding*, 340-41.
44. Joseph Butler, "On Personal Identity," in *Body, Mind, and Death*, ed. Antony Flew, (New York: Macmillan, 1964), 167.
45. Oliver Sacks, *The Man Who Mistook His Wife for a Hat*, (London: Picador, 1986), 104.
46. See Taylor, *Sources of the Self*, 171.
47. Kant, *Kritik der reinen Vernunft*, 370-436.
48. Merleau-Ponty, *Phénoménologie de la perception*, 481.
49. Ibid., 487.
50. See Jonathan Glover, *I: The Philosophy and Psychology of Personal Identity*, (Harmondsworth: Penguin, 1988), 68.
51. Quoted in Marx W. Wartofsky, *Conceptual Foundations of Scientific Thought: an introduction to the philosophy of science*, (London: Collier-Macmillan, 1968), 336.
52. See Nagel, *The View from Nowhere*, 41-42.
53. Ludwig Wittgenstein, *Tractatus logico-philosophicus*, in *Werkausgabe*, 8 vols., (Frankfurt-am-Main: Suhrkamp, 1984), 1.67.
54. Ibid., 1.68.
55. Merleau-Ponty, 467.
56. Ludwig Feuerbach, "Die Naturwissenschaft und die Revolution," in *Theorie-Werkausgabe*, 6 vols., ed. Erich Thies, (Frankfurt-am- Main: Suhrkamp, 1975), 4.253, 263.
57. Feuerbach, "Einige Bemerkungen über den 'Anfang der Philosophie' von Dr. J. F. Reiff," in vol. 9 of *Gesammelte Werke*, 18 vols., ed. Werner Schuffenhauer, (Berlin: Akademie, 1970), 151.
58. Arthur Schopenhauer, *Die Welt als Wille und Vorstellung*, in *Sämtliche Werke*, 5 vols., ed. W. F. von Lohneysen, (Frankfurt-am- Main: Suhrkamp, 1986), 1.217- 18.
59. Parfit, *Reasons and Persons*, 216.
60. Ibid., 214.
61. Ibid., 260.

62. Ibid., 265-6.

63. Ibid., 451.

64. Mead, *Mind, Self, and Society*, 164.

65. Quoted in Karl Miller, *Doubles: Studies in Literary History*, (Oxford: Oxford University Press, 1985), 355-56.

66. Mead, 142-44.

67. See Glover, *I*, 34.

68. Ibid., 34-5.

69. Quoted in ibid., 43-44. Notable, however, is Henry Harris's criticism of the anatomical basis of these philosophical exercizes. In "Whose brain is it, anyway?" (*The Times Higher Education Supplement*, 18 December, 1992), he writes: "It is difficult to know precisely what is meant by 'two streams of consciousness,' but it is certainly not the case that in these split-brain patients the complete panoply of mental functions is duplicated. A more realistic description of the situation is that elements of the 'stream of consciousness' that are normally co-ordinated in the two halves of the brain are now no longer so. The net result is impairment (usually very serious) of cerebral function, not enhancement or *de novo* duplication."

70. Parfit, 246.

71. R. D. Laing, *The Divided Self*, (Harmondsworth: Penguin, 1965), 19-20.

72. Ibid., 69.

73. Douglas R. Hofstadter, *Gödel, Escher, Bach: An Eternal Golden Braid*, (Harmondsworth: Penguin, 1980), 388.

74. Manfred Frank, *Was ist Neostrukturalismus?* (Frankfurt-am-Main: Suhrkamp, 1984), 304.

75. Schopenhauer, *Die Welt als Wille und Vorstellung*, in *Sämtliche Werke*, 1.139.

76. See Frank, *Was ist Neostrukturalismus?* 275.

77. Gilbert Ryle, *The Concept of Mind*, (Harmondsworth: Penguin, 1963), 28.

78. Ibid., 105-6.

79. See Hans-Georg Gadamer, *Wahrheit und Methode*, 2nd ed., (Tübingen: Mohr, 1965), 250-90.

80. Merleau-Ponty, *Phénoménologie de la perception*, 437.

81. See Hofstadter, *Gödel, Escher, Bach*, especially chapters 14 and 15.

82. Ibid., 697.

83. Nagel, *The View from Nowhere*, 128.

84. Douglas R. Hofstadter, "A Conversation with Einstein's Brain," in *The Mind's I*, ed. Hofstadter and Dennett, 455.

85. Ryle, 159.

86. Ibid., 186.

87. See Frank, *Was ist Neostrukturalismus?* 252.

88. Maturana and Varela, *Autopoiesis and Cognition*, 35.

89. A brain is not simply a fixed configuration of circuitry, as a computer is. The dendritic spines by which one neuron is connected to the synaptic knobs of other neurons and which thus constitute the pathways by which one neuron can "trigger" another to fire, are capable – given certain conditions – of themselves breaking contact or making new contact. So-called "Hebb synapses" are presumed to be strengthened every time that the firing of one neuron is followed by the firing of a certain other one and weakened whenever

it is not. Such modifications in the wiring up of our neurons, it is argued, are vital in learning and the laying-down of long-term memories. The acquisition of skills is thus probably a result of patterns of neural activity tending to flow along particular pathways, termed (by Hebb) "assemblies of neurons." It remains a matter of lively controversy whether *all* memories – memories of individual items and of skills alike – really are stored in the form of such structural changes. There are indeed various types of memory, such as face-recognition, which do seem to be located in different areas of the brain, and much is still uncertain regarding the manner of their storage. Nonetheless, one of the key areas of the brain as far as memory formation is concerned – the hippocampus – is known to exhibit this plasticity to an exceptionally high degree.

90. Rose, *The Making of Memory*, 137-38.

91. In itself, my self-narrative contains no internal criteria for establishing its truth or falsity (except consistency and logical possibility). It is only through external criteria – my interaction with the world and with people who make contrary claims – that faulty memories can be eliminated or modified.

92. Jean-Paul Sartre, *Being and Nothingness*, trans. Hazel E. Barnes, (London: Methuen, 1958), xxxiii, 202. I have slightly altered the translation of Sartre's "un être qui échappe à la connaissance et qui la fonde."

93. Ibid., 198.

94. Ibid., 34.

95. Hegel, *Wissenschaft der Logik*, in *Werke*, 5.52.

96. See also Feuerbach, "Wider den Dualismus von Leib und Seele, Fleisch und Geist" (1846), in *Theorie-Werkausgabe*, 4.173.

97. Taylor, *Sources of the Self*, 47-48.

98. The fact that our interpretation of ourselves is couched in narrative has been seen as indicative of a further source of temporal self-difference: namely, as a narrative, our self- understanding is inescapably *propositional* in nature, articulated in a language composed of a differential system of signs. This differentiality entails that the meaning of a sign is something that is permanently deferred or delayed, dependent on what it is *not* (a potentially infinite chain of absent signs, themselves in turn dependent upon what *they* are not). It is always open to possible modification by later signs, and as something which can be repeated in any number of different contexts the meaning of a sign is never immune from change. Meaning is felt by some to be much more fluid than was traditionally understood, dispersed and unstable rather than fixed and self-identical, and this applies in particular to the meaning of *me*, the sense of the signs making up *my* narrative. Derrida's radical attack on semantic identity makes complete self-understanding impossible, even in principle: constructed out of language as I am, I am a victim of the fact that (my) meaning can only ever be provisionally pinned down. The subject/object split is not just a spatial difference, therefore; there is a temporal deferral or postponement too, infecting self-presence with lateness.

99. Mead, *Mind, Self, and Society*, 174.

100. Hegel, *Phänomenologie des Geistes*, in *Werke*, 3.23, 584-85.

101. Sartre, *Being and Nothingness,* 62.

102. Kant, *Kritik der reinen Vernunft*, 174.

103. Hume, *A Treatise of Human Nature*, in *Philosophical Works*, 1.534.
104. G. C. Lichtenberg, *Sudelbücher*, ed. Franz H. Mautner, (Frankfurt-am-Main: Insel, 1984), 528.
105. Quoted in Glover, *I*, 50.
106. Parfit, *Reasons and Persons*, 225.
107. See John Passmore, *A Hundred Years of Philosophy*, 2nd edn, (Harmondsworth: Penguin, 1968), 262.

PART TWO: OF LAUGHTER

Chapter 2: Self as Structure

1. Glover, *I*, 197.
2. I. Eibl-Eibesfeldt, *Grundriß der Vergleichenden Verhaltensforschung*, 6th edition, (Munich: Piper, 1980), 206-9.
3. Vivian Mercier, *The Irish Comic Tradition*, (London: Oxford University Press, 1962), 107.
4. These jokes are all taken from Trevor Griffiths's play *Comedians*, (London: Faber and Faber, 1979), 41, 47.
5. Christie Davies, "Stupidity and Rationality: Jokes from the Iron Cage," in *Humour in Society: Resistance and Control*, ed. C. Powell and G. E. C. Paton, (London: Macmillan, 1988), 18- 19.
6. John Hind, *The Comic Inquisition: Conversations with Great Comedians*, (London: Virgin, 1991), 126.
7. Delia Chiaro, *The Language of Jokes: Analysing verbal play*, (London: Routledge, 1992), 8.
8. Hind, 61, 65.
9. Christine Brooke-Rose, "Ill wit and good humour: women's comedy and the canon," in *Comparative Criticism: An Annual Journal*, ed. E. S. Shaffer, (Cambridge: Cambridge University Press, 1988), 127.
10. Immanuel Kant, *Anthropologie in pragmatischer Hinsicht*, ed. Wolfgang Becker, (Stuttgart: Reclam, 1983), 198.
11. But see also the reaction of Susan Purdie, *Comedy: The Mastery of Discourse*, (Hemel Hempstead: Harvester Wheatsheaf, 1993), 140. Purdie writes: "It is possible even for sophisticated 'ideologically sound' joking to reinforce these deeply rooted patterns of male and female power – for example, the joking about 'men's little willies' which is based on the construction of 'proper' masculinity as large-willied, so that a lack in that area is comically degrading." Although this hits part of the truth, however, such jokes may equally well be understood as aimed not at small-willied men but at *all* men insofar as they are hung-up about being well- hung. They can thus be taken as showing that male potency itself is but a pose, an imposture.
12. Quoted in Arthur Koestler, *The Act of Creation*, (London: Arkana, 1989), 53.
13. Steve Linstead, "'Jokers Wild': Humour in Organisational Culture," in *Humour in Society*, ed. Powell and Paton, 126.

14. See Purdie, *Comedy*, 64-66.

15. Linstead, 142.

16. Quoted in George E. C. Paton, "The Comedian as Portrayer of Social Morality," in *Humour in Society*, ed. Powell and Paton, 214.

17. G. W. F. Hegel, *Ästhetik*, 2 vols., ed. F. Bassenge, (Berlin: Aufbau, 1965), 2.552.

18. Koestler, *The Act of Creation*, 86.

19. Arthur Koestler, "Association and Bisociation," in *Play – Its Role in Development and Evolution*, ed. J. S. Bruner, A. Jolly and K. Sylva, (Harmondsworth: Penguin, 1976), 647.

20. George Meredith, "An Essay on Comedy," in *Comedy*, ed. Wylie Sypher, (Baltimore: Johns Hopkins University Press, 1980), 48.

21. Quoted in *The Times*, 21 March, 1990.

22. Henri Bergson, *Le Rire*, (Paris: Presses Universitaires de France, 1940), 4-5.

23. Quoted in David Esrig, *Commedia dell'arte: eine Bildgeschichte der Kunst des Spektakels*, (Nördlingen: Greno, 1985), 163.

24. Wayne Booth, *The Rhetoric of Fiction*, (Chicago: University of Chicago Press, 1961), 304.

25. On irony, see D. C. Muecke, *Irony and the Ironic*, (London: Methuen, 1982), especially 40.

26. See David Farley-Hills, *The Comic in Renaissance Comedy*, (London: Macmillan, 1981), 35

27. Don DeLillo, *White Noise*, (London: Pan/Picador, 1986), 36.

28. Ibid., 67, 215.

29. Muecke, 48.

30. See the account given by Michel Foucault, *Discipline and Punish. The Birth of the Prison*, trans. Alan Sheridan, (Harmondsworth: Peregrine, 1979), 200-9.

31. Jean-Paul Sartre, "L'acteur comique," in *Un théâtre de situations*, (Paris: Gallimard, 1973), 208.

32. Plato, *The Republic*, trans. Francis M. Cornford, (Oxford: Clarendon Press, 1941), 83.

33. Ibid., 330-31.

34. Baudelaire, "De l'essence du rire," in *Oeuvres complètes*, 1.373.

35. Bonaventura, *Nachtwachen*, ed. Wolfgang Paulsen, (Stuttgart: Reclam, 1990), 126.

36. See Ernst Robert Curtius, *Europäische Literatur und lateinisches Mittelalter*, (Bern: Francke, 1948), 421-23.

37. René Girard, *La Violence et le sacré*, (Paris: Grasset, 1972), 120.

38. Ibid., 24, 404.

39. James George Frazer, *The Golden Bough: A Study in Magic and Religion*, abridged edition, (London: Macmillan, 1922), 575.

40. Wylie Sypher, "The Meanings of Comedy," in *Comedy*, ed. Sypher, 242.

41. Michael D. Bristol, *Carnival and Theater*, (London: Methuen, 1985), 152.

42. Ibid., 154.

43. Mikhail Bakhtin, *Rabelais and his World*, trans. Hélène Iswolsky,

(Bloomington: Indiana University Press, 1984), 266.

44. C. L. Barber, *Shakespeare's Festive Comedy*, (Princeton: Princeton University Press, 1959), 22.

45. Joachim Ritter, "Über das Lachen" (1940), in *Subjektivität*, (Frankfurt-am-Main: Suhrkamp, 1979), 79.

46. Helmuth Plessner, *Lachen und Weinen*, (Munich: Leo Lehnen,1950), 105, 121.

47. Jean-Pierre Dupuy, "Tangled Hierarchies: self-reference in philosophy, anthropology and critical theory," trans. Mark Anspach, in *Comparative Criticism* (1990), ed. Shaffer, 113.

48. Francis M. Cornford, *The Origin of Attic Comedy* (1914), ed. T. H. Gaster, (New York: Doubleday, 1961), 11.

49. Girard, *La Violence et le sacré*, 131, 144.

50. La Rochefoucauld, *Maximes et Réflexions diverses*, (Paris: Gallimard, 1976), 73.

51. Plato, *Euthyphro. Apology. Crito. Phaedo. Phaedrus*, with an English translation by H. N. Fowler, (London: Heinemann, 1923), 75.

52. Cornford, *The Origin of Attic Comedy*, 134ff.

53. See K. J. Dover, *Aristophanic Comedy*, (Berkeley: University of California Press, 1972), 116-17.

54. I. F. Stone, *The Trial of Socrates*, (London: Pan/Picador, 1989), 178.

55. François Rabelais, *Oeuvres complètes*, ed. Guy Demerson and others, (Paris: Seuil, 1973), 38.

56. Sypher, "The Meanings of Comedy," in *Comedy*, ed. Sypher, 229-30.

Chapter 3: Self as Individual

1. David Bevington, introduction to *Henry IV, Part 1*, ed. David Bevington, (Oxford: Oxford University Press, 1987), 65-66.

2. Barber, *Shakespeare's Festive Comedy*, 214.

3. Northrop Frye, *An Anatomy of Criticism*, (Princeton: Princeton University Press, 1957), 183.

4. Quoted in the introduction to *The Merry Wives of Windsor*, ed. G. R. Hibbard, (Harmondsworth: Penguin, 1969), 42.

5. Ibid., 42-43.

6. Enid Welsford, *The Fool: His Social and Literary History* (1935), (New York: Doubleday, 1961), 213, 215.

7. Wolfgang Iser, "Das Komische: ein Kipp-Phänomen," in *Das Komische*, ed. Wolfgang Preisendanz and Rainer Warning, (Munich: Fink, 1976), 398-402.

8. Sandra Billington, "'Suffer Fools Gladly': The Fool in Medieval England and the Play *Mankind*," in *The Fool and the Trickster*, ed. Paul V. A. Williams, (Cambridge: Brewer, 1979), 54.

9. Sypher, "The Meanings of Comedy," in *Comedy*, ed. Sypher, 220.

10. V. A. Kolve discusses this in *The Play Called Corpus Chrisi*, (London: Edward Arnold, 1966), 126ff.

11. Ibid., 138.

12. Ibid., 181, 184.

13. Bakhtin, *Rabelais and his World*, 90- 91.

14. Dover, *Aristophanic Comedy*, 33.

15. Frye, *An Anatomy of Criticism*, 172.

16. See Rainer Warning, "Elemente einer Pragmasemiotik der Komödie," in *Das Komische*, ed. Preisendanz and Warning, 306-7.

17. Sigmund Freud, "Der Witz und seine Beziehung zum Unbewußten" (1905), in *Psychologische Schriften*, in *Studienausgabe*, 10 vols., ed. A. Mitscherlich, A. Richards, J. Strachey, (Frankfurt-am-Main: S. Fischer, 1970), 4.96.

18. Bristol, *Carnival and Theater*, 70.

19. François Rabelais, *Oeuvres complètes*, 627.

20. Victor Turner, "Comments and Conclusions," in *The Reversible World: Symbolic Inversion in Art and Society*, ed. B. A. Babcock, (Ithaca: Cornell University Press, 1978), 281.

21. Wolfgang Preisendanz, "Negativität und Positivität im Satirischen," in *Das Komische*, ed. Preisendanz and Warning, 415.

22. Leo Rosten, *The Joys of Yiddish*, (Harmondsworth: Penguin, 1971), xvii. Rosten further writes: "Humour also serves the afflicted as compensation for suffering, a token victory of brain over fear," xxiii.

23. Sandy Cohen, "Racial and Ethnic Humor in the United States," in *Amerikastudien/American Studies* 30, no. 2,(1985): 207-8.

24. Ibid., 208.

25. See Anton Zijderveld, *Humor und Gesellschaft. Eine Soziologie des Humors und des Lachens*, trans. Diethard Zils, (Graz: Styria, 1976), 189.

26. Cohen, 208.

27. Martin Amis, *Money*, (Harmondsworth: Penguin, 1985), 171.

28. DeLillo, *White Noise*, 68.

Chapter 4: Self as Subject

1. In its concern with the comedy of fantasy, this chapter is a shorter variation on the chapter "The Cognitive Mask" in my *Madness, Masks, and Laughter*. The theoretical perspective, however, is a different one.

2. Baudelaire, "De l'essence du rire," in *Oeuvres complètes*, 1.384-85.

3. Quoted in Otto Rommel, "Die wissenschaftlichen Bemühungen um die Analyse des Komischen," in *Wesen und Formen des Komischen im Drama*, ed. R. Grimm and K. L. Berghahn, (Darmstadt: Wissenschaftliche Buchgesellschaft, 1975), 13.

4. Dover, *Aristophanic Comedy*, 30.

5. Italo Calvino, *Cosmicomics*, trans. William Weaver, (London: Abacus, 1982), 43.

6. Ibid., 44.

7. Ibid., 46.

8. Coveney and Highfield, *The Arrow of Time*, 65.

9. F. H. Bradley, *Appearance and Reality*, 9th imp., (Oxford: Clarendon Press, 1930), 189-90.

10. Martin Amis, *Time's Arrow*, (Harmondsworth: Penguin, 1992), 61, 63.

11. Kurt Vonnegut, *Slaughterhouse-Five*, (New York: Dell/Laurel, 1991), 74.

12. W. H. Auden, "Notes on the Comic," in *The Dyer's Hand and Other Essays*, (New York: Random, 1962), 371-73.

13. Friedrich Nietzsche, *Nachgelassene Fragmente*, in *Werke*, 8.3.66.

14. Hegel, *Ästhetik*, 1.122.

15. This applies equally to Newtonian conceptions of absolute time, where the instants are autonomous and logically prior to the events that "fill" them, and to relational conceptions, according to which time would not be passing if nothing were happening. Relativistic notions of space and time as a four-dimensional manifold likewise attribute one dimension to time.

16. P. F. Strawson, *The Bounds of Sense*, (London: Methuen, 1966), 126-27.

17. David Mayer III, *Harlequin in his Element: The English Pantomime, 1806- 1836*, (Cambridge, Mass.: Harvard University Press, 1969), 40.

18. Ibid., 112-14.

19. Albert Camus, *The Myth of Sisyphus*, trans. Justin O'Brien, (Harmondsworth: Penguin, 1975), 26, 32, 50.

20. Nietzsche, *Die Geburt der Tragödie*, in *Werke*, 3.1.53.

21. A. J. Greimas, *Sémantique structurale*, (Paris: Larousse, 1966), 71.

22. Ibid., 70.

Chapter 5: Self as Living Organism

1. See, for example, Søren Kierkegaard, *Concluding Unscientific Postscript*, trans. David F. Swenson and Walter Lowrie, (Princeton: Princeton University Press, 1941), 147-51.

2. Quoted in Giacomo Oreglia, *The Commedia dell'arte*, trans. Lovett F. Edwards, (London: Methuen, 1968), 108.

3. Gerburg Treusch-Dieter, "Das Gelächter der Frauen," in *Lachen, Gelächter, Lächeln*, ed. Kamper and Wulf, 115.

4. Kierkegaard, 150.

5. Edgar Allan Poe, *Comedies and Satires*, ed. David Galloway,(Harmondsworth: Penguin, 1987), 161.

6. Ibid., 77 -78.

7. Ibid., 78 - 79.

8. Norman Holland, *Laughing: A Psychology of Humour*, (Ithaca: Cornell University Press, 1982), 85.

9. Michel de Montaigne, *Essais*, 3 vols., ed. A. Micha, (Paris: Garnier-Flammarion, 1969), 1.285- 87.

10. Lichtenberg, *Sudelbücher*, 231.

11. Kierkegaard, 400.

12. See Aristotle, *Poetics I*, translated with notes by Richard Janko, (Cambridge, Indianapolis: Hackett Publishing Company, 1987), xxiii .

13. Ibid., 59.

14. Ibid., xix.

15. Northrop Frye, "The Argument of Comedy" (1949), in *Comedy: Developments in Criticism*, ed. D. J. Palmer, (London: Macmillan, 1984), 78 -79.

16. Schopenhauer, *Die Welt als Wille und Vorstellung*, in *Sämtliche Werke*, 2.132-33.

17. Eric Bentley, "On the Other Side of Despair" (1964), in *Comedy:*

Developments in Criticism, ed. Palmer, 141.

18. Quoted in Sypher, "The Meanings of Comedy," in *Comedy*, ed. Sypher, 205.

19. Holland, *Laughing*, 32.

20. Rabelais, *Oeuvres complètes*, 126-27.

21. Ibid., 170.

22. Mercier, *The Irish Comic Tradition*, 63.

23. Voltaire, *Candide, ou l'optimisme*, ed. André Morize, (Paris: Didier, 1957), 14.

24. Lucian, *On Funerals*, in vol. 4 of *Works*, with a translation by A. M. Harmon, (London: Heinemann, 1953), 121.

25. Erasmus, *Praise of Folly*, trans. Betty Radice, (Harmondsworth: Penguin, 1971), 141.

26. DeLillo, *White Noise*, 99-100.

27. Ibid., 216.

28. Ibid., 38.

29. Ibid., 266.

30. Ibid., 228-29.

31. Mercier, 50.

32. Zijderveld, *Humor und Gesellschaft*, 149.

33. Bentley, "On the Other Side of Despair," in *Comedy: Developments in Criticism*, ed. Palmer, 148.

34. Lewis Carroll, *Alice's Adventures in Wonderland and Through the Looking-Glass*, ed. Roger Lancelyn Green, (Oxford: Oxford University Press, 1982), 170.

35. Christian Morgenstern, *Alle Galgenlieder*, (Zurich: Diogenes, 1981), 32. The German reads:

> Ein Knie geht einsam durch die Welt.
> Es ist ein Knie, sonst nichts!
> Es ist kein Baum! Es ist kein Zelt!
> Es ist ein Knie, sonst nichts.
>
> Im Kriege ward einmal ein Mann
> erschossen um und um.
> Das Knie allein blieb unverletzt –
> als wär's ein Heiligtum.
>
> Seitdem geht's einsam durch die Welt.
> Es ist ein Knie, sonst nichts.
> Es ist kein Baum, es ist kein Zelt.
> Es ist ein Knie sonst nichts.

36. Poe, *Comedies and Satires*, 32, 35, 36

37. Ibid., 38.

38. See W. H. Auden, *Collected Poems*, ed. E. Mendelson, (London: Faber and Faber, 1976), 437.

39. Quoted in Walter Redfern, *Puns*, (Oxford: Basil Blackwell, 1984), 128.

40. Bakhtin, *Rabelais and his World*, 151.

41. Rabelais, *Oeuvres complètes*, 698.

42. Samuel Beckett, *Murphy*, (London: Pan/Picador, 1973), 154.

43. Jonathan Swift, *Gulliver's Travels*, ed. Paul Turner, (Oxford: Oxford

University Press, 1986), 214.

44. Quoted in Tony Staveacre, *Slapstick: The Illustrated Story of Knockabout Comedy*, (London: Angus and Robertson, 1987), 170.

45. Ibid., 166, 170.

46. Quoted in Redfern, 63.

47. Tobias Smollett, *The Adventures of Roderick Random*, ed. Paul-Gabriel Boucé, (Oxford: Oxford University Press, 1979), 182, 148.

48. Rabelais, 379.

49. Sigmund Freud, "Der Humor" (1927), in *Studienausgabe*, 4.275- 282.

50. Nelson, *Comedy*, 73.

51. William McDougall, *An Outline of Psychology*, (London: Methuen, 1923), 169.

52. See R. C. Solomon, "Emotionen und Anthropologie: Die Logik emotionaler Weltbilder," in *Logik des Herzens. Die soziale Dimension der Gefühle*, ed. G. Kahle, (Frankfurt-am-Main: Suhrkamp, 1981), 233.

53. Quoted in Bristol, *Carnival and Theater*, 181.

54. Bakhtin, *Rabelais and his World*, 298-99.

55. Michel Foucault, *Madness and Civilization: A History of Insanity in the Age of Reason*, trans. Richard Howard, (London: Tavistock, 1971), 17.

56. Laing, *The Divided Self*, 51.

57. Ibid., 150.

58. Ibid., 176.

59. Ibid.

60. Mayer III, *Harlequin in his Element*, 41.

61. See also chapter 2 .

62. Frazer, *The Golden Bough*, 301.

63. Cornford, *The Origin of Attic Comedy*, 11.

64. See Girard, *La Violence et le sacré*, 430-32.

65. Gilbert Murray, "Excursus," in Jane Ellen Harrison, *Themis: a study in the social origins of Greek religion*, 2nd edition, (Cambridge: Cambridge University Press, 1927), 341.

66. Frye, *An Anatomy of Criticism*, 192.

67. See Susan Purdie, *Comedy*, chapter 8.

68. Mercier, *The Irish Comic Tradition*, 50-51.

69. Ibid., 48.

70. Quoted in Anthony Burgess's introduction to James Joyce, *A Shorter Finnegans Wake*, (London: Faber and Faber, 1966), 16.

71. James Joyce, *Finnegans Wake*, 2nd ed., (London: Faber and Faber, 1960), 4, 6.

72. Rabelais, *Oeuvres complètes*, 226.

73. Ibid., 678- 97.

74. *The Rig Veda. An Anthology*, trans. Wendy Doniger O'Flaherty, (Harmondsworth: Penguin, 1981), 52.

75. Ibid. See the eighth stanza of the same burial hymn.

76. Oreglia, *The Commedia dell'arte*, 69-70.

77. Rabelais, 93.

78. Ibid., 71-72.

79. Ibid., 630-31.

80. See Staveacre, *Slapstick*, 171-72.

81. Friedrich Dürrenmatt, "Theaterprobleme," in *Theater: Essays, Gedichte und Reden,* in *Werkausgabe,* 30 vols., (Zurich: Diogenes, 1985), 24.62.

82. See Jurzik, "Die zweideutige Lust am Lachen," in *Lachen, Gelächter, Lächeln,* ed. Kamper and Wulf, 43.

83. Rabelais, 88.

84. Giovanni Boccaccio, *The Decameron,* trans. G. H. McWilliam, (Harmondsworth: Penguin, 1972), 49.

85. Ibid., 55

86. David Kunzle, "The World Upside Down," in *The Reversible World,* ed. Babcock, 60, 64.

87. Lucian, *Menippus, or the Descent into Hades,* in *Works 4,* 99.

88. Lucian, *Cataplus: The Downward Journey, or the Tyrant,* in *Works,* vol. 2, with a translation by A. M. Harmon, (London: Heinemann, 1953), 33.

89. Lucian, *Menippus,* 103.

90. Jane H. M. Taylor, "The *Danse macabre*: reflections on black humour, with illustrations," in *Comparative Criticism* (1988), ed. Shaffer, 154.

91. Ibid., 149.

92. Swift, *Gulliver's Travels,* 195.

93. In the seventh of Bonaventura's *Nachtwachen,* the truthfulness is the confessional veracity of religious repentance, as the heralding of the day of reckoning (a practical joke, as it happens) has the entire local populace hysterically baring all before the Almighty and disclosing their most secret vices.

94. Richard Brautigan, *The Hawkline Monster,* (London: Arena, 1987), 86-87.

95. Ibid., 80.

96. Schopenhauer, *Die Welt als Wille und Vorstellung,* in *Sämtliche Werke,* 1.381.

97. Georges Bataille, *L'érotisme,* in vol. 10 of *Oeuvres complètes,* (Paris: Gallimard, 1987), 101.

98. Rabelais, *Oeuvres complètes,* 158.

99. Mercier, *The Irish Comic Tradition,* 53-55.

100. See *Early Greek Philosophy,* translated and edited by Jonathan Barnes, (Harmondsworth: Penguin, 1987), 271.

101. Bataille, *L'érotisme,* 106.

102. John Donne, *A Selection of His Poetry,* ed. John Hayward, (Harmondsworth: Penguin, 1950), 29.

103. Cornford, *The Origin of Attic Comedy,* 15.

104. Ibid., 276.

105. Schopenhauer, 2.562.

106. Ibid., 1.450; 2.727-28.

107. Nelson, *Comedy,* 72.

108. Samuel Beckett, *Endgame,* (London: Faber and Faber, 1964), 18.

109. Schopenhauer, 2.132.

110. Martin Amis, *The Rachel Papers,* (Harmondsworth: Penguin, 1984), 156.

111. Amis, *Money,* 323.

Chapter 6: Self as Body

1. Petronius, *The Satyricon,* and Seneca, *The Apocolocyntosis,* trans. J. P. Sullivan, (Harmondsworth: Penguin, 1977), 150.
2. Ibid.
3. *Priapea: Poems for a Phallic God,* translated and edited by W. H. Parker, (London: Croom Helm, 1988), 20.
4. Ibid., 87, 119, 157.
5. Amis, *The Rachel Papers,* 101.
6. Martin Amis, *London Fields,* (Harmondsworth: Penguin, 1990), 316, 317, 330.
7. See Alain Daniélou, *Shiva et Dionysos: La religion de la Nature et de l'Eros,* (Paris: Fayard, 1979), chapter 1.
8. Ibid., 72. The translation is taken from Eugene Monick, *Phallos: Sacred Image of the Masculine,* (Toronto: Inner City Books, 1987), 29.
9. Daniélou, chapter 1.
10. Paul V. A. Williams, "Exú: The Master and the Slave in Afro-Brazilian Religion," in *The Fool and the Trickster,* ed. Williams, 118. Candomblé and Candomblé de caboclo are practised in the State of Bahia in northeast Brazil. They were both originally introduced by the African slaves brought by the Portuguese, but whereas Candomblé is a mixture of purely African religions, Candomblé de caboclo contains borrowings from the indigenous Brazilian cultures as well as from European Catholicism. Exú plays a similar role in both traditional Candomblé and Candomblé de caboclo.
11. Herman te Velde, *Seth, God of Confusion: A Study of his Role in Egyptian Mythology and Religion,* trans. G. E. van Baaren-Pape, (Leiden: E. J. Brill, 1967), 54.
12. Paul Radin, *The Trickster: A Study in American Indian Mythology,* (New York: Schocken, 1972), 18-19.
13. Ibid., 19.
14. See, for example, *Priapea,* ed. Parker, 97:

> Commoditas haec est in nostro maxima pene,
> laxa quod esse mihi femina nulla potest.

15. Rabelais, *Oeuvres complètes,* 219, 398.
16. Quoted in Bakhtin, *Rabelais and his World,* 316.
17. Wilhelm Fliess, *Über den ursächlichen Zusammenhang von Nase und Geschlechtsorgan,* (Halle, 1910).
18. Rabelais, 163.
19. Laurence Sterne, *The Life and Opinions of Tristram Shandy, Gentleman,* ed. Graham Petrie, (Harmondsworth: Penguin, 1967), 225.
20. Poe, *Comedies and Satires,* 29.
21. Quoted in the introduction to Nikolai Gogol, *Diary of a Madman and Other Stories,* trans. and intro. Ronald Wilks, (Harmondsworth: Penguin, 1972), 10.
22. Ibid., 49-50.
23. Ibid., 51.
24. Philip Roth, *The Breast,* (Harmondsworth: Penguin, 1985), 13.
25. Baudelaire, "De l'essence du rire," in *Oeuvres complètes,* 1.390-91.
26. Poe, 91.
27. Ibid., 97.

28. Amis, *Money*, 185.

29. In *The Observer*, 2 Sept., 1990.

30. Bakhtin, *Rabelais and his World*, 26.

31. Samuel Beckett, *Watt*, (London: Picador, 1988), 37.

32. Lenny Bruce, *The Essential Lenny Bruce*, ed. John Cohen, (London: Papermac, 1987), 34-35.

33. Ibid., 200.

34. Quoted in Redfern, *Puns*, 173.

35. Ibid., 22.

36. Zijderveld, *Humor und Gesellschaft*, 157-58.

37. Bakhtin, 148.

38. Rabelais, *Oeuvres complètes*, 322.

39. Radin, *The Trickster*, 25-26.

40. Amis, *Money*, 36.

41. Curtius, *Europäische Literatur und lateinisches Mittelalter*, 431

42. Amis, *The Rachel Papers*, 80-81.

Chapter 7: Self as Rational Unity

1. Bruce Robinson, *Withnail and I, and How to Get Ahead in Advertising*, (London: Bloomsbury, 1989), 147.

2. Ibid., 149.

3. Ibid., 172.

4. Ibid., 157.

5. Ibid., 168- 69.

6. Joyce, *Finnegans Wake*, 3.

7. Plato, *Timaeus*, with a translation by R. G. Bury, (London: Heinemann, 1929), 249.

8. This arises because the nervous systems of arthropods such as insects and crustacea include – besides the high concentration of neurons in the head ganglion (the "brain") – a number of other relatively autonomous ganglia or neuron-clusters distributed around the body.

9. *Canu Maswedd yr Oesoedd Canol. Medieval Welsh Erotic Poetry*, ed. and trans. Dafydd Johnston, (Cardiff: Tafol, 1991), 28-29. I cannot speak Welsh, but the original sounds so good that here it is anyway:

> Casaf rholbren wyd gennyf,
> corn cod, na chyfod na chwyf;
> calennig gwragedd-da Cred,
> cylorffon ceuol arffed,
> ystum llindag, ceiliagwydd
> yn cysgu yn ei blu blwydd,
> paeledwlyb wddw paladflith,
> pen darn imp, paid â'th chwimp chwith;
> pyles gam, pawl ysgymun,
> piler bôn dau hanner bun,
> pen morlysywen den doll,
> pŵl argae fal pawl irgoll.   (lines 9-20)

10. Ibid., 30-31 (lines 29-30).

11. Ibid. (lines 41-2).
12. Ibid. (lines 37-8).
13. Quoted in Kurt Vonnegut, *Slaughterhouse-Five*, 2.
14. *Medieval Welsh Erotic Poetry*, 28-31 (lines 6, 15, 29, 24).
15. Ibid., 42-3 . Here, again, is the Welsh :

y llwyn sur, llawn yw o serch,
fforest falch iawn, ddawn ddifreg,
ffris ffraill, ffwrwr dwygaill deg,
breisglwyn merch, drud annerch dro,
berth addwyn, Duw'n borth iddo.   (lines 46-50)

16. Denis Diderot, *Les Bijoux Indiscrets*, in vol. 3 of *Oeuvres complètes*, (Paris : Hermann , 1978), 43 .
17. Ibid., 52, 220.
18. Ibid., 64.
19. Ibid., 98.
20. Ludovico Ariosto, *Orlando Furioso*, trans. Guido Waldman, (Oxford: Oxford University Press, 1974), 282.
21. See Ritter, "Über das Lachen," 78 .
22. Purdie, *Comedy*, 84.
23. Clearly, conceptions of suffering and sympathy depend upon an immense complex of psychological and sociological variables, and the barrier separating malicious mirth from pity and concern will be correspondingly flexible.
24. Sacks, *The Man Who Mistook His Wife for a Hat*, 53-54 (italics omitted).
25. Hegel, *Ästhetik*, 2 . 553 .
26. Baudelaire, "De l'essence du rire," in *Oeuvres complètes*, 1. 380 .
27. Amis, *The Rachel Papers*, 132.
28. Ibid., 139.
23. Ibid., 148.
30. Ibid., 176.
31. Ibid., 96.
32. Amis, *Money*, 60, 330, 100.
33. Ibid ., 18 , 329 .
34. Ibid., 362.
35. Ibid., 267.
36. Ibid., 268.
37. Rose, *The Making of Memory*, 137- 38.
38. Lewis Carroll, *Alice*, 15.
39. Ibid., 16.
40. Ibid., 18.
41. Ibid.
42. Ibid., 40- 41.
43. Ibid., 45.
44. Staveacre, *Slapstick*, 5.
45. For an early example of love's lunacy, how about the following silly exchange from the medieval French *Farce Nouvelle Nommée la Folie des Gorriers*, which shows two gallants outdoing one another in going out of their (own) minds:

Le Second : Plus regarde, et moins me congnoys;
Je ne suis plus moy, se me semble.
Le Premier: Je ne scay a qui je ressemble;
Je ne suis point.
Le Second : Dea! qui peust ce estre?
Le Premier: Je ne suis ne varlet ne maistre,
Et ne sçay se je suis ou non.
Le Second : Ce ne suis pas.
Le Premier: Ce ne suis mon.
Point ne suis moy certainement.
Le Second : Mais qu'en ditz-tu, par ton serment?
Suis je?
Le Premier: Tu es. Et moy? Non, rien.
Le Second : Par sainct Jacques, je te voy bien.
Tu es toy, et moy riens quelzconques.
Le Premier: Et qu'es tu donc?
Le Second : Je ne fuz oncques.
Le Premier: Tu n'ez ......Tu es, je le congnois.
Et moy, non.
Le Second: Tu te mescongnoys.
Tu as esté et si seras,
Non pas moy.
Le Premier: Tu en mantiras.
Je le voy bien, car tu es toy,
Et congnoys que ne suis pas moy ...   (lines 426- 45)

46. Parfit, *Reasons and Persons*, 246.

47. Radin, *The Trickster*, 8.

48. Dante, *The Divine Comedy. Hell*, trans. Dorothy L. Sayers, (Harmondsworth: Penguin, l949), 229.

49. Miller, *Doubles*, 57- 58.

50. See, for example, Jean-Paul Sartre, *Being and Nothingness*, 202: "we run after a possible which our very running causes to appear, which is nothing but our running itself, and which thereby is by definition out of reach. We run towards ourselves and we are – due to this very fact – the being which can not be reunited with itself."

51. See Purdie, *Comedy*, 45.

52. Davies, "Stupidity and Rationality: Jokes from the Iron Cage," in *Humour in Society*, ed. Powell and Paton, 25, 26.

53. Ibid., 22.

54. Ibid., 11.

55. Amélie Oksenberg Rorty, "The Deceptive Self: Liars, Layers, and Lairs," in *Perspectives on Self-Deception*, ed. Brian P. McLaughlin and Amélie Oksenberg Rorty, (Berkeley: University of California Press, 1988), 23.

56. See my *Madness, Masks,and Laughter*, chapter 2.

57. Ibid., chapter 5.

58. Plato, *The Republic*, 80, 83.

59. Ibid., 329.

60. See Bristol, *Carnival and Theater*, 113.

61. See Chapter 1, n. 65.

62. Beckett, *Watt*, 146.
63. Ibid., 209.

Chapter 8: Self as Persona

1. Baudelaire, "De l'essence du rire," in *Oeuvres complètes*, 1.396.
2. See *Madness, Masks, and Laughter*, chapters 4 and 5.
3. Plautus, *The Pot of Gold and Other Plays*, trans. E. F. Watling, (Harmondsworth: Penguin, 1965), 58.
4. Ibid., 64, 65.
5. Ibid., 252.
6. Ibid., 169-70.
7. Miguel de Cervantes Saavedra, *The Adventures of Don Quixote*, trans. J. M. Cohen, (Harmondsworth: Penguin, 1950), 122.
8. Tobias Smollett, *Roderick Random*, 51-52.
9. Hegel, *Wissenschaft der Logik*, in *Werke*, 5.96.
10. Though this is – nowadays at least – a notoriously unreliable criterion for ascertaining sexual identity.
11. Peter Brand, "Disguise in Renaissance Comedy, with Illustrations," in *Comparative Criticism* (1988), ed. Shaffer, 86.
12. At one point Viola – threatened with violence – admits to the audience: "A little thing would make me tell them how much I lack of a man" (3.4).
13. Parfit, *Reasons and Persons*, 254-55.
14. Ibid., 255.
15. Ibid., 260.
16. Girard, *La Violence et le sacré*, 88, 91.
17. Terence Cave, *Recognitions: A Study in Poetics*, (Oxford: Clarendon Press, 1988), 489.
18. Molière's *Amphitryon* has:

Mercure :	Qui frappe?	
Amphitryon:	Moi.	
Mercure:	Qui, moi?	
Amphitryon:	Ah! ouvre.	(Act 3, scene 2)

Kleist's version has the same:

Merkur:	Wer klopfet?	
Amphitryon:	Ich.	
Merkur:	Wer? Ich!	
Amphitryon:	Ah! Öffne.	(Act 3, scene 2)

19. Ryle, *The Concept of Mind*, 189.
20. In their film *A Chump at Oxford*.

Conclusion: Changing the Subject

1. Quoted by Roy Porter in *A Social History of Madness: Stories of the Insane*, (London: Weidenfeld and Nicolson, 1987), 3.
2. Amélie O. Rorty, "The Deceptive Self: Liars, Layers, and Lairs," in

Perspectives on Self-Deception, ed. McLaughlin and Rorty, 16-17.

3. Hofstadter, *Gödel, Escher, Bach*, 43-45.

4. Nozick, *Philosophical Explanations*, 4, 98.

5. Hilary Putnam, *Reason, Truth and History*, (Cambridge: Cambridge University Press, 1981), 111.

6. Locke, *An Essay Concerning Human Understanding*, 671.

7. See Rainer Warning, "Komik und Komödie als Positivierung von Negativität (am Beispiel Molière und Marivaux)," in *Positionen der Negativität*, ed. Harald Weinrich, (Munich: Fink, 1975), 341-67.

8. For Bertolt Brecht, indeed, the element of distance – the overcoming of empathy and identification – characteristic of the comic mode is what makes possible the *Verfremdung* that allows things to be seen as if with new eyes, questioning standpoints normally taken for granted and alerting us to the possibility of difference and change.

9. Purdie, *Comedy*, 5.

10. Linstead, "'Jokers Wild': Humour in Organisational Culture," in *Humour in Society*, ed. Powell and Paton, 142 (italics omitted).

11. See *Madness, Masks, and Laughter*, Introduction.

12. For accounts of the paradox of surprise, see Patrick Hughes and George Brecht, *Vicious Circles and Infinity: An Anthology of Paradoxes*, (Harmondsworth: Penguin, 1978), 35-53.

13. A little bit of sophistry creates the necessary parallels. If true, the statement undermines itself by infringing the law of identity. It must therefore be false. If false (i.e. I am the producer of this sentence), it is – in a rather contrived sense – true, for I am in fact the producer of *this* sentence ("I am the producer of this sentence"), and not of the sentence "I am not the producer of this sentence." The sentence is true to the extent that I cannot be the producer of a meaningful sentence that denies that I am its producer.

14. Hofstadter, "Reflections," in *The Mind's I*, ed. Hofstadter and Dennett, 278.

15. Nagel, *The View from Nowhere*, 128-29.

16. Hegel, *Wissenschaft der Logik*, in *Werke*, 5.124.

17. Ibid., 6.75. cf.: "Die abstrakte Identität mit sich ist noch keine Lebendigkeit, sondern daß das Positive an sich selbst die Negativität ist, dadurch geht es außer sich und setzt sich in Veränderung," 6.76.

18. Ibid., 6.75-6: "Er [der Widerspruch] gilt überhaupt, sei es am Wirklichen oder in der denkenden Reflexion, für eine Zufälligkeit, gleichsam für eine Abnormität und vorübergehenden Krankheits-paroxysmus. ... Er ist aber ... nicht bloß als eine Abnormität zu nehmen, die nur hier und da vorkäme, sondern ist das Negative in seiner wesenhaften Bestimmung, das Prinzip aller Selbstbewegung."

Bibliography

Comic Works

Amis, Martin. *London Fields*. Harmondsworth: Penguin, 1990.
Amis, Martin. *Money*. Harmondsworth: Penguin, 1985.
Amis, Martin. *The Rachel Papers*. 1973; Harmondsworth: Penguin, 1984.
Amis, Martin. *Time's Arrow*. Harmondsworth: Penguin, 1992.
Apollinaire, Guillaume. *L'Enchanteur pourrissant*. Edited by Michel Décaudin. Paris: Gallimard, 1972.
Ariosto, Ludovico. *Orlando Furioso*. Translated by Guido Waldman. Oxford: Oxford University Press, 1974.
Aristophanes. *The Knights. Peace. The Birds. The Assemblywomen. Wealth*. Translated by Alan H. Sommerstein and David Barrett. Harmondsworth: Penguin, 1978.
Aristophanes. *Lysistrata. The Acharnians. The Clouds*. Translated by Alan H. Sommerstein. Harmondsworth: Penguin, 1973.
Aristophanes. *Plays*. With an English translation by B. B. Rogers. 3 vols. Cambridge: Harvard University Press (Loeb Classical Library), 1960-63.
Aristophanes. *The Wasps. The Poet and the Women. The Frogs*. Translated by David Barrett. Harmondsworth: Penguin, 1964.
Auden, W. H. *Collected Poems*. Edited by Edward Mendelson. London: Faber and Faber, 1976.
Barnes, Peter. *The Ruling Class*. 1969; London: Heinemann, 1980.
Beaumarchais. *Théâtre*. Paris: Flammarion, 1965.

Beaumont, Francis. *The Knight of the Burning Pestle*. Edited by
 Michael Hattaway. London: Ernest Benn, 1969
Beckett, Samuel. *Endgame*. London: Faber and Faber, 1958.
Beckett, Samuel. *Murphy*. London: Pan/Picador, 1973.
Beckett, Samuel. *Waiting for Godot*. London: Faber and Faber, 1956.
Beckett, Samuel. *Watt*. 1953; London: Picador, 1988.
Boccaccio, Giovanni. *The Decameron*. Translated by G. H.
 McWilliam. Harmondsworth: Penguin, 1972.
Bonaventura. *Nachtwachen*. Rev. ed. Edited by Wolfgang Paulsen.
 Stuttgart: Reclam, 1990.
Brautigan, Richard. *The Hawkline Monster*. 1974; London: Arena,
 1987.
Brecht, Bertolt. *Stücke 1-10*. In *Werke*. 24 vols. Edited by W. Hecht et
 al. Frankfurt-am-Main: Suhrkamp, 1989–.
Bruce, Lenny. *The Essential Lenny Bruce*. Edited by John Cohen.
 London: Papermac, 1987.
Bruno, Giordano. *Candelaio*. Edited by Giorgio Barberi Squarotti.
 Turin: Einaudi, 1964.
Buckingham, George Villiers, 2nd duke of. *The Rehearsal*. In *Three
 Restoration Comedies*, edited by G. G. Falle. New York: St
 Martin's Press, 1964.
Bürger, Gottfried August. *Wunderbare Reisen zu Wasser und zu Lande,
 Feldzüge und lustige Abenteuer des Freiherrn von
 Münchhausen*. Frankfurt-am-Main: Insel, 1976.
Calvino, Italo. *Cosmicomics*. Translated by William Weaver. London:
 Sphere/Abacus, 1982.
Carroll, Lewis. *Alice's Adventures in Wonderland and Through the
 Looking-Glass*. Rev. ed. Edited by Roger Lancelyn Green.
 Oxford: Oxford University Press, 1982.
Cervantes Saavedra, Miguel de. *The Adventures of Don Quixote*.
 Translated by J. M. Cohen. Harmondsworth: Penguin, 1950.
Chaucer, Geoffrey. *Canterbury Tales*. Rev. ed. Edited by A. C. Cawley.
 London: Dent, 1975.
Corneille, Pierre. *L'Illusion comique*. Edited by Marc Fumaroli. Paris:
 Larousse, 1970.
Dante Alighieri. *The Divine Comedy. Hell*. Translated by Dorothy L.
 Sayers. Harmondsworth: Penguin, 1949.
DeLillo, Don. *White Noise*. London: Picador, 1985.
Diderot, Denis. *Les Bijoux Indiscrets*. In vol. 3 of *Oeuvres complètes*.
 Paris: Hermann, 1978.
Everyman. Edited by A. C. Cawley. Manchester: Manchester
 University Press, 1961.
Farce nouvelle nommée la Folie des Gorriers. In *Recueil général des
 Sotties*. 3 vols. Edited by E. Picot. Paris: Didot, 1902-12.
Fielding, Henry. *Completed Works*. 16 vols. Edited by W. E. Henley.

London: Heinemann, 1903.

Gogol, Nikolai Vasilevich. *Diary of a Madman and Other Stories.* Translated by Ronald Wilks. Harmondsworth: Penguin, 1972.

Gogol, Nikolai Vasilevich. *The Government Inspector.* Translated by D. J. Campbell. London: Sylvan Press, 1947; London: Heinemann, 1980.

Grabbe, Christian Dietrich. *Scherz, Satire, Ironie und tiefere Bedeutung.* Edited by Alfred Bergmann. Stuttgart: Reclam, 1970.

Graves, Robert. *Collected Poems 1959.* London: Cassell, 1959.

Griffiths, Trevor. *Comedians.* Rev. ed. London: Faber and Faber, 1979.

Gryphius, Andreas. *Absurda Comica oder Herr Peter Squenz.* Edited by Herbert Cysarz. Stuttgart: Reclam, 1954.

Holberg, Ludvig. *Jeppe vom Berge, oder Der verwandelte Bauer.* Translated by Hermann Engster. Stuttgart: Reclam, 1980.

Jarry, Alfred. *Tout Ubu.* Edited by Maurice Saillet. Paris: Livre de Poche, 1985.

Johnston, Dafydd, trans. *Canu Maswedd yr Oesoedd Canol. Medieval Welsh Erotic Poetry.* Cardiff: Tafol, 1991.

Jonson, Ben. *Works.* 11 vols. Edited by C. H. Herford, P. Simpson, and E. Simpson. Oxford: Clarendon Press, 1925-52.

Joyce, James. *Finnegans Wake.* 1939; London: Faber and Faber, 1960.

Joyce, James. *A Shorter Finnegans Wake.* Edited by Anthony Burgess. London: Faber and Faber, 1966.

Kleist, Heinrich von. *Sämtliche Werke und Briefe.* Rev. ed. 2 vols. Edited by Helmut Sembdner. Munich: Hanser, 1977.

Lesage, Alain-René. *Le Diable boiteux.* Edited by Roger Laufer. Paris: Gallimard, 1984.

Lucian. *Works. Vol.2.* With an English translation by A. M. Harman. London: Heinemann (Loeb Classical Library), 1953.

Lucian. *Works. Vol.4.* With an English translation by A. M. Harman. London: Heinemann (Loeb Classical Library), 1953.

Machiavelli, Niccolò. *Mandragola.* Edited by G. Davico Bonino. Turin: Einaudi, 1980.

Mankind. In *The Macro Plays: The Castle of Perseverance. Wisdom. Mankind.* Edited by Mark Eccles. London: Oxford University Press, 1969.

Marlowe, Christopher. *The Complete Plays.* Edited by J. B. Steane. Harmondsworth: Penguin, 1969.

Middleton, Thomas. *A Chaste Maid in Cheapside.* Edited by Alan Brissenden. London: Ernest Benn, 1968.

Middleton, Thomas. *A Mad World, My Masters.* Edited by Standish Henning. Lincoln: University of Nebraska Press, 1965.

Molière. *Oeuvres complètes.* Paris: Seuil, 1962.

Morgenstern, Christian. *Alle Galgenlieder.* Zurich: Diogenes, 1981.

Nestroy, Johann. *Der böse Geist Lumpazivagabundus oder das liederliche Kleeblatt. Der Talisman. Freiheit in Krähwinkel.* Edited by Thomas Rothschild. Munich: Goldmann, 1983.

Oreglia, Giacomo. *The Commedia dell'Arte.* Translated by Lovett F. Edwards. London: Methuen, 1968.

Orton, Joe. *The Complete Plays.* London: Eyre Methuen, 1976.

Parker, W. H., trans. *Priapea: Poems for a Phallic God.* London: Croom Helm, 1988.

Petronius. *The Satyricon.* And Seneca. *The Apocolocyntosis.* Translated by J. P. Sullivan. Harmondsworth: Penguin, 1977.

Plautus. *The Pot of Gold and other plays.* Translated by E. F. Watling. Harmondsworth: Penguin, 1965.

Plautus. *Works.* 5 vols. With an English translation by Paul Nixon. Cambridge: Harvard University Press (Loeb Classical Library), 1930-38.

Poe, Edgar Allan. *Comedies and Satires.* Edited by David Galloway. Harmondsworth. Penguin, 1987.

Rabelais, François. *Oeuvres complètes.* Edited by Guy Demerson et al. Paris: Seuil, 1973.

The Rig Veda. An Anthology. Translated by Wendy Doniger O'Flaherty. Harmondsworth: Penguin, 1981.

Robinson, Bruce. *Withnail and I.* And *How to Get Ahead in Advertising.* London: Bloomsbury, 1989.

Rochester, John Wilmot, 2nd earl of. *Complete Poems and Plays.* Edited by Paddy Lyons. London: Dent, 1993.

Roth, Philip. *The Breast.* 1972; Harmondsworth: Penguin, 1985.

Shakespeare, William. *As You Like It.* 2nd ed. Edited by Agnes Latham. London: Methuen, 1975.

Shakespeare, William. *Comedy of Errors.* Edited by R. A. Foakes. London: Methuen, 1962.

Shakespeare, William. *Henry IV, Part 1.* Edited by David Bevington. Oxford: Oxford University Press, 1987.

Shakespeare, William. *The Second Part of King Henry IV.* Edited by A. R. Humphreys. London: Methuen, 1966.

Shakespeare, William. *The Merchant of Venice.* 7th ed. Edited by John Russell Brown. London: Methuen, 1961.

Shakespeare, William. *The Merry Wives of Windsor.* Edited by G. R. Hibbard. Harmondsworth: Penguin, 1969.

Shakespeare, William. *A Midsummer Night's Dream.* 3rd ed. Edited by Harold F. Brooks. London: Methuen, 1979.

Shakespeare, William. *The Poems.* Edited by F. T. Prince. London: Methuen, 1960.

Shakespeare, William. *Twelfth Night.* 2nd ed. Edited by J. M. Lothian and T. W. Craik. London: Methuen, 1975.

Shakespeare, William. *The Winter's Tale.* Edited by Ernest Schanzer.

Harmondsworth: Penguin, 1969.

Simpson, N. F. *One Way Pendulum: A Farce in a New Dimension.* 1960; London: Faber and Faber, 1988.

Smollett, Tobias. *The Adventures of Roderick Random.* Edited by Paul-Gabriel Boucé. Oxford: Oxford University Press, 1979.

Sorel, Charles. *Le berger extravagant, ou Parmi des fantaisies amoureuses on void les impertinences des Romans et de la poesie.* Paris: T. du Bray, 1628.

Sterne, Laurence. *The Life and Opinions of Tristram Shandy, Gentleman.* Edited by Graham Petrie. Harmondsworth: Penguin, 1967.

Stoppard, Tom. *Jumpers.* 2nd ed. London: Faber and Faber, 1986.

Stoppard, Tom. *Rosencrantz and Guildenstern are Dead.* London: Faber and Faber, 1967.

Swift, Jonathan. *Gulliver's Travels.* Edited by Paul Turner. Oxford: Oxford University Press, 1986.

Swift, Jonathan. *Poems.* Rev. ed. 3 vols. Edited by Harold Williams. Oxford: Clarendon Press, 1958.

Tourneur, Cyril. *The Revenger's Tragedy.* Edited by Brian Gibbons. London: Ernest Benn, 1967.

Valentin, Karl. *Kurzer Rede langer Sinn. Texte von und über Karl Valentin.* Edited by Helmut Bachmaier. Munich: Piper, 1990.

Voltaire. *Candide, ou L'optimisme.* Edited by André Morize. Paris: Didier, 1957.

Vonnegut, Kurt. *Slaughterhouse-Five.* 1966; New York: Dell / Laurel, 1991.

Wakefield Pageants in the Towneley Cycle, The Edited by A. C. Cawley. Manchester: Manchester University Press, 1958.

Zuckmayer, Carl. *Der Hauptmann von Köpenick.* Frankfurt-am-Main: Fischer Taschenbuch, 1961.

Theoretical Works

Aristotle. *Poetics I.* Translated by Richard Janko. Cambridge: Hackett Publishing Company, 1987.

Audeni W. H. *The Dyer's Hand and Other Essays.* New York: Random, 1962.

Babcock, Barbara A., ed. *The Reversible World: Symbolic Inversion in Art and Society.* Ithaca: Cornell University Press, 1978.

Bakhtin, Mikhail. *Rabelais and his World.* Translated by Hélène Iswolsky. Bloomington: Indiana University Press, 1984.

Barber, C. L. *Shakespeare's Festive Comedy: A Study of Dramatic Form and its Relation to Custom.* Princeton: Princeton University Press, 1959.

Barnes, Jonathan, trans. *Early Greek Philosophy*. Harmondsworth: Penguin, 1987.

Barrow, John D. *Theories of Everything. The Quest for Ultimate Explanation*. London: Vintage, 1992.

Bataille, Georges. *L'érotisme*. In vol. 10 of *Oeuvres complètes*. Paris: Gallimard, 1987.

Baudelaire, Charles. "De l'essence du rire." In *Oeuvres complètes*. 11 vols. Edited by J. Crépet. Paris: Conard, 1923.

Bergson, Henri. *Le Rire*. Paris: Presses Universitaires de France, 1940.

Billington, Sandra. "'Suffer Fools Gladly': The Fool in Medieval England and the Play *Mankind*." In *The Fool and the Trickster*, edited by Paul V. A. Williams. Cambridge: Brewer, 1979.

Booth, Wayne. *The Rhetoric of Fiction*. Chicago: University of Chicago Press, 1961.

Bradley, F. H. *Appearance and Reality*. 9th impression. Oxford: Clarendon Press, 1930.

Brand, Peter. "Disguise in Renaissance Comedy, with Illustrations." In *Comparative Criticism: An Annual Journal*, edited by E. S. Shaffer. Cambridge: Cambridge University Press, 1988.

Bristol, Michael D. *Carnival and Theater: Plebeian culture and the structure of authority in Renaissance England*. London: Methuen, 1985.

Brooke-Rose, Christine. "Ill wit and good humour: women's comedy and the canon." In *Comparative Criticism: An Annual Journal*, edited by E. S. Shaffer. Cambridge: Cambridge University Press, 1988.

Bruner, Jerome S., Alison Jolly and Kathy Sylva, eds. *Play – Its Role in Development and Evolution*. Harmondsworth: Penguin, 1976.

Camus, Albert. *The Myth of Sisyphus*. Translated by Justin O'Brien. Harmondsworth: Penguin, 1975.

Cave, Terence. *Recognitions: A Study in Poetics*. Oxford: Clarendon Press, 1988.

Chadwick, Henry. *Augustine*. Oxford: Oxford University Press, 1986.

Chiaro, Delia. *The Language of Jokes: Analysing verbal play*. London: Routedge, 1992.

Cohen, Sandy. "Racial and Ethnic Humor in the United States." In *Amerikastudien/American Studies* 30 (1985).

Cornford, F. M. *The Origin of Attic Comedy*. Edited by T. H. Gaster. 1914; New York: Doubleday, 1961.

Coveney, Peter, and Roger Highfield. *The Arrow of Time. The Quest to Solve Science's Greatest Mystery*. London: Flamingo, 1991.

Culler, Jonathan. *Structuralist Poetics*. London: Routledge and Kegan Paul, 1375.

Curtius, Ernst Robert. *Europäische Literatur und lateinisches Mittelalter*. Bern: Francke, 1948.

Daniélou, Alain. *Shiva et Dionysos: La religion de la Nature et de l'Eros.* Paris: Fayard, 1979.

Dante Alighieri. *Literary Criticism of Dante Alighieri.* Translated by R. S. Haller. Lincoln: University of Nebraska Press, 1973.

Dover, K. J. *Aristophanic Comedy.* Berkeley: University of California Press, 1972.

Dupuy, Jean-Pierre. "Tangled Hierarchies: self-reference in philosophy, anthropology and critical theory." Translated by Mark Anspach. In *Comparative Criticism: An Annual Journal,* edited by E. S. Shaffer. Cambridge: Cambridge University Press, 1990.

Dürrenmatt, Friedrich. "Theaterprobleme." In *Theater: Essays, Gedichte und Reden.* Vol. 24 of *Werkausgabe.* 30 vols. Zurich: Diogenes, 1985.

Eibl-Eibesfeldt, I. *Grundriß der vergleichenden Verhaltensforschung.* 6th ed. Munich: Piper, 1980.

Elster, Jon, ed. *The Multiple Self.* Cambridge: Cambridge University Press, 1986.

Erasmus. *Praise of Folly.* Translated by Betty Radice. Harmondsworth: Penguin, 1971.

Esrig, David. *Commedia dell'arte: eine Bildgeschichte der Kunst des Spektakels.* Nördlingen: Greno, 1985.

Evanthius. *De fabula.* Edited by G. Cupaiuolo. Naples: Società Editrice Napoletana, 1979.

Farley-Hills, David. *The Comic in Renaissance Comedy.* London: Macmillan, 1981.

Feuerbach, Ludwig. "Einige Bemerkungen über den 'Anfang der Philosophie' von Dr. J. F. Reiff." In vol. 9 of *Gesammelte Werke.* 18 vols. Edited by Werner Schuffenhauer. Berlin: Akademie, 1970.

Feuerbach, Ludwig. *Theorie-Werkausgabe.* 6 vols. Edited by Erich Thies. Frankfurt-am-Main: Suhrkamp, 1975.

Fichte, Johann Gottlieb. *Grundlage der gesamten Wissenschaftslehre.* 1794; Hamburg: Felix Meiner, 1988.

Fichte, Johann Gottlieb. *Über den Begriff der Wissenschaftslehre.* In vol. 2 of *Gesamtausgabe,* edited by R. Lauth and H. Jacob. Stuttgart: Friedrich Frommann, 1965.

Flew, Antony, ed. *Body, Mind, and Death.* New York: Macmillan, 1964.

Fliess, Wilhelm. *Über den ursächlichen Zusammenhang von Nase und Geschlechtsorgan.* Halle, 1910.

Foucault, Michel. *Discipline and Punish: The Birth of the Prison.* Translated by Alan Sheridan. Harmondsworth: Penguin, 1979.

Foucault, Michel. *Madness and Civilization: A History of Insanity in the Age of Reason.* Translated by Richard Howard. London: Tavistock, 1971.

Frank, Manfred. *Die Unhintergehbarkeit von Individualität*. Frankfurt-am-Main: Suhrkamp, 1986.

Frank, Manfred. *Was ist Neostrukturalismus?* Frankfurt-am-Main: Suhrkamp, 1984.

Frazer, James George. *The Golden Bough: A Study in Magic and Religion.* Abridged edition. London: Macmillan, 1922.

Freud, Sigmund. *Studienausgabe*. 10 vols. Edited by A. Mitscherlich, A. Richards, and J. Strachey. Frankfurt-am-Main: S. Fischer, 1969-72.

Frye, Northrop. *An Anatomy of Criticism*. Princeton: Princeton University Press, 1957.

Gadamer, Hans-Georg. *Wahrheit und Methode*. 2nd ed. Tübingen: Mohr, 1965.

Girard, René. *La Violence et le sacré*. Paris: Grasset, 1972.

Glasgow, R. D. V. *Madness, Masks, and Laughter: An essay on comedy*. London: Associated University Presses, 1995.

Glover, Jonathan. *I: The Philosophy and Psychology of Personal Identity*. Harmondsworth: Penguin, 1988.

Gregory, Richard L. *Mind in Science: A History of Explanations in Psychology and Physics*. Harmondsworth: Penguin, 1984.

Greimas, A. J. *Sémantique structurale*. Paris: Larousse, 1966.

Grimm, R., and K. L. Berghahn, eds. *Wesen und Formen des Komischen im Drama*. Darmstadt: Wissenschaftliche Buchgesellschaft, 1975.

Hampshire, Stuart. *Thought and Action*. London: Chatto and Windus, 1959.

Harris, Henry. "Whose Brain Is It, Anyway?" In *The Times Higher Education Supplement*, 18 December, 1992.

Harrison, Jane Ellen. *Themis: a study in the social origins of Greek religion*. 2nd ed. Cambridge: Cambridge University Press, 1927.

Hegel, G. W. F. *Ästhetik*. 2nd ed. 2 vols. Edited by Friedrich Bassenge. Berlin: Aufbau, 1965.

Hegel, G. W. F. *Werke*. 20 vols. Edited by E. Moldenhauer and K. M. Michel. Frankfurt-am-Main: Suhrkamp, 1986.

Heidegger, Martin. *Sein und Zeit*. 1927; Tübingen: Niemeyer, 1986.

Hind, John. *The Comic Inquisition: Conversations with Great Comedians*. London: Virgin, 1991.

Hobbes, Thomas. *Leviathan*. Edited by C. B. Macpherson. Harmondsworth: Penguin, 1968.

Hofstadter, Douglas R. *Gödel, Escher, Bach: An Eternal Golden Braid*. Harmondsworth: Penguin, 1980.

Hofstadter, Douglas R., and Daniel C. Dennett, eds. *The Mind's I: Fantasies and Reflections on Self and Soul*. Harmondsworth: Penguin, 1982.

Holland, Norman. *Laughing: A Psychology of Humour*. Ithaca: Cornell
    University Press, 1982.
Howarth, W. D., ed. *Comic Drama: The European Heritage*. London:
    Methuen, 1978.
Hughes, Patrick, and George Brecht. *Vicious Circles and Infinity: An
    Anthology of Paradoxes*. Harmondsworth: Penguin, 1978.
Hume, David. *The Philosophical Works*. 4 vols. Edited by T. H. Green
    and T. H. Grose. 1886. Reprint; Darmstadt: Scientia Verlag
    Aalen, 1964.
Joubert, Laurent. *Traité du Ris*. 1579; Geneva: Slatkine Reprints, 1973.
Kamper, D., and Chr. Wulf, eds. *Lachen, Gelächter, Lächeln*.
    Frankfurt-am-Main: Syndikat, 1986.
Kant, Immanuel. *Anthropologie in pragmatischer Hinsicht*. Edited by
    Wolfgang Becker. Stuttgart: Reclam, 1983.
Kant, Immanuel. *Kritik der reinen Vernunft*. Hamburg: Felix Meiner,
    1956.
Kierkegaard, Søren. *Concluding Unscientific Postscript*. Translated by
    David F. Swenson and Walter Lowrie. Princeton: Princeton
    University Press, 1941.
Koestler, Arthur. *The Act of Creation*. 1964; London: Arkana, 1989.
Kolve, V. A. *The Play Called Corpus Christi*. London: Edward Arnold,
    1966.
Kristeva, Julia. *The Kristeva Reader*. Edited by Toril Moi. Oxford:
    Basil Blackwell, 1986.
Laing, R. D. *The Divided Self: An Existential Study in Sanity and
    Madness*. 1959; Harmondsworth: Penguin, 1965.
Laing, R. D. *Self and Others*. 2nd ed. Harmondsworth: Penguin, 1971.
Rochefoucauld, La. *Maximes et Réflexions diverses*. 2nd ed. Edited by
    Jean Lafond. Paris: Gallimard, 1976.
Lewin, Roger. *Complexity: Life at the Edge of Chaos*. New York:
    Collier-Macmillan, 1992.
Lichtenberg, G. C. *Sudelbücher*. Edited by Franz H. Mautner
    Frankfurt-am-Main: Insel, 1984.
Locke, John. *An Essay Concerning Human Understanding*. Edited by
    P. H. Nidditch. Oxford: Clarendon Press, 1975.
McDougall, William. *An Outline of Psychology*. London: Methuen,
    1923.
McGinn, Colin. *The Character of Mind*. Oxford: Oxford University
    Press, 1982.
McLaughlin, Brian P., and Amélie Oksenberg Rorty, eds. *Perspectives
    on Self-Deception*. Berkeley: University of California Press,
    1988.
Maturana, Humberto R., and Francisco J. Varela. *Autopoiesis and
    Cognition: The Realization of the Living*. Dordrecht: Reidel,
    1980.

Mayer III, David. *Harlequin in his Element: The English Pantomime, 1806-36*. Cambridge: Harvard University Press, 1969.

Mead, George H. *Mind, Self, and Society*. Edited by Charles W. Morris. Chicago: University of Chicago Press, 1962.

Mercier, Vivian. *The Irish Comic Tradition*. London: Oxford University Press, 1962.

Merleau-Ponty, Maurice. *Phénoménologie de la perception*. Paris: Gallimard, 1945.

Miller, Karl. *Doubles: Studies in Literary History*. Oxford: Oxford University Press, 1985.

Monick, Eugene. *Phallos: Sacred Image of the Masculine*. Toronto: Inner City Books, 1987.

Montaigne, Michel de. *Essais*. 3 vols. Edited by A. Micha. Paris: Garnier-Flammarion, 1969.

Muecke, D. C. *Irony and the Ironic*. 2nd ed. London: Methuen, 1982.

Nagel, Thomas. *The View from Nowhere*. Oxford: Oxford University Press, 1986.

Nelson, T. G. A. *Comedy: The Theory of Comedy in Literature, Drama and Cinema*. Oxford: Oxford University Press, 1990.

Nietzsche, Friedrich. *Werke. Kritische Gesamtausgabe*. 20 vols. Edited by G. Colli and M. Montinari. Berlin: de Gruyter, 1967–.

Nozick, Robert. *Philosophical Explanations*. Oxford: Clarendon Press, 1981.

Palmer, D. J., ed. *Comedy: Developments in Criticism*. London: Macmillan, 1984.

Parfit, Derek. *Reasons and Persons*. Oxford: Oxford University Press, 1986.

Passmore, John. *A Hundred Years of Philosophy*. 2nd ed. Harmondsworth: Penguin, 1968.

Penrose, Roger. *The Emperor's New Mind*. London: Vintage, 1990.

Plato. *Euthyphro. Apology. Crito. Phaedo. Phaedrus*. With an English translation by H. N. Fowler. London: Heinemann (Loeb Classical Library), 1923.

Plato. *The Republic*. Translated by Francis M. Cornford. Oxford: Clarendon Press, 1941.

Plato. *Timaeus. Critias. Cleitophon. Menexenus. Epistles*. With an English translation by R. G. Bury. London: Heinemann (Loeb Classical Library), 1929.

Plessner, Helmuth. *Lachen und Weinen*. Munich: Leo Lehnen, 1950.

Porter, Roy. *A Social History of Madness: Stories of the Insane*. London: Weidenfeld and Nicolson, 1987.

Powell, Chris, and George E. C. Paton, eds. *Humour in Society: Resistance and Control*. London: Macmillan, 1988.

Preisendanz, Wolfgang, and Rainer Warning, eds. *Das Komische.* Munich: Fink, 1976.

Priest, Stephen. *Theories of the Mind*. Harmondsworth: Penguin, 1991.

Prigogine, Ilya, and Isabelle Stengers. *Order out of Chaos*. London: Flamingo, 1985.

Purdie, Susan. *Comedy: The Mastery of Discourse*. Hemel Hempstead: Harvester Wheatsheaf, 1993.

Putnam, Hilary. *Reason, Truth and History*. Cambridge: Cambridge University Press, 1981.

Radin, Paul. *The Trickster: A Study in American Indian Mythology*. New York: Schocken, 1972.

Redfern, Walter. *Puns*. Oxford: Basil Blackwell, 1984.

Ritter, Joachim. "Über das Lachen." 1940. In *Subjektivität*. Frankfurt-am-Main: Suhrkamp, 1979.

Rose, Steven. *The Making of Memory*. London: Bantam, 1992.

Rosten, Leo. *The Joys of Yiddish*. Harmondsworth: Penguin, 1971.

Ryle, Gilbert. *The Concept of Mind*. Harmondsworth: Penguin, 1963.

Sacks, Oliver. *The Man Who Mistook His Wife for a Hat*. London: Picador, 1986.

Sartre, Jean-Paul. "L'acteur comique." In *Un théâtre de situations*. Paris: Gallimard, 1973.

Sartre, Jean-Paul. *Being and Nothingness: An Essay on Phenomenological Ontology*. Translated by Hazel E. Barnes. London: Methuen, 1958.

Schopenhauer, Arthur. *Sämtliche Werke*. 5 vols. Edited by W. F. von Löhneysen. Frankfurt-am-Main: Suhrkamp, 1986.

Schrödinger, E. *What is Life?* Cambridge: Cambridge University Press, 1946.

Shaffer, Jerome A. *Philosophy of Mind*. Englewood Cliffs, N. J.: Prentice-Hall, 1968.

Solomon, R. C. "Emotionen und Anthropologie: Die Logik emotionaler Weltbilder." In *Logik des Herzens. Die soziale Dimension der Gefühle*, edited by G. Kahle. Frankfurt-am-Main: Suhrkamp, 1981.

Staveacre, Tony. *Slapstick: The Illustrated Story of Knockabout Comedy*. London: Angus and Robertson, 1987.

Stone, I. F. *The Trial of Socrates*. London: Pan/Picador, 1989.

Strawson, Peter F. *The Bounds of Sense*. London: Methuen, 1966.

Strawson, Peter F. *Individuals*. London: Methuen, 1959.

Sypher, Wylie, ed. *Comedy*. 1956; Baltimore: Johns Hopkins University Press, 1980.

Taylor, Charles. *Sources of the Self: The Making of the Modern Identity*. Cambridge: Cambridge University Press, 1989.

Taylor, Jane H. M. "The *Danse Macabre*: reflections on black humour, with illustrations." In *Comparative Criticism*, edited by E. S. Shaffer. Cambridge: Cambridge University Press, 1988.

te Velde, Herman. *Seth, God of Confusion: A Study of his Role in Egyptian Mythology and Religion.* Translated by G. E. van Baaren-Pape. Leiden: E. J. Brill, 1967.

Vesey, Godfrey. *Personal Identity.* London: Macmillan, 1974.

Warning, Rainer. "Komik und Kömodie als Positivierung von Negativität (am Beispiel Molière und Marivaux)." In *Positionen der Negativität*, edited by Harald Weinrich. Munich: Fink, 1975.

Wartofsky, Marx W. *Conceptual Foundations of Scientific Thought: an introduction to the philosophy of science.* London: Collier-Macmillan, 1968.

Welsford, Enid. *The Fool: His Social and Literary History.* 1935; New York: Doubleday, 1961.

Williams, Bernard. "Imagination and the Self." In *Studies in the Philosophy of Thought and Action*, edited by P. F. Strawson. London: Oxford University Press, 1968.

Williams, Paul V. A. "Exú: The Master and the Slave in Afro-Brazilian Religion." In *The Fool and the Trickster*, edited by Paul V. A. Williams. Cambridge: Brewer, 1979.

Wittgenstein, Ludwig. *Werkausgabe.* 8 vols. Frankfurt-am-Main: Suhrkamp, 1984.

Wright, Elizabeth. *Psychoanalytic Criticism: Theory in Practice.* London: Methuen, 1984.

Young, J. Z. *Philosophy and the Brain.* Oxford: Oxford University Press, 1987.

Zijderveld, Anton. *Humor und Gesellschaft. Eine Soziologie des Humors und Lachens.* Translated from the Dutch by Diethard Zils. Graz: Styria, 1976.

Index

Girard, R., 69-70, 73-74, 83, 133-34, 195

Gödel, K., 40-41, 42, 207

Goethe, J. W. von, 64

Gogol, Nikolai, 174; "Diary of a Madman," 184; *The Government Inspector*, 89-90, 195; "The Nose," 157, 161

Gonad, Buster (and his unfeasibly large testicles), 154-55

Goodies, The, 138

Grabbe, Christian Dietrich: *Scherz, Satire, Ironie und tiefere Bedeutung*, 71, 120-21

Greimas, A. J., 101-2

Gryphius, Andreas: *Herr Peter Squenz*, 125-26, 128

Gwilym, Dafydd ap, 167-68, 224

Harlequin (*commedia dell'arte*), 72, 80, 94-95, 137-38, 185, 204

Harlequin (English pantomime), 87, 95, 100, 131

Hazlitt, W., 79

Hegel, G. W. F., 15, 45, 48, 61, 174, 189-90

Heidegger, M., 13, 26, 39, 106

Heraclitus, 47

Hermes, 153, 154, 182, 185

Hobbes, T., xi, 57, 65

Hofstadter, D. R., 41-42

Holbein, H., 140

Holberg, Ludvig: *Jeppe from the Hill*, 129-30

Holland, N., 111

Homer: *Margites*, 161; *Odyssey*, 151

Hood, T., 124

Hume, D., 21, 33, 49-50

Hutcheson, F., 65

Iamblichus, 110

Ionesco, Eugene, 111

Iser, W., 81-82

Janko, R., 110

Jarry, Alfred, 161, 163; *Ubu enchaîné*, 115; *Ubu roi*, 115, 138

Johnston, D., 168

Jonson, Ben, 134

Joubert, L., 155

Joyce, James: *Finnegans Wake*, 123, 136-37, 144, 162, 167

Julian of Norwich, 68

Kant, I., viii-ix, 22-23, 26, 48-49, 58, 94, 99-100

Keystone Kops, 111

Kierkegaard, S., 106, 107, 110

Kleist, Heinrich von: *Amphitryon*, 198-99; *Der zerbrochne Krug*, 71

Koestler, A., 63

Kolve, V. A., 84-85

Kristeva, J., 5-6

Laing, R. D., 35-36

La Rochefoucauld, 74

Laurel and Hardy, 66, L95, 199-200

Lee, N., 201

Leno, Dan, 192-93

Lesage, A.-R.: *Le Diable Boiteux*, 159

Lichtenberg, G. C., 49-50, 110

Linstead, S., 205

The Living Corpses, 129

Locke, John, x-xi, 18, 24-25, 203

Locrine, 127-28

Lord of Misrule, 72, 77, 79, 81

Lucian: *Cataplus*, 141; *On Funerals*, 117; *Menippus, or the Descent into Hades*, 140-41, 142

Lucifer. *See* Devil

Luguru (Tanzania), 120

Luther, M., 68

McGinn, C., 12-13

Machiavelli, Niccolò: *Mandragola*, 130

Man Bites Dog, 115

Mankind, 82-83, 155, 171-72

Manning, Bernard, 57

Marlowe, Christopher: *Doctor Faustus*, 71, 72, 131; *Jew of Malta*, 112

Marx, K., 5, 202

Maturana, H., 16-17, 18, 43

Mayer, David, III, 100

Mead, G. H., 5-6, 31, 32, 47, 50

John Wilmot, 152
Rorty, A. O., 183
Rose, S., 43-44, 211
Rosten, L., 91, 218
Roth, Philip: *The Breast*, 157
Ryle, G., 38, 42, 47, 182, 199

Sacks, Oliver, 25, 173-74
Sade, Marquis de, 143, 144
Sadowitz, Gerry, 58
Sartre, J.-P., 26, 44-45, 48, 67, 68, 72, 182, 226
Satan. *See* Devil
scapegoat, 68, 69-70, 73-76, 78-80, 83-85, 132-35
Schlegel, A. W., 24, 94
Schlegel, F., 94
Schopenhauer, A., 29, 37, 111, 143, 146, 148
Schrödinger, E., 15
Searle, J., 8-9
Seth, 153
Shakespeare, William, 81; *As You Like It*, 192; *Comedy of Errors*, 134-35, 195-97; *Hamlet*, 111; *Henry IV, Part 1*, 77-79, 124, 127; *Henry IV, Part 2*, 77-79, 119, 124; *King Lear*, 111; *The Merchant of Venice*, 172; *The Merry Wives of Windsor*, 77, 79-80, 134; *A Midsummer Night's Dream*, 126; "Phoenix and Turtle," 144-45; *Romeo and Juliet*, 125; *Twelfth Night*, xiv, 81, 82, 83, 193-94, 196, 204; *A Winter's Tale*, 131-33
Sheela-na-gig, 144
Sidney, P., 111
Silenus, 75-76
Simpson, N. F.: *One Way Pendulum*, 46-47, 116, 138, 177
Siva, 153, 185
Smollett, Tobias: *Roderick Random*, 124, 161, 189
Socrates, 22, 34, 36, 74-76, 83, 203-4, 206
Sophocles, 161
Sorel, Charles: *Le Berger Extravagant*, 139

Staveacre, T., 179
Sterne, Laurence: *Tristram Shandy*, 155-56, 161
Stone, I. F., 75
Stoppard, Tom: *Jumpers*, 120; *Rosencrantz and Guildenstern are Dead*, 107-8, 126-27, 190-91, 200
Strawson, P. F., 10-11
Stubbes, P., 72
Swift, Jonathan, 123; *Gulliver's Travels*, 123, 142, 162
Sypher, W., 70, 83

Taylor, C., 3-4, 6, 11, 47
Taylor, J., 142
Totentanz. See *danse macabre*
Tourneur, C.: *The Revenger's Tragedy*, 112-13
Tractatus Coislinianus, 110
Trappola (of *commedia dell'arte*), 106
Trickster (Winnebago), 153-54, 163, 168, 181
True Romance, 115
Turner, V., 88

Valentin, Karl, 108
Vice (figure in morality plays), 71, 72, 77, 79, 83
Viz, 154-55, 180
Voltaire: *Candide*, 116
Vonnegut, Kurt: *Slaughterhouse-Five*, 97-98

wake (Irish), 120, 125, 136-37
Welsford, E., 81
Whitehead, A. N., 27
Winnebago Trickster. *See* Trickster
Wittgenstein, L., 25, 28, 48
Wood, Victoria, 58

Xenophon, 75

Young, J.Z., 16

Zeus, 86, 135, 154
Zuckmayer, Carl: *Der Hauptmann von Köpenick*, 89

.